PEOPLE IN PAIN

FOREWORD BY *Margaret Mead*

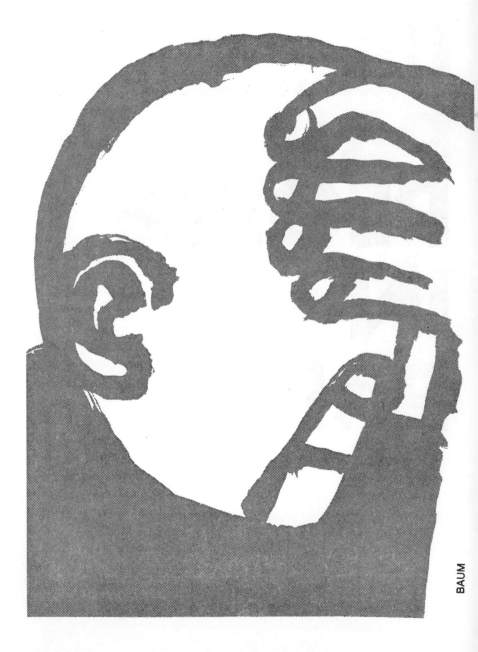

BAUM

PEOPLE IN PAIN

�֍�֍�֍✷✷✷✷✷✷✷✷✷✷✷✷✷✷✷✷✷✷✷✷✷✷✷✷✷✷✷✷✷✷✷

Mark Zborowski

Jossey-Bass Inc., Publishers
615 Montgomery Street • San Francisco • 1969

PEOPLE IN PAIN
   by Mark Zborowski

Copyright © 1969 by Jossey-Bass, Inc., Publishers

Copyright under Pan American and Universal
Copyright Conventions

Jossey-Bass, Inc., Publishers
615 Montgomery Street
San Francisco, California 94111

Library of Congress Catalog Card Number 70-92888

Standard Book Number SBN 87589-046-6

Manufactured in the United States of America
       Composed and printed by York Composition Company, Inc.
       Bound by Chas. H. Bohn & Co., Inc.

JACKET DESIGN BY WILLI BAUM, SAN FRANCISCO

FIRST EDITION

Code 6920

THE JOSSEY-BASS BEHAVIORAL SCIENCE SERIES

General Editors

WILLIAM E. HENRY, *University of Chicago*

NEVITT SANFORD, *Wright Institute, Berkeley*

Special Adviser in Social Welfare
MARTIN B. LOEB, *University of Wisconsin*

Foreword

People in Pain is a study of the way in which different peoples, with contrasting histories, responded to their new culture and yet kept some of the attitudes, weaknesses, and strengths of their own historical cultures. Mark Zborowski has chosen to study the response to pain, a form of human experience so sharp, so unmistakable, so immediate, that members of any culture can recognize, empathize, or identify with another human being in pain. The cry of genuine anguish knows no linguistic boundaries, and fortitude under the needle and the knife needs no interpreters. When he began this study almost twenty years ago, Zborowski came to it, not with the memory of his childhood, but with the disciplined awareness of a mature man with a wife and son of his own, who had experienced, as a new immigrant, the very mixture of welcome and rebuff that had been the setting within which the earlier immigrants came. He lived the process of Americanization. One of the groups that he has studied here—and I myself was one of his subjects—is what we technically call old Americans, Americans who have been here so long that there are no ties, except in names and genealogies, with the old world. I believe he has come to understand old Americans, as an adult becoming an American, as well as he understands the Jews who, before World War II, lived in determinedly nonconforming enclaves in Eastern Europe.

How do Americans learn to become Americans, when first they come from other shores, when they rear their children here, when they become grandparents? How much of what was learned in Ireland, in Poland, in Italy survives, and how? When the furniture in the home is changed, when the language is spoken without an accent, when the food from the old country is eaten only on holidays—have the new Americans become, in essence, old Americans? This is a question of very present importance to America, a country to which so many millions have come as strangers and stayed to become citizens, a country in which the struggle to accept more and more unlike strangers still goes on. We have moved from the narrowness of the sixteenth and seventeenth centuries, when American Indians were hunted like some alien, hardly human creatures of the forest, and African slaves were bought and sold at their masters' pleasure. We have passed through periods of deaths, too many to count, of the Chinese coolies who built the Great Pacific Railroad and of prejudice against those very close to the original settlers but differing only in some detail of greater skill or trade—like the most maligned Scots, or the Irish, denigrated for their Catholicism. Today we are experiencing a particularly bitter phase of the struggle as we reach the end; last ditchers fight with the greatest endurance.

In this period of regained and new identities, when Americans are stimulated not only by what is going on at home but also by the

Foreword

unprecedented speed of changes abroad—in Asia and Africa, the Caribbean and South America—the question of how fast and in what ways each of us changes becomes doubly important. Zborowski's first book was a study of a people who for hundreds of years, living among strangers, cut off from a homeland to which they could not return, kept their identity. They were Eastern European Jews, described so vividly in *Life Is With People*.[1] For that book he drew on the experience of his own childhood and adolescence, on that of a group of American collaborators who had themselves made the transition differently or today had only grandparental reminiscences to go by, and on the records of many highly verbal informants who could describe the old ways of the *shetl* in Eastern Europe. Typists and clerks who handled the pages of the manuscript wrote their memories and their grandparents' memories on the margins and backs of the pages. Young people who had hardly suspected the richness of their heritage had it returned to them in warmth and humor.

Anthropological work depends upon a combination of the stranger's trained eye and ear and the enjoyment that the natives have in seeing their own lived but only slightly appreciated culture clarified before their eyes. This work done in hospitals, among men and women suffering from recent or present illness and pain, was a collaboration as surely as if Zborowski were the welcomed anthropological visitor in the remote mountains of New Guinea. He listened to them, he treated them as whole human beings, he was unconstrained, as doctors and nurses so often cannot be because of the exigencies and emergencies of treatment. He was the one person who had time to listen; they talked, and he learned, and they learned, he about them and they about themselves—which is the way good anthropology works.

Among those sensitive scientists who came to us as a result of the political disturbances which drove the gifted from Western Europe to enrich our universities and our laboratories, Zborowski is one who has had especially good opportunities to study us and to learn to know

[1] Zborowski, Mark, and Elizabeth Herzog. *Life Is With People: The Jewish Little-Town of Eastern Europe.* New York: International Universities Press, 1952. Reprinted New York: Schocken, 1962.

us. And he has also had the parallel opportunity to approach, through the penetrating revelation of the response to pain, first and second and third generations from other countries.

In *People in Pain* we stand together, Eastern European Jews, whom Zborowski knows as one of them, old Americans in whose allegiances he found his new allegiance, Irish and Italians, whose forebears came here as he had done. It is all spread out before us to illuminate our view of our mixed and contrasting American heritage. And it is here to warn us of how deep the old roots go into the past and that the recalcitrancy of a patient, or a parent, may not be best understood by branding him as uncooperative or ignorant. The first report on this study, "Cultural Components in Responses to Pain,"[2] had become a classical reason for teaching physicians, nurses, social workers, and teachers how to understand their patients, clients, and pupils, who often puzzle and exasperate them. Now we have the whole book, and we need it. In the new climate of today, when a more sensitive conscience is responding to better-documented suffering, humiliations, and frustrated hope, we need this record of differences among those who are all, after all, Americans.

MARGARET MEAD
The American Museum
of Natural History

New York
September, 1969

[2] Zborowski, Mark. "Cultural Components in Responses to Pain," *Journal of Social Issues,* 1952, *8*(4), 16–30.

To

Regina and George

Preface

People in Pain is the result of several years of research to investigate pain as a cultural experience. This project was undertaken under the sponsorship of the United States Public Health Service and The Institute for Intercultural Studies at the American Museum of Natural History.

My book is about people in pain. The people were patients at the Veterans Administration Hospital, Bronx, New York. I express my deep gratitude to them for being willing to accept the additional suffering of my presence and many questions and for being willing to share with me their feelings and emotions, the expressions of which constitute the major part of my book.

Margaret Mead was my guide, consultant, and informant at all stages of the study. No words can adequately express my feelings of indebtedness to her for years of friendship, scholarly advice, and moral encouragement. Lois Mark, anthropologist, and Dorly Wang, social psychologist—both members of the research team—contributed professional skills and personal loyalty to the collection of the data and their analysis. Jack Cohen, chief psychologist at the Veterans Administration Hospital, did the complex, statistical computations that form the basis for the cross-cultural comparisons offered in my concluding chapter. In his work Cohen was assisted by the research team and by George Zborowski, who spent long hours translating qualitative material into computable data.

Throughout the study I benefited greatly from consultation with the late Laurence Frank and Harold G. Wolf, who were always ready to share with me their ideas in the field of culture and pain.

With appreciation I acknowledge the cooperation of the administrators and medical and paramedical staffs of the Veterans Administration Hospital in facilitating my study by providing space, equipment, and help in the selection of patients.

The scope of the intellectual and moral contribution of my wife, Regina, cannot be assessed in words. I hope that by dedicating the book to her and to our son I can suggest the full debt of my feelings.

MARK ZBOROWSKI
Mount Zion Hospital

San Francisco
September, 1969

Contents

Contents

PEOPLE
IN
PAIN

Introduction

People in Pain is the result of a three-year research project entitled "Cultural Components in Response to Pain." The study was initiated in an attempt to contribute to the understanding of the phenomenon of pain by focusing on behavioral responses to pain, with the assumption that these responses present identifiable regularities patterned along cultural models common to groups of people of a similar ethnic origin.

In contrast to other studies on pain, this research was not

1

concerned with the complexity of the pain experience from the neurological, physiological, or medical point of view, which is beyond the professional interests and competence of its initiators. Neither was the aim of the research to offer direct insights into the psychology of pain, despite the realization that such variables as patients' personality or emotional life experiences are of utmost importance in influencing attitudes and behavior in pain; the investigation of this type of problem would be in the domain of experts in the field of psychology and psychiatry. The sole objective of the project was to contribute to the understanding of people's responses to pain by providing information derived from a study based on concepts drawn from the sciences of human culture and society, with the help of research methods and techniques appropriate for the study of men as social beings. This conceptual frame of the study (which is developed in greater detail in Chapter One) refers to the cultural patterning of physiological phenomena in man's life, to the dynamics of transmission of cultural values and norms within the society, to the diversity and relativity of cultural patterns, and to the place of cultural manifestations in the integrated cultural whole. The methods and techniques employed in the research will be best understood from a description of the organization of the project and its activities.

The actual research extended over a period of three years (1951–1954) and consisted of three main phases: the exploratory stage, the gathering of data, and, finally, the analysis of the collected material. In the exploratory phase main efforts were directed toward the definition of research problems through discussions with experts, through surveys of work done in the field of pain as reflected in the literature, and through acquaintance with opinions and feelings about the problems of pain as held by people most directly involved in its management, that is, practitioners in various branches of medicine.

From examination of the literature it became apparent that the main contribution to the study of pain has been made by medical and paramedical specialists, who have investigated human suffering from the point of view of neurophysiology or pathology, with emphasis either on laboratory experiments or on clinical data.

2

Introduction

These studies provided important bases for the understanding of the physiobiological background of the pain experience but offered little help relative to the objectives of the investigation. The psychiatric and psychological publications, although offering stimulating and provocative analyses of the dynamics of "psychogenic pain" (for example, Engel, 1959, 1961) or the concept of pain in relation to pleasure in a psychoanalytic model (Szasz, 1957), referred primarily to individual case material without incorporating in the discussion the cultural background of the patients in its relation to behavior in pain.

On the other hand, the anthropological and ethnographic material, rich in first-hand reports on initiation rites, mutilations, and health practices among primitive peoples, offered even less than the medical literature, because it provided mainly descriptions of situations associated with pain without an analysis of the participants' attitudes and behavior. In this respect modern anthropologists have followed the path of early explorers, travelers, and missionaries, who left detailed narratives of native cultures and societies and frequently depicted behavior in pain; but in most cases their examples served only to cite so-called barbaric customs of savages unaffected by the beneficial influence of Christianity and Western civilization. It would be futile to look in these descriptions for a scientific analysis of attitudes or emotions associated with customs of self mutilation, torture, or pain endured during illness.

The study and the formulation gained most from information obtained in direct conversations and interviews with practitioners in the field of medicine, who shared their impressions and experiences derived from dealing with pain in everyday practice. Preliminary interviews were conducted with staff physicians of one of the major Health Insurance Plan clinics in the New York City metropolitan area, which was selected because of its multiethnic membership. This group of doctors was approached with the assumption that, because the majority of their group membership belonged to three large ethnic minorities—Jewish, Irish, and Italians —they had had ample opportunity to observe the differences among their patients and would therefore be able to formulate impressions as to the nature of these differences. This assumption was proven

3

correct, and the contribution of the physicians was of major importance in the subsequent planning of the research design.

The doctors' views were important as a source of factual information and impressions about behavioral differences among members of various ethnic groups. Moreover, they were the first group of informants to offer an example of attitudes toward behavior in pain that, as further studies have shown, are prevalent in our society. They were also the first, in my experience, to differentiate between correct and incorrect behavior in pain according to criteria held by their profession and, as was later found, by the society at large. Without explicitly showing approval or disapproval, they expressed their values in describing their patients' behavior as overexaggerated, overemotional, and hysterical or as stolid, mature, or masculine. According to their opinions, some groups of patients took their pain well, whereas others were "nuisances" and "alarmists." In other words, to denote their patients' actual behavior, they employed qualifying adjectives that implied definite value judgments.

Because these conversations and interviews centered predominantly on problems of differences among patients along ethnic lines, the doctors were at first most hesitant in expressing their impressions. Members of the medical profession are reluctant to differentiate patients according to religion, race, or nationality. In conformity with the traditions of medical ethics, the patient is to be viewed only as "a human being in need of help. He has to be given medical care regardless of religion, color, or ethnic background." Accordingly, the patient's behavior in the process of treatment has to be evaluated exclusively in terms of his participation in, and response to, the therapeutic process; any deviation from the pattern of behavior expected in illness and treatment should be considered only in the light of individual idiosyncrasies and, where necessary, should be interpreted with the help of psychology or psychiatry.[1] Therefore, it is not surprising that a number of doctors

[1] Later observations have shown that it is against the hospital moral code and, often, against hospital practice to attribute incorrect or uncooperative behavior to the patient's membership in a specific social, cultural,

Introduction

at first expressed strong disapproval when asked about ethnic differences in responses to pain. Some even implied a racist character of the research. They insisted that patients are individuals whose responses to pain are determined by their individual pain thresholds or temperaments, which have no relation to their being Jews, Poles, or Greeks. Moreover, they suggested that they were not interested and, frequently, not even informed of a patient's ethnicity, since it has no bearing on his illness or treatment.

However, when the doctors became convinced that the objectives of the research were not threatening their professional and moral integrity, many offered information that reflected their actual impressions formed during years of medical practice among the multinational and multicultural population of New York City. With many reservations, insisting that their comments were only impressions that might be totally wrong, the medical people stated that their Jewish and Italian patients tended to be more emotional and that they tended to exaggerate their pain more than other nationalities. Furthermore, they ventured the generalizations that Mediterranean people have a lower threshold of pain than Nordic people; Anglo-Saxons take their pain better than Jews and Italians, who are complaining and demanding; and Irish patients are stolid, whereas Jews are overemotional. They also offered observations to the effect that there seems to be a difference in behavior in pain according to generation; that is, although immigrant Jews and Italians tend to behave in an emotional manner, American-born patients are just like other American patients—rational and unemotional.

All these comments, despite their impressionistic and unscientific nature, suggested a number of directions to be taken in the final organization of the research design. They indicated: (1) an apparent similarity in manifest behavior among certain ethnic groups despite evident differences in their cultural traditions, for

---

or national group. An overemotional patient is identified as a "mental case" rather than as a Puerto Rican, Jew, or Italian. Consequently, exaggerated behavior was responded to by the ward administration by a transfer to the psychiatric ward or, at best, by some punitive measures.

5

example, Italians and Jews; (2) diversities in behavior along generational lines, thus indicating an acceptance of a general model of responding to pain, which is that of the American patient; (3) conflicts between the expectations of the doctor and the actual behavior of the patient who tends to prefer expressive responses to pain.

The next steps taken in the study were a direct outcome of the results obtained during the exploratory phase. Four groups of patients were selected for an intensive study of their responses to pain: patients of Jewish, Italian, Irish, and Old American origin.[2] These groups were chosen for the following reasons:

The Old Americans were selected because, although they are a demographic minority, their behavior patterns are those of the social and cultural majority in this country. They seem to represent the cultural ideal that serves as an acculturation model for the descendants of immigrants who tend to adopt the American way of life. As the preliminary interviews suggested, members of the medical and nursing professions tended to approve this kind of behavior and expected from their patients general conformity with such a mode of behavior at home or in the hospital. Jews and Italians were selected because of the similarity of their behavioral responses, despite the obvious differences in their cultural traditions and folkways. Thus they offered the opportunity for a better understanding of the dynamics involved in the cultural patterning of responses to pain. Patients of Irish origin were selected because, although their behavior was singled out by the physicians as similar to that of the Old American, a number of comments were made that suggested a peculiar attitude toward pain. They tend to neglect painful symptoms and to en-

---

[2] The term *Old American* is used to refer to patients of Anglo-Saxon origin, usually of Protestant creed, whose ancestors have dwelt in the United States more than three generations. The term, although far from being entirely satisfactory, is nevertheless accepted among a number of students of American sociology and seems to be preferable to the terms *Core American* or *Yankee*. Old American denotes the social group that seems to set the cultural model of our society as reflected in its values and structure.

6

dure them for exceptionally long periods of time without seeking medical help.[3]

Where could these four groups of patients be studied in the most economical and the least time-consuming manner? Where could one find sufficient numbers of Irish, Jewish, Italian, and Old American patients suffering from pain assembled in one convenient place? Furthermore, where could one find an age distribution among patients that would make it possible to study them along generational lines? These were some of the practical problems that arose after the objectives of the study were formulated and the ethnic groups to be studied were defined. The solution was a large Veterans Administration hospital in the New York City metropolitan area. This institution, by definition, offered medical care to all people who had served in the armed forces, which can be considered as the most adequate representation of the ethnic composition of the country's male population. Moreover, because every veteran is entitled to hospital treatment, it was safe to assume that the hospital would contain people who had participated in World War I, World War II, and the Korean War—in other words, people between the ages of 20 up to 65 and over, including immigrants, children of immigrants, and even grandchildren of immigrants.

Thus, the selection of a Veterans Administration hospital offered certain basic advantages; however, it also had a number of shortcomings, the most important of which was the limitation of the research and its conclusions to male patients only.[4] Another disadvantage of this hospital was the fact that the majority of its population was of lower and lower-middle economic background, prohibiting an investigation of possible class variations among patients of higher economic and social groups.[5]

[3] Originally it was planned to study patients of Polish origin, but subsequently it became evident that their number in available patient populations was too small for meaningful conclusions.

[4] This limitation was only partly remedied by a few interviews with occasional women patients who had served in the armed forces during World War II as WACs or WAVEs or nurses. Their number was, however, too small to draw any significant conclusions.

[5] Subsequent statistical analysis has shown that we overestimated the importance of a broader socioeconomic spectrum.

7

The research techniques used were those traditionally employed by anthropologists in the field. Because the study was oriented toward sociocultural objectives and, because the conceptual bases for the study were drawn from anthropological theory, it was only logical to use methods proper to this science: participant observation and formal and informal interviews. The hospital being the social and institutional setting where patients perceived and responded to pain, the researcher assumed the role of a participant observer in order to study all the aspects of a patient's life in the hospital that were directly and indirectly related to his responses to pain. These observations were recorded in a diary form for further reference.

Data collected in the process of direct observation were complemented by information secured in intensive interviews, which offered the patient the opportunity to describe freely his attitudes, behavior, or feelings in association with pain experience. Moreover, the interviewee was asked to provide information relative to patterns prevalent in his group as reflected in the experiences of members of his family, friends, and neighbors. In our research on pain the patient assumed the role of a cultural informant and contributed data as to generalized standards of attitudes and behavior according to their social acceptance and expectancy. In addition, the interviews supplied information and insights as to the role of interpersonal relationships, such as husband-wife or parent-children, in situations associated with pain and how they affect, or are affected by, the experience. Not only pain in association with illness was discussed during the interviews, but also pain caused by injuries, accidents, sports, or work. Following the assumption that responses to pain are part of a total pattern, data pertaining to pain relief and associated attitudes toward doctors, medications, surgery, and hospitalization were of primary importance. Furthermore, the interview provided insights in the more general areas of the informant's cultural life, such as family structure, communication patterns, or values with reference to body, work, and time orientation. In other words, although the interview focused on various aspects of the pain experience, it also offered information pertaining to the patient's cultural background, as well as clues to his eth-

Introduction

nic identification and emotional involvement with his group's traditions.

The interview was informal, free, and unstructured, although directed toward the objectives of the study. No questionnaire was used, because the aim of the researcher was to ensure the spontaneous character of the association flow, unhampered by the rigidity of a priori constructed schedules. The interviewer attempted to create an atmosphere of a team situation, in which the interviewee was not a passive subject but an active participant in a research process. This goal was achieved by informing the patient about the objectives of the study and about its possible implications for medical care.

Interviews were taped in preference to hand recording, which is selective and incomplete, and which usually misses a great deal of the emotional tone of the verbal expression. Also, the use of tape allowed for a better concentration on the communication process, which was unimpaired by the interruptions and delays that frequently accompany hand recording.[6]

Data collected in the process of observation and interviewing of patients were further complemented, wherever possible, with specific information provided by doctors, nurses, or members of the family. This comparison was made not only to check the accuracy of the informant but mainly to compare his own report about the experience with the way the same experience was seen through the eyes of other people involved in it, professionally and personally. The collateral information was most illuminating for the investigation of attitudes and feelings about various types of behavior as manifested by different ethnic groups of patients.

[6] The frequently expressed objection to the use of a recording apparatus is that it intimidates the interviewee and thus inhibits his spontaneity. These objections seem to be based on a confusion between speaking into a microphone and using a microphone. The experience has shown that after the initial minutes of recording, the presence of the microphone is completely forgotten by both participants in the interview, and their communication remains unimpaired and entirely satisfactory. The quotations that are abundantly used in the forthcoming chapters are a sufficient argument in favor of the use of a recording machine. Needless to say, the tape recorder was used with the full consent of the patient.

People in Pain

These interviews and observations were made on 242 respondents, among whom 146 were patients of Irish, Jewish, Italian, and Old American origin. The remaining 96 included patients whose ethnic origin was wrongly identified, doctors and specialists from various hospital services, nurses, therapists and other hospital staff members, and, finally, a group of healthy people who provided interesting data on attitudes toward pain when the person was not affected directly by the discomfort of pain and illness.

A major methodological question was the selection of patients according to their pathology. The opinion of doctors, which was based on their clinical experiences, suggested that responses to pain are strongly influenced by the type of disease that causes it. This influence is sensory as well as psychological; some diseases are likely to provoke more actual pain and associated anxieties than others. Thus, they felt, it was advisable to select patients of different ethnic backgrounds with identical diagnoses, thus keeping the pathological factor constant. The view of the anthropologist was somewhat different. Although accepting the significance of the pathological variable, he attributed to the cultural component a far greater importance, which could be substantiated only by comparing the behavior of patients with different diagnoses. To test both hypotheses, the research operations were conducted among two groups of patients: one suffering from an identical illness and the other chosen at random among patients with different diagnoses. The first group included patients from neurological wards with the diagnosis of herniated discs, which is usually associated with severe pains; in the other group were people suffering from headaches, cancer, heart diseases, various disabilities, amputees with phantom pains, and so on. In the first group the pathology variable was kept constant; in the second this variable was disregarded.

The original aim of the project was to develop a *qualitative* study of responsive patterns to pain, that is, to assess the cultural pattern of patients' statements, actions, and feelings as they were expressed in the interviews or observed on the ward, without quantitative consideration. The original methodological assumption was that the accuracy of the final generalizations would be substantiated not by statistical quantifications of specific responses, but by the regularities and qualitative interrelations between items of information obtained in a series of interviews with the patients. Every individual was assumed to be a carrier of his group's cultural traditions and attitudes and therefore capable of offering significant insight into the pattern that should emerge from information obtained from other individuals from his cultural group. Data that at first did not seem consistent with information obtained from other interviews were not viewed as affecting the validity of the conclusion but, on the contrary, as helping to understand better the pattern in terms of the deviation from it. Thus, when some Italians denied emotionality in response to pain, this information did not weaken the generalization about tears as part of the Italian pattern of responses to pain, but indicated that the pattern was undergoing changes in a new social setting in which other cultural forces were at work and acting against the continuation of traditional patterns developed in a different geographical, historical, or social environment.

Of course, this emphasis on the quality, rather than the quantity, of information does not negate the considerable methodological significance of statistical analysis. On the contrary, a proper research design should include, wherever possible, both methods in order to ensure the validity and precision of final findings. When time permits and financial resources are available, it is most advisable to check, with the help of statistical techniques, conclusions derived from a qualitative study offering, in addition to factual information, the "emotional tone" of the cultural phenomenon. The techniques of observation and unstructured interviews can be supplemented by special techniques aimed at the collection of data that could lend themselves to quantifications, controls, and tests of statistical significance.

A step in this direction was also taken in our study. Although it was designed as a qualitative study, the uniformity and consistency of information obtained in the interviews suggested the possibility of quantification of some of the data as an additional research tool and as a numerical illustration of final conclusions.

To obtain series of responses in numbers sufficient for meaningful quantifications, specific items were isolated from the interviews and were integrated into a structured questionnaire, which was administered to an additional group of patients. The data obtained from the interviews and from the questionnaires provided the numerical material that could be handled by statistical methods. The results of these procedures are summarized in Chapter Six.

The results of the qualitative analysis of the data obtained through observation and in the interviews are reported in the subsequent chapters. Their interpretation is based on what people *do* and *say* about their pain experience, as well as on how this experience is seen by members of the patients' social environments. The conclusions are supported and illustrated by the patients' own words, which are quoted verbatim in extensive citations. Instead of speaking *for* the patients, I felt that it would be better to let them speak directly to the reader, thus preserving the authenticity of their attitudes and emotions as reflected in their own words. I have supplied only conceptual comments and explanations in order to cement together all the data into an integrated, patterned whole.

In this connection a question might be raised concerning the universality of the conclusions. Assuming that they are correct in terms of the attitudes and behavior of the interviewed patients in this particular hospital, how can one be sure that they are true for other Italians, Irish, Jews, or Old Americans? The question raised is that of the representativeness of the interviewed group of patients and, consequently, of the universal validity of the study. For some social scientists the validity of the findings is strictly a function of sampling techniques: if it can be shown that the selected groups of patients are statistically representative samples of the corresponding ethnic populations in the country, then the generalizations based on their statements might be considered reliable.

The study cannot offer this type of validation, for no sampling technique was used, either in the selection of the hospital or in its population. The only criteria for selection of patients for the interviews were ethnic origin and the presence of pain. It can be added that the patients were self-selected according to sex, socio-

Introduction

economic status, and military service—they were male veterans of lower and lower-middle class. Accordingly, there was no proof whatsoever regarding their statistical representativeness. They can be considered only as a series of clinical cases; therefore, the reliability of the study is comparable to that of any study based on an extensive case material. Nevertheless, the anthropological field techniques and theory do not necessarily require careful sampling techniques in the selection of informants in order to study cultural manifestations or patterns, because, "Any member of a group, provided that his position within that group is properly specified, is a perfect sample of the group-wide pattern."[7] Every Irish, Italian, or Old American patient represents the culture in which he was brought up; which was transmitted to him by his parents, teachers, and peers; and which he has learned in his native group. As long as his position in his society is identified by information pertaining to sex, social and economic background, education, age, marital status, emotional preferences and values, life history, and of other variables, the data he offers are sufficiently valid to serve as a basis for reconstruction of certain aspects of the general pattern. When Irish informants, old or young, foreign or American-born, teachers or laborers, married or single, mention the habit of drinking and its role in their family or social life, the anthropologist does not feel that he needs a representative sample of the Irish population for the generalization that alcohol plays an important role in Irish culture, not because of the number of Irishmen who say it but because Irishmen say it.

[7] Mead (1953). The question of representativeness and validity of anthropological studies has been for many years the element of discord between anthropologists and sociologists. Dr. Mead's article, from which the above statement is quoted, offers comprehensive discussion of methodological differences between sociologists and anthropologists concerning the validity of their observations.

13

CHAPTER 1

The Cultural Dimensions of Pain

For centuries the discussion of pain and its problems was the prerogative of two groups of students: those concerned with man's body, that is, the physicians, and those who probed his mind and soul, that is, the philosophers and theologians. The first group dealt with pain in the process of healing; the second was concerned with the moral and metaphysical implications of suffering. Although the contribution of the latter is beyond the scope of the present study, the work of medical experts is its starting point. The ultimate goal of this presentation is to add to the discussion of pain initiated by students of the human body the contribution of methods and concepts drawn from the science of man and his culture.

The physician's preoccupation with pain is obvious. It is without question the most frequent and compelling reason why a patient comes to his door. Relief of pain remains one of the major aspects of medical practice, for fear of pain is second only to the fear of death. Out of the physician's need to alleviate this sensation —which has become the symbol of human anguish and sorrow— have emerged the scientific investigations into its nature. Specialists in medical and allied professions have directed their skill and knowledge toward research on pain; physicians, neurologists, physiologists, and psychologists have devised ingenious experiments in order to find answers to such questions as: Is pain an emotional phenomenon or a physiological sensation? Are there specific neural pathways that bring the sensation of pain to the brain, or is the pain a result of intensive stimulation of any sensory nerve? Is it possible to measure its threshold and intensity, or is perception of pain purely subjective and beyond quantitative investigation?

After years of research and experimentation, some physiologists and neurologists came to a conclusion, formulated by James D. Hardy, Harold D. Wolff, and Helen Goodell (1952), that pain is "a specific sensation with its own structural, functional, and perceptual properties." As with other sensations, such a vision, sound, or smell, they concluded that pain had a specific sensory equipment and could be classified according to quantitative and qualitative criteria, depending on where and how it originated. According to this group, pain had a measurable threshold of perception; that is, under normal conditions the same measurable amount of a painful stimulus would evoke a minimum of perceptible pain. This threshold of pain perception was, according to these scientists, identical for all humans regardless of sex, age, or race. It is important to note, however, that although some physiologists have accepted the sensory aspects of this theory, the controversy continues (Sternbach, 1968, pp. 27–43), with a special emphasis on the differences between "experimental" and "pathological" (clinical) pain.

People in Pain

Beecher, who was involved with the study of pain-relieving properties of drugs and had observed a good deal of pain among hospital patients, objected to the use of experimental pain for measurements and generalizations. He considered the pathological pain felt by patients totally different from the pain perceived by trained and instructed subjects in a laboratory setting. According to Beecher (1952), the qualitative difference between experimental and pathological pain was so great that "the study of either can apply only slightly to the other." The main reason for this difference, he felt, was the role of the emotional associations of patients in pain, which are of such magnitude that they overshadow the quantitative aspects of the sensation and make meaningless any laboratory findings.[1]

Beecher's emphasis on emotions associated with pathological pain suggested that the neurophysiological analysis of the sensation seemed to explain only part of the total phenomenon. There is more to pain than a sensation that is perceived and transmitted to the brain. The individual not only perceives pain but also feels it and reacts to it. When Aristotle defined pain as the "antithesis of pleasure," and when Freud discussed the concept of the "pleasure principle" in terms of avoidance of pain, both were mainly concerned with the emotional experiences associated with the sensation. The physiology of sound does not explain the listener's emotional reactions to a violin concerto; neither does the theory of color perception offer much insight into the feelings experienced in front of a painting. Similarly, a purely physiological theory alone cannot bring us closer to the understanding of a patient's state of mind when he calls a physician because of pain in his chest. The scientific classification of sensory qualities of pain into burning, pricking, or aching throws only a faint light on behavior that can vary from Spartan stoicism to hysteria or tears. In fact, Hardy, Wolff, and Goodell, in analyzing the nature of pain, were quite aware of the role of emotion in association with the sensation of pain. In view of the complexity of the phenomenon, they suggested

---

[1] Sternbach (1968) was able to demonstrate that by introducing the element of anxiety in the experimental situation, the qualitative aspects of pain perception were significantly altered.

16

The Cultural Dimensions of Pain

the concept of pain experience, of which "the pain sensation is but a part . . . and may not even be the major feature" (Hardy et al., 1952, p. 239). The pain experience of an individual includes both the sensation and his reaction to it—what he "feels, thinks, or does about it" (Wolff and Wolf, 1951, p. 11)—in other words, his emotions and behavior when in pain. In a laboratory setting an attempt can be made to observe and investigate pain as a "pure" sensation. In everyday life, however, pain is a total experience encompassing sensory and reactive patterning, which are interdependent and inseparable.

One set of reactions to pain stems from the biological heritage of man. Such reactions are often described as "instinctive" because of their reflex nature, independent of human consciousness; thus, with other reflex activities, they belong to human anatomy and physiology. Painful stimulations can provoke such physiological manifestations as changes in respiration, perspiration, or circulation of blood; blushing; changes in heartbeat; or a sudden muscular contraction. Like other reflexes, these reactions can be provoked experimentally, without involving the will or mind. Successful attempts have been made to determine the relationship of such physiological reactions to the intensity of stimulation, and to analyze their nature and changes under the influence of various environmental agents or among different individuals. It has been found, for instance, that, unlike the threshold of pain, reactions to the sensation are highly variable with age and sex. These studies lie within the province of the physiologists and neurologists; their results are as yet primarily of academic interest to the clinician attempting to evaluate the severity of his patient's pain. As long as a physician must depend on a patient's subjective description of his suffering—and, so far, it is still his chief source of information—he is mainly concerned with reactions to pain different from those provoked in a laboratory.

In evaluating a patient's complaints, the practitioner is confronted less with the actual sensation of pain than with its expression in the patient's verbal presentation. Reflex reactions such as wincing, twitching of muscles, or changes in color or skin are helpful in determining the presence of pain and, to a certain extent, its severity; but the specific qualities of the sensation—such as its actual intensity, location, or duration—are greatly obscured by the patient's emotions and anxieties, which are reflected in his behavior during the examination or in his selection of words used to describe the pain. When a patient speaks of "excruciating" or "intolerable" pain, he is not reproducing his objective sensory experience, but is describing his subjective feelings in response to it. In other words, the patient's verbal report is but one aspect of his actual reactions to pain—reactions that are quite different from those defined as involuntary reflexes. These reactive patterns, which are expressed in the patient's description of his experience, are part of his cognition and can frequently be controlled by will and reason. They are influenced by factors that are beyond the traditional interests of medicine and neurophysiology, although members of these professions may contribute pertinent observations and insights, derived from years of experience and practice, into their nature (Hardy et al., 1952, p. 297). In fact, these patterns stem from the patient's total life experience as an individual and as a member of society; accordingly, their analysis requires the use of concepts and methods drawn from sciences concerned with a broader study of man's attitudes and behavior. For convenience, in order to distinguish such cognitive reactions from those identified as involuntary reflexes and studied in the laboratory of the neurophysiologist, we will refer to them as "responses" to pain, rather than as "reactions."[2] These responsive patterns are manifested on emotional and behavioral levels, where behavior is frequently the manifestation of feelings and attitudes stimulated by the presence of pain. Feelings of anxiety, depression, or anger, which are observed daily among patients at home or in the hospital, are expressed in actions, gestures, sounds, and words that are directly related to the individual's perceptions of discomfort and misery.

The direct observation of individuals in pain suggests the arrangement of behavioral responses in five general groups: (1)

---

[2] A comparable distinction between *response* and *reaction* has been made by Dubos (1965, p. xviii).

motor responses (twisting, wriggling, movement of the body or its parts, walking, jumping, clenching teeth); (2) vocal responses (moaning, groaning, crying, screaming); (3) verbal responses (complaining, cursing, talking about pain, asking for help); (4) social responses (withdrawal from people, changes in communication patterns, changes in social manners or personal appearance); (5) the absence of manifest behavior (hiding of pain or suppressing external signs of pain). Needless to say, an individual's behavior in pain may be a combination of any of these types of responses. Frequently, the type of response manifested by a person in pain depends on specific social situations; for instance, the presence or absence of manifest behavior may depend on whether the person is at home or in the hospital, alone or with his friends.

Physicians who deal with people in pain, and who are daily confronted with the puzzling problem of the wide range of individual responses, frequently attribute differences in patients' behavior to three main causes: (1) the sensory attributes of pain, such as intensity, duration, or location; (2) the nature of the disease; and (3) individual psychological factors. Unquestionably these observations are quite valid. The severity of pain may influence the responsive patterns; certain pathological conditions may stimulate greater anxieties and worries; and some personalities, such as hypochondriacs, display behavior quite different from that of normal patients. However, these explanations are not fully satisfactory. In the first place, because there are no objective criteria for the severity of pain, it is difficult to evaluate its relation to the response. Moreover, research done in this area seems to show that there is no direct relationship between the intensity of the sensation and the response to it (Hardy et al., 1952, pp. 239, 246). With regard to the pathology of pain, it is common knowledge that the same painful disease can provoke quite different responses among different individuals, suggesting that there is only a limited direct relationship between the type of disease and the patient's emotions. Confronted with these objections, physicians frequently reduce all differences in responsive patterns of their patients to differences in their personalities, leaving the exploration of this aspect of the pain experience to psychology. The contribution of psychology to the understanding of the significance of the personality factor in pain experience has been of major importance (Engel, 1959, 1961; Petrie, 1960); however, referring the solution of the problem to individual psychology alone does not seem to be the final answer.

A number of students of pain phenomena have observed uniformities in response to pain among individuals who were members of identifiable groups characterized by certain common traits. Thus, Libman found that "prizefighters, Negroes, and American Indians, as groups, failed to react to noxious stimuli of intensity great enough to induce reaction of discomfort in the average white city dweller" (Wolff and Wolf, 1951, p. 15). Chapman (1944) has also observed differences in reaction to pain among different ethnic groups: "For a comparison of ethnic groups a series of 18 Negroes and a corresponding number of so-called Northern Europeans of the same age and sex were studied . . . Not only did the Negro perceive pain on a lower level, but he also reacted relatively nearer his pain perception level than did the Northern European . . . The group of Italians and individuals of Russian-Jewish extraction tested had both pain perception and pain reaction values which corresponded more nearly to those of the Negro."[3] Ploss, one of the first students of sex in society, made a number of observations about labor pains expressed by French, German, Jewish, and Indian women (1876, Vol. 2, p. 625).

Explorers and travelers frequently admired the absence of usual responses to pain among members of primitive societies, and the behavior of citizens of ancient Sparta has remained an example of stoicism and impassivity in pain.

All these observations seem to emphasize the similarities in behavior among members of the same ethnic groups. People respond to their pain not only as individuals, but also as Italians, Jews, Negroes, or Nordics. The common denominator of these individuals is their ethnicity, that is, their national origin and com-

---

[3] Hardy et al. have expressed their doubts as to differences in the levels of perception (1952, p. 119); however, they did not question the observation regarding differences in reactions to pain.

mon cultural and social heritage. Thus the students of pain have introduced in their observations another dimension, the sociocultural one, which is quite distinct in its dynamics from the physiological and the psychological interpretations of the pain experience. The physiology of pain acquires cultural and social attributes, and its analysis calls for investigation, not only in laboratories and clinics, but also in the complex maze of society.

The introduction into pain research of variables of a sociocultural nature is not totally unexpected. The physiology of pain is but a part of the general physiology of human life, and the interdependence between human physiology and culture is apparent in every aspect of the process of living. What is living if not, to a great extent, a series of adaptive responses to the stimuli of hunger, sex, or changes in temperature? Directly or indirectly, most of what a man feels or does can be traced to the need to satisfy these basic needs. In this respect man is part of the rest of the animal world. Like other animals, man eats to satisfy his hunger, seeks shelter when he is cold, and copulates in response to the sex impulse. The same physiological forces that govern the life of animals rule the life of man; people and animals differ only as to their particular ways of responding to the calls of life. The difference lies in the specific forms of eating, mating, or building shelters.

Despite the recent advances in ethological studies, much about the dynamics of animal behavior in response to physiological stimuli remains unknown, and our ignorance is hidden behind the convenient term of "instinctive" behavior. On the other hand, relatively more is known about human behavior, and a large part of what is known can be explained in terms of man's society and culture.

There are many definitions of culture, and all of them are probably true to the extent that they emphasize one or another of its aspects (Kroeber and Kluckhohn, 1964). One definition, offered by Kluckhohn (1944), is especially pertinent to this discussion: "By 'culture,' anthropology means the total way of life of a people, the social legacy the individual acquires from his group." Moreover, "Every culture is designed to perpetuate the group and its solidarity, to meet the demands of individuals for an orderly way of life and for satisfaction of biological needs."

Despite the power of the physiological stimulus, the human response is seldom spontaneous and direct. Under normal conditions people do not eat whenever they feel pangs of hunger; neither do they mate whenever they experience the impact of the sexual desire. Whatever the intensity of the impulse, man tends to follow definite norms that regulate patterns of food consumption or mating habits in his society. These norms not only prescribe the appropriate time, place, or way of eating or mating, but they also contain rules for abstinence from responding to the call of the impulse. Certain foods cannot be eaten even under the threat of starvation (for example, pork among Jews or Moslems), and even the most powerful sexual attraction cannot excuse an incestuous relationship. Malinowski (1944), in one of his essays devoted to the functional interpretation of culture, said: "Not even the simplest need, nor yet the physiological function most independent of environmental influences, can be regarded as completely unaffected by culture . . . there is no human activity which we could regard as purely physiological that is 'natural' or untutored."[4] The "cultured" nature of physiological activities implies that they have to be learned, not only on the level of reflex conditioning, but also on the level of interpersonal relationships through word and example. Children in the process of growing up in a society learn from their elders what, where, and when they should eat; whom and how they should marry; and what type of clothing they should wear for protection from cold and rainy weather. In this process of learning the rules of "their" way of life, they obtain from parents, teachers, and peers specific information as to the manner of responding to physiological impulses, as well as pertinent value judgments. They are taught which type of response is good and which is bad; what is right and what is wrong. Furthermore, together with these value judgments, they also acquire the knowledge of social sanctions for incorrect behavior. The learning of cultural norms of responding

[4] A most stimulating discussion of the relationship between physiology and culture was offered by Frank (1948).

22

to physiological needs implies learning of value judgments associated with the principles of reward and punishment. These judgments, and anticipation of approval or disapproval with its sanctions, color every aspect of human behavior; they become part of the individual's code of manners and morals; and they shape his attitudes toward his own and other people's behavior. In consequence, people develop not only behavioral, but also attitudinal, response patterns to physiological stimuli that are part of the biological process of life.

Very early in his life the child discovers the correct way to control the pressures of his bladder and colon. He soon knows the punishment for an incorrect response to them and, along with other playmates and adults, mocks the unfortunate youngster who happens to have an "accident."

The satisfaction of physiological needs fulfills the basic biological function of survival—individual or group. An animal responds to hunger in order not to die of starvation; he seeks shelter in order not to freeze to death; by mating he preserves his species. So does man. However, in human societies the response to the physiology of life acquires an additional significance. People eat not only to live but also to celebrate religious or social events; they marry not only to produce children, but also to acquire an adult status in society; they build a house not only for protection, but also for financial prestige. In other words, in man's society, biological processes vital for his survival acquire a social and cultural significance. Intake of food, sexual intercourse, and shelter seeking— all universal physiological phenomena—become institutions regulated by cultural and social norms, thus fulfilling not only biological but also social and cultural functions. Metabolic changes and endocrinal activities in human organisms may stimulate hunger or sexual desire, but society and culture dictate to man the food he may eat, the social setting and circumstances for eating, and the adequate partner for mating. At times the impact of this demand can be as strong as that of a biological need, or even stronger. For social reasons man will eat even when he is not hungry or marry even when he is physically impotent. On the other hand, he will fast or submit himself to freezing weather in order to observe a religious ritual, therefore responding to a cultural norm that may be contrary to the biological impulse. Thus every human response to a physiological stimulus is to be examined as a whole phenomenon, in its biological *and* sociocultural context. This comprehension of biological and cultural significance is essential for the understanding of those aspects of human experience that remain puzzling if viewed only within the physiological frame of reference. And this principle, which is true for the study of hunger or sex, holds true also for the study of pain.

The biological importance of pain seems to be obvious. Its role in the preservation of life has been emphasized in many scientific studies.[5] Its primary function is to warn the organism against dangers threatening its integrity. Painful agents of a mechanical, chemical, thermal, or electrical nature, such as sharp objects, poison, fire, or shock—the "noxious stimuli," as the physiologist calls them—carry a potential danger of destruction. Their contact with the pain nerves produces the sensation of pain, which provokes a state of alarm. This state of alarm is manifested in protective activities of reflex nature, so-called flight-or-fight reactions, which are directed toward avoidance of the course of pain and thus tend to preserve the body from injury. The organism either tries to withdraw from the noxious stimulus (for example, by contraction of muscles) if it is exterior to the body, or expel it (by coughing or vomiting) if the painful agent has penetrated the digestive or respiratory system. If withdrawal or expulsion is impossible, the organism mobilizes all its resources to fight the danger and to counteract its implications. On a cognitive level the sensation provokes a state of anxiety, which stimulates the need to take steps to protect life from the threatening agent. The theory of the life-preserving function of pain seems to be supported by laboratory findings that the perception of pain (its threshold) begins on the level of tissue damage (Hardy et al., 1952, p. 244). The sensation of pain does not indicate a potential danger, but rather the actual begin-

[5] Some clinicians who have observed the harmful effects of pain upon patients doubt the validity of this observation (Leriche, 1939).

ning of destruction. Thus on the biological level the function of pain is to mobilize automatic and cognitive activities directed toward the defense of the organism from noxious agents that may present a threat to the survival of the individual.[6]

The biological significance of this sensation is so great that the state of alarm and anxiety, with the associative protective reactions, can be provoked not only in direct contact with the noxious stimulus; the flight-or-fight reactions can be manifested by the organism even when the actual sensation of pain is absent. In such cases the function of the noxious stimulus is fulfilled by the mere presence of objects associated with pain—the so-called symbols of pain. Any sensory perception (sight, smell, or hearing) of the pain symbol may have the same effect as perception of pain and is sufficient to suggest danger and prepare the organism for protective activities. One withdraws his hand from the fire when he touches a flame, and he also avoids all possible contact with burning objects. Furthermore, symbols of pain are not necessarily mere pain carriers. Social situations or even words can serve to arouse alarm and anxiety reactions, for example, in a dark alley or during a quarrel.[7]

[6] Sternbach (1968, p. 9) questions the "simple tissue-damaging definition of pain stimuli, which implies an adaptational, protective survival model" in view of "false alarm" and damage without pain.

[7] The fact that pain may affect the emotional state to such an extent that even a slight suggestion of it might provoke anxiety manifestations is possibly because pain, more than any other sensation, is associated with fear of death. Although hunger and thirst may be also linked with the possibility of death, this relationship seems to be less direct. There are no alarm or anxiety responses to symbols of starvation similar to those manifested in the presence of symbols of pain. Fear of pain is comparable to the fear of death, because the immediate and direct significance of both phenomena for the survival of the individual are very similar. However, it is important to note that *anxiety* responses are manifested only when there is a cognitive interpretation of the significance of the sensation as message of death and destruction. When pain is perceived on a level that precludes a cognitive interpretation—for instance, when the cortical functions of the brain are artificially interrupted—anxiety responses are absent. This has been observed, for instance, in patients who have undergone lobotomy. These patients frequently report that they feel pain, but it does not bother them (Freeman and Watts, 1950). As a result of an operation that had caused the impairment of the

People in Pain

The response to symbols of pain is learned from the collective experience accumulated in the traditions of the human race: a man will avoid the blade of a knife because somewhere, sometime, a member of the human family was injured by it, and this information was passed on from generation to generation, from man to man, from mother to child. We do not have to learn from individual experience the effects of the atom bomb in order to take protective measures; the fate of Hiroshima will forever remain in the collective memory of the human race. The cultural traditions of human societies eliminate the need for individual experience as the only source of knowledge, and many of these traditions refer to the symbols of pain.

The fact that cultural definitions of symbols of pain can be transmitted to members of the society along with other cultural information has a considerable significance for human survival. An animal deprived of its ability to perceive pain will perish sooner or later because of the inability to identify the agents of danger in its environment. On the other hand, a man whose sensory equipment for pain perception is impaired can adjust himself to life merely by following the collective social experience. Medical literature is rich in examples of excellent adaptation to life made by

---

anxiety-provoking mechanism, pain lost its biological significance on the cognitive level. For this very reason, lobotomy has been suggested for relief of intractable pain.

The close relationship between pain on the one hand and life and death on the other is also apparent in the fact that in certain situations pain whose primary function is to provoke apprehension also serves the function of an anxiety-allaying device. Thus, for instance, many patients have expressed their satisfaction with the fact that they feel pain in the injured parts of their body because it gave them the assurance that the injured leg or arm was not dead. On the contrary, they were more worried about numbness and absence of the sensation than about the possible discomfort caused by pain. Along these lines one could interpret certain aspects of phantom pain manifested by amputees and some paraplegics as a denial of death of their limbs (Sternbach, 1968).

Thus pain is also a symbol of living. As long as one suffers, he is still alive, for suffering is an attribute of life and reality. "Pinching" is the antithesis of sleep and death. Pain, therefore, is necessary for self-awareness, which is a purely human characteristic. To paraphrase the famous saying: I suffer, therefore I exist—*Dolo ergo sum.*

individuals with congenital inability to perceive pain (for example, Kunkle and Chapman, 1943).[8]

The passing on of information pertaining to symbols of pain is part of the social process of transmission of cultural traditions and, accordingly, is associated with value judgments and attitudes. The individual obtains information as to the potential dangers associated with an object, as well as criteria that allow him to judge situations and circumstances under which the same object may lose its threatening nature and might even become beneficial. Thus man is able to discriminate between an incendiary flame bringing destruction and death and a fire bringing warmth and comfort; he learns to avoid a club but to use a stick as one of his first agricultural implements. Thus symbols of pain may become symbols of comfort, according to the functions man assigns to them in the process of cultural development. Moreover, pain itself, a sensation that seems to be abhorred by all living creatures who are able to show their reactions by sound or motion, is evaluated by man, in terms of "good" or "bad," according to its function as defined by human culture. A dagger is to be avoided because its purpose is to cause injury and death; a bread knife is good because it is useful to man; a lancet is accepted, despite its pain-carrying quality, be-

[8] However, the loss of sensitivity to pain among people who previously have been able to perceive it frequently has harmful consequences. Thus serious burns and bone fractures have been observed among paraplegics people who have partially lost their sensory abilities as a result of a spinal injury. Unable to feel pain caused by a burning cigarette or heavy pressure on their legs, they may suffer serious damage to their skin tissues or bone structure. Some of them would not notice the injury for several days and would consult the physician only after having noticed visually the infection or inflammation caused by the neglected wound.

Interestingly enough, similar observations have been reported among schizophrenics in the stage of acute catatonia. However, here the mechanism is reversed. Although the sensory equipment does not seem to be impaired at all, and the patient is able to perceive pain, he does not respond to the noxious stimulus with the usual reactions of withdrawal. Like the lobotomized patients, he may feel pain, but it does not seem to bother him; therefore he suffers burns or other injuries. This phenomenon is another illustration of the relationship between pain, life, and reality. In the process of withdrawal from reality, the patient ignores also its symbols, one of which is pain.

cause the pain it brings is a necessary part of medical treatment. Pain inflicted by an injection needle is good and acceptable; pain caused by an accidental prick of a sewing needle is bad because it is seen only as an injury. The cultural significance attributed to pain, symbols of pain, and situations associated with pain makes them acceptable or avoidable regardless of the actual intensity of the sensation.

The acceptance of pain does not mean that the feeling quality of the sensation has changed. The sensation is always unpleasant (although in some cases one may "enjoy" even its unpleasantness, such as in childbirth or in masochistic experiences), but the displeasure of pain is tolerated when cultural tradition calls for its acceptance. Thus the original cognitive response to the sensory phenomenon is modified by the cultural meaning attributed to it. Pain is no more just "pain," an objective, physiological sensation; it acquires cultural properties that make for its acceptance or nonacceptance and for its avoidance or tolerance.

Discrimination between acceptable and nonacceptable pain, pain symbols, and pain situations, according to their cultural meaning, may bring about a phenomenon that plays an important role in the total pain experience and that can be traced to the conflict between the animal heritage of man and his human legacy—his culture. It is the conflict between the automatic reflex reactions to the sensation, which are inherited by man in the process of his biological evolution, and the cognitive responses learned in the process of cultural development. The automatic reflex of withdrawal from the jab of a needle will be present regardless of whether the needle is used for harmful or therapeutic purposes; but the cultural association in man's mind will determine whether the reflex reaction will be freely manifested or voluntarily suppressed. Whether a man controls or follows his reflexes depends on his ability to evaluate the significance of the stimulus in terms of his cultural criteria and attitudes. The behavior of a patient in a dental chair or in a medical laboratory is an illustration of the consequences of this conflict. On the one hand, the patient tends to display reflex signs of alarm and anxiety, such as a tendency to withdraw, changes in heartbeat, or excessive perspiration; on the other hand, he tolerates the dental treatment or the penetration of the hypodermic needle.[9]

A major element in the conflict between reflex tendencies and responses, which is influenced by the attitudes of acceptance or nonacceptance of pain, is man's preparedness for the experience. In other words, does the individual expect pain under given circumstances or not? Certain life situations are always associated with pain: childbirth, operations, war, or specific athletic activities. People confronted with these situations are rationally prepared for their painful implications. Those pains are frequently considered as normal or natural. Women expect pain in labor, and prizefighters expect it in the ring. The anticipation of pain allows man to prepare himself to respond to it in accordance with his attitudes of acceptance or nonacceptance. When a dentist tells his patient that "it will hurt now," the patient who accepts pain associated with dental treatment will brace himself and grab the arms of the chair, thus getting ready to suppress the tendencies to withdraw his head or push away the dentist's instrument. On the contrary, when pain is perceived suddenly and unexpectedly, and when its impact is not anticipated, chances are that the individual's behavior will be characterized by uninhibited manifestations of alarm and anxiety, with all their behavioral concomitants. Here again, the cultural traditions define situations in which one should or should not expect pain. One anticipates pain during a football match but hardly in a chess game; soldiers expect pain on the battlefield but not in the training camp.[10] People working in industries expect painful

---

[9] One might speculate that fainting spells during injections or in the dental chair can be attributed to the inability of the individual to solve the conflict between the reflex reactions and the cognitive responses. The patient responds to the difficulty of the situation by withdrawing his consciousness from the struggle to solve the conflict.

[10] The investigation of pain in a laboratory situation among trained and instructed subjects is possible partly because of their anticipation of pain. The situation of pain is culturally defined as a research setting without harmful effects for the subject. This definition is transmitted to the subject as part of the training, and he can prepare himself to face the test without the usual emotional responses and is able to control his reflex reactions to the noxious stimulus—the dolorimeter and its painful effects.

accidents and injuries in the process of work; this expectancy not only does not stop them from working, but also allows them not to pay too much attention to pain associated with the injuries. These are occupational hazards, and a worker is not supposed to be over-concerned with pain and, certainly, is not expected to get too vocal in case of an accident. Similarly, in everyday life people are expected to experience a certain amount of aches and pains: tooth-aches, headaches, bellyaches, aching muscles, and so on. In many societies such pains are considered normal. In other words, they are seen as a part of living, without grave implications for the survival of the individual, because the cultural traditions have suppressed the alarm-provoking element of these painful sensations. On the other hand, if a certain anticipated pain is associated with harmful consequences, it may elicit a totally different pattern of behavior. For instance, if in a given society pain in the left side of the chest is associated with heart trouble and is viewed as a possible indication of death, it might be appropriate not only to release all the reflex reactions but even to amplify them by introducing additional, cul-turally accepted manifestations, such as complaints, moaning, or even tears. In such a situation the actual intensity of the sensation is of little significance in determining the reactive patterns. The meaning attributed to the pain in terms of anticipated conse-quences, and the norms of correct behavior in such situations, will determine the conduct of the patient.

The fact that pain is expected does not necessarily mean that it is automatically accepted. In the United States, labor pains are expected but not accepted. Therefore a number of clinical measures are taken to minimize the painful sensation. In other countries, labor pains are both expected and accepted.[11] If "pain expectancy" can be defined as the anticipation of pain in associa-tion with a specific physical, social, or cultural situation, "pain ac-

---

[11] "Birth is 'natural,' no drugs being given, and this is the procedure also in Drente and generally throughout The Netherlands. At present, how-ever, there is considerable controversy going on between the Leiden school, which advocates the use of drugs, and Utrecht, which opposes such use" (Keur and Keur, 1955).

ceptance" is the willingness to tolerate this sensation. Both attitudes will have their influence on the tendency to inhibit or to amplify the reflex reactions by emotional and behavioral responses. By extension, the same attitudes will influence the reactions and responses with regard to the pain symbols.

So far the role of cultural traditions with reference to the biological significance of pain and its symbols has been discussed in terms of the human race, without taking into consideration the cultural diversity among men. The subject of the discussion was the interrelation between man, culture, and pain experience. However, the family of man is not homogeneous; neither is human culture. People differ not only as persons, but also as individuals belonging to racial, ethnic, and cultural systems. They are divided in countless societies and groups, and each of them has its own culture—customs, traditions, habits, and ethical and moral codes. What is acceptable in one group may be rejected in another. What is considered good by a Negro in central Africa is bad for an inhabitant of Harlem. Headhunting is a legitimate part of the native culture of Borneo, but it is severely punished by the Dutch administration of the island. The Jewish ritual of circumcision was considered abominable by ancient Romans, but it is accepted as a hygienic operation in contemporary American culture. War is seen as a necessary evil by Western societies that are unable to solve their conflicts peacefully, but it is rejected by the Eskimos, for whom laughter, not lethal weapons, is considered the most efficient means to defeat an enemy. Each human group has its own moral and ethical criteria, which are part of its cultural legacy. They are part of its religious system, its social organization, or its economy. They might be absolute and universal in terms of the society that accepts them, but their nature is relative and even parochial when seen in the light of the diversity of human groups and cultures.

Cultural relativity, which allows for the acceptance of a pattern of behavior in one group and its rejection in another, is also expressed in attitudes toward pain. The only universal feeling about pain is that no normal human likes it. This feeling of dislike is universal because it is part of the biological heritage of the en-

31

tire human race, like the feelings of hunger or sex, which are common to all men. Everyone, regardless of his race or culture, will tend to manifest similar reflex reactions to a painful stimulus. However, human societies differ greatly in their attitudes of expectancy and acceptance of a particular pain experience or of its symbol. The first American Indians who met the white man did not run away from their guns, because they did not associate them with pain. Later, although anticipating their destructive power, they learned to face them with admirable impassivity. Pain inflicted by an injection needle is expected and usually accepted in Western cultures, but members of primitive tribes will resist inoculation because they are not familiar with its therapeutic function. Tortures that are part of initiation rites are accepted by members of Indian societies because they lead to social status and prestige, but they are rejected by Western societies as barbaric and sadistic. The pain-accepting behavior of the Christian martyrs was never understood by the citizens of Rome, just as the Christians could not accept the self-mutilations of the worshipers of the god Attis.

Furthermore, cultural traditions dictate to members of a given society not only whether they should expect and tolerate pain in a given situation, but also the correct conduct during the pain experience or when faced with the symbols of pain. These traditions contain rules and norms for appropriate behavior in the process of suffering, and the society will expect the individual to conform to these precepts. These rules may vary according to age, sex, status, or any other social criterion. Thus behavior that is appropriate for women or children may be unbecoming of men. According to contemporary norms, soldiers should not cry, but the Greek heroes of the Trojan War shed tears without shame or guilt. Incorrect behavior in pain, like any other deviation from the social norm, meets with disapproval and even with specific sanctions. If pain tolerance is expected from a male, his inability to control his emotions or reactions is qualified as "sissy," feminine, or even cowardly.

The norms for behavior in pain are directly related to the conflict between the reflex reactions and responses. Should one inhibit the instinctive reactions, or is it better not to interfere with the natural tendencies of the body? Should one control the manifestations of the flight-or-fight pattern, or should he amplify them consciously? The answers to these questions are contained in every culture system. Every member of the society is expected to live up to the standards set by his culture. Frequently his inability to comply is penalized not only by his fellow members, but also by his own feelings of shame and guilt for not being able to behave "like a man," "like a trooper," or "like an adult."

Along the same lines, the mores and customs of peoples define for different classes of individuals in the society general standards for appropriate behavior in pain. In addition, they set specific rules according to the situation in which pain is experienced and according to its cause. American Indians were supposed to be able "to take" any kind of pain, whereas in many primitive tribes men are expected to tolerate ritual pain silently but are allowed to groan and moan when their pain is caused by illness. Occasional pain exclamations, which are expected in a hospital, are certainly out of place during a football game, although the latter pain may be more intense. The culture of a group of people defines for its members each type of correct behavior, whether in religious ritual, in courtship, or in pain. A well-trained individual knows the answers to the very brief formula: who does what, where, when, and how.[12]

People usually tend to comply with cultural patterns of conduct. One of the significant aspects of growing up in a society is the process of internalization of social and cultural values by the child. Daily, on countless occasions, the parents pass on to their children moral precepts, rules of correct behavior, and good man-

---

[12] The ability to respond correctly to pain according to cultural standards has nothing to do with sensitivity to pain; it is only a matter of tolerance. The fact that a prizefighter takes pain better than another member of the society does not mean that his pain threshold is higher; it only means that his expected and actual tolerance of pain is greater than the next fellow's. Sensitivity and tolerance are frequently confused, especially by some doctors who speak of higher or lower threshold of pain among different groups of patients. The sensitivity to pain among all patients is probably more or less the same, but the absence or presence of certain manifest reactions to pain is an indication of tolerance, which usually results from the norms of correct behavior in the social group to which the patient belongs.

ners. They do so by word and by example, supporting their instructions with appropriate manipulation of various expressions of their approval and disapproval and rewarding their offspring for doing things the right way and punishing them for doing them wrong. Finally these principles and standards penetrate so deeply into the child's consciousness that they become his "second nature," and the tendency to follow the parental teachings acquires an almost automatic character. Moreover, these patterns are reinforced in the later years of life in the process of interaction with other members of the society who, having received similar training, exercise a strong influence in the same direction. Various cultural institutions—religious, social, legal, or economic—provide a number of direct and indirect media of pressure for preventing the individual from deflection from the social and cultural norms. Probably the most powerful pressure is accomplished by public opinion and by self. Most likely, such thoughts as "What will people say?" and "How will I feel if . . . ?," by provoking feelings of shame and guilt, have kept more people from transgression than the fear of hell or jail.

Nevertheless, despite all parental, social, and personal forces, the absolute and complete compliance with The Way by every individual in the society is an ideal that is hardly ever attained. In their everyday activities people *tend* to conform to the ideal rules and codes set up by parents, teachers, or priests, but more than once they deviate and commit transgressions, sins, and crimes. The range of these deviations is very wide because of the number of cultural rules covering every possible phase of human life, and they may vary from the wrong use of a knife during a meal to its wrong use in interpersonal relationships. The sanctions vary accordingly: in one case the consequence may be a dirty look or a slap; in another, capital punishment. Some deviations are considered normal —for a child, a woman, a senile man, or even for everybody. Other deviations are crimes, depending on how much they threaten the order and welfare of the society. These diversions may vary from an occasional transgression to a consistent deviant pattern of life that is expressed in many, if not all, aspects of the individual's activities. Every society has its deviants, who may be called non-conformists, queers, or criminals. Some of them are tolerated within the society; others are isolated or exiled, again according to the basic criterion of the welfare of the group. *Salus populi suprema lex* ("The welfare of the people is the ultimate law") was the basic principle of the Roman law, and this principle is true for every human group, whether it is so articulated or not. Deviation from correct patterns of behavior in pain are treated similarly. People may mock someone who cries from pain in a society in which tolerance of pain is highly valued, and some government may severely punish a soldier's inability to resist tortures inflicted in order to extract important military information.

The reasons for human deviance from the ideal pattern are probably the same as those responsible for the existence of human individualities, which are seldom alike. They are attributable to constitutional, genetic, mental, or environmental factors. Thus, for instance, the same family structure that molds a child into solid cultural forms may contain elements that produce the opposite result, because of specific emotional tensions within the family. One of the patients interviewed in the process of our study displayed attitudes and behavior in pain different from those of other members of his group. The interview revealed that he felt such hostility toward his older brother that he decided "to do everything differently"; since this brother did behave according to group standards, the interviewed patient assumed a totally different attitude. In most cases, however, the reasons for individual deviance are so deeply seated that only a profound and intensive psychological analysis might help understand its dynamics. Yet, certain bases for nonconformity can be traced to tensions and conflicts inherent to the very nature of the cultural development of human society. Cultures are not static. Human ways and customs are constantly changing, and from generation to generation old patterns of life are being altered and new ones introduced. Fainting spells were the privilege of women fifty years ago; now their marital or parental difficulties are expressed in psychosomatic headaches or allergies, and the analyst's telephone number has replaced the vial of smelling salts. A

generation or two ago a child was to be "seen and not heard"; today the emphasis is on "free expression." One of the characteristic
traits of cultural change is that individuals who have introduced
or adopted new ways and forms are frequently considered to be
deviants and nonconformists. The first women who claimed the
right to vote were deviants, and so were the first Romans who accepted the Gospel; now women's voting is as normal as that of
men, and Rome is the capital of Christianity.

The changes in cultural patterns do not occur only as a
result of processes intrinsic to the culture itself, such as technologi-
cal, political, or social developments. In many instances they are
results of the meeting of different cultures in the process of interactions of human societies. Contact between cultures is a universal
phenomenon in man's history, and probably it is as old as the
human race. In trade or in war, in conquest or in immigration,
peoples of different cultures get to know one another; learn their
respective customs, mores, and folkways; and frequently incorpo-
rate them into their own, traditional ways of life. Manus children
in New Guinea today play American baseball, which has its indirect origin in the ritualistic ball games of North American Indians.
The presence of American soldiers in New Guinea during World
War II has significantly altered the ways of the life of the natives
of New Guinea in a short period of twenty years, as witnessed by
Mead (1956) during her field trips to that island. In the process
of cultural contact, some individuals of one society may be eager
to accept alien ways, against the conservative feelings of the majority, who will attempt to preserve their own pattern intact. In the
eyes of the conservative group the reformer is frequently seen as
deviant. In the same vein, societies that include a large proportion
of settlers from other ethnic and cultural groups view the behavior
of newcomers as deviant from the patterns of the majority, whereas
members of minority groups consider as deviants those individuals
who for various reasons adopt the majority's attitudes and behavior. In czarist Russia the comportment of German colonists was a
continual source of jokes; the Orthodox Jewish minority in Wil-

liamsburg consider their Americanized brothers traitors to their cultural tradition.

At times the deviance from the original pattern is only superficial and is manifested only on the behavioral level, while the individual who has adopted the new patterns is emotionally still strongly attached to the old values and standards. This situation is especially frequent when the group as a whole tends to be assimilated by the host culture and tends to adjust to the patterns of the majority. As will be shown, a number of patients who were born in the United States of immigrant parents manifested a behavior similar to that of other American patients, although at the same time they expressed attitudes toward pain or illness that were analogous to the attitudes of immigrants. Frequently, deviations from old, national cultural patterns are associated with strong feelings of guilt, which, at times, may be expressed indirectly in manifestations of defensiveness and hostility toward the native group and its values. Nevertheless, deviance from the accepted patterns is a phenomenon inseparable from the cultural life of a society.

The differences in behavioral and attitudinal patterns that are observable among certain individuals are at times due also to the fact that the societies to which they belong are complex and diversified. Frequently they are composed of many occupational, educational, economic, and other groups. Within the general cultural framework, these groups may have their own subculture characterized by their own code of behavior and attitudes. Thus, for instance, members of the upper class may have manners and habits different from those of the lower class, although both classes belong to the same ethnic group. Professors may have customs different from workers, and people who live in the North may have customs that are laughed at in the South. It is a common observation among doctors that upper-class patients behave differently in illness from lower-class patients, who are usually less educated and lack a certain medical sophistication. All these factors, individual as well as collective, psychological as well as cultural and social, contribute to the phenomenon of variance from the ideal pattern of behavior in people's responses to pain and other biophysiological phenomena.

So far the discussion of the cultural and social influences on people's behavior in pain has been related to its biological function of the preservation of life. However, the observation was made earlier that pain, like any other manifestation in life, acquires also an independent sociocultural prominence in the life of the society. Although this second function loses its direct relationship with processes of a strictly biological nature, it still plays an important role in the total pain experience, because the individual in pain is frequently bound to interpret his suffering also in the light of its social and cultural meaning.

The most obvious sociocultural bearing of pain is implied in the word itself, which has derived from the Latin word *poena* ("punishment"), which can be traced to the Sanscrit root *pu,* meaning purification.[13] Inflicttion of pain is one of the oldest, al-

---

[13] It is interesting to observe that, to my knowledge, *only* the English language has adopted this word to describe directly the quality of the physical sensation, along with the Anglo-Saxon *ache,* which usually describes a dull sensation "arising from disorders that might be relieved" (*Webster's Dictionary of Synonyms,* 1942). The original Latin word *dolor* was not incorporated into English (unless for poetical usage) but is the main word in French, Spanish, and other languages derived from the Latin, along with the word *mal,* which has a connotation of *evil* and *wickedness,* while the word *peine* preserved its punitive meaning (punishment or penalty). On the other hand, the French have retained the emotional connotation associated with *pain* and *punishment,* that is, anguish and anxiety, which also existed in the original Latin.

The word *suffering,* which derives from the Latin *suf-ferro* ("to be under a burden," "to support") acquired the connotation of *bearing* and was integrated into both English and French in this meaning. However, the English have added to it also the implication of *tolerance, patience,* and *power to resist* (*Webster*), while the French, who at times might use it to express tolerance, express by it the notion of *abeyance* and a *state of suspense* (*petit Larousse*).

Pain in German (*Schmerz*), Russian (*bol*), Polish (*ból*), or Hebrew (*K'eyv*) does not have a punitive implication at all. However, in all these languages it is used as in English or French to denote mental anguish and anxiety.

In Hebrew the word *k'eyv* is closely associated with illness, and one of its synonyms is a state of *weakness* and *abandonment.* (Gur, *Dictionary of Hebrew Language.* Tel Aviv, 1948, p. 246). The Polish word for suffering

though certainly not universal, forms of punishment. In the process of teaching children correct behavior, and in forcing adults to comply with group norms, the unpleasant quality of pain sensation and the biological fear of it have fulfilled an important social function. In many societies parental and national authorities were, and still are, based on infliction of pain. From the symbolic slap to the deadly bastinado, from the Cross to the Iron Maiden, pain was associated with obedience, guilt, and punishment. The whip was the symbol of the Egyptian pharaoh, who used slave labor to build pyramids, and it is still being freely applied in contemporary labor camps. The British schoolmaster and the eastern European Jewish melamed are in agreement on the pedagogical value of physical punishment. It is no wonder that for us one of the first associations with pain is guilt, sin, and transgression. Pain that may be a punishment for a transgression of man's laws and regulations becomes, by extension of the social experience, also a chastisement for sins against Divine injunctions and commandments. Pain was one of the first punishments for the Original Sin of man and woman. This manifestation of the Lord's justice and anger became responsible for the question uttered by many people in pain: "What have I done that I deserve this misery?" For a true believer, whether Jew, Catholic, or Protestant, pain is an expression of a supernatural castigation for consciously or unconsciously committed sins. But suffering is not merely a punishment, but also a form of redemption; after pain has been inflicted and suffered, a man has paid his debt to man or God and consequently is pure again. The Son of God himself redeemed by pain the sins of humanity. Thus the pain experience was incorporated into the religious life of the society as a vehicle of atonement. Christians and pagans alike have accepted

---

(*cierpiec*) is very closely related to the Russian word *tyerpyenye*, which primarily means *patience* and *power to resist*. On the other hand, the Russian equivalent of suffering is *stradanye*, which is derived from *strada*, meaning labor during harvesttime.

These semantic comments illustrate quite well different cultural attitudes toward pain and its significance in different societies. The language, which is the "mirror of the nation," reflects very directly cultural values held by people who speak it.

this function of pain: not only Christ suffered pain, but also the Syrian Adonis, the Egyptian Horus, and the Greek Dionysus. Pain became an integral part of creeds and rituals, and among peoples in many parts of the world infliction of sufferings by self or others is one of the most dramatic religious experiences. Thus one of the primary sociocultural functions of pain is its punitive and purifying significance.

The unpleasant quality of the sensation of pain is exploited by society for cultural purposes. In addition, the biological tendency to avoid pain fulfills an important function. The ability to control pain and to suppress the flight-or-fight reactions became a major test for such qualities as strength of character, of masculinity, or of class. The transition from adolescence into adulthood, from lay status into a sacred one, or from a civilian group into a military order is frequently associated with rituals of initiation, of which ability to tolerate pain is one of the main features. To pass the required steps, the initiate is expected to control all his reflex reactions aimed at the avoidance of pain.[14] The infliction of pain, actual or symbolic, is frequently part of ceremonies of admittance to secret societies and special social groups, whether in primitive Africa or in a fraternity in an American college. Mutilation marks, scars, and tattoos are signs of adulthood, manhood, social status, and prestige. The mutilations of the South American Indian serve the same social function as the saber scar on the face of a Prussian officer. Both

[14] The following description of initiation rites among South American Indians is a good illustration of these functions of the pain experience:

"A *Mbaya* boy of about 13 attained warrior's status through a ceremony. Having painted himself red and white and wearing all his feather, bead, and metal ornaments, he changed for a whole night and day beating a drum. At sunset a shaman pricked the boy's penis and jabbed his body with a jaguar bone awl, causing blood to flow abundantly. The boy was expected to remain passive. His blood was smeared all over the body. . . .

"There is some evidence in the literature that certain Guiacuru groups imposed this ordeal on young children who likewise had to show their courage by not flinching. The lower lip was perforated by a famous warrior during early childhood. At puberty they jabbed the boy's genitals and pulled out one of the two remaining crowns of hair on his tonsured head. The adolescent was now regarded as an adult and was allowed to wear bracelets and a belt of animal or human hair" (Steward, 1946, pp. 321–322).

have shown their strength of character in enduring pain, thus gaining entrance in their chosen class of people.

Furthermore, pain became a symbol of grief and mourning through its association with misery and unhappiness. By self-inflicting pain, relatives, friends, or subjects show to the community the extent of their despair at the loss of a beloved father, husband, friend, or ruler. In many societies self-mutilation is part of the mourning ceremonies. The ancient Syrians have mourned the seasonal death of their god Adonis by mutilating parts of their body, and primitive Australians "would cut and gash themselves with sharp instruments until their heads and bodies streamed with blood" to deplore the death of a member of their community.[15] Mourners, lovers, martyrs, and heroes, at various times and in various societies, have expressed grief, love, or devotion by suffering pain for the sake of a friend, fatherland, or god.

In each social situation in which pain plays a major role the behavior of the individual or group is strictly standardized according to the customs of the culture. The initiation ordeal is usually experienced in silence and impassivity, but funeral rites are often associated with screams, tears, and wailing.[16]

In each of the described circumstances the responses to pain fulfill one more function in addition to those that were discussed. They also *carry a message* to the community. In responding to pain by screams or in suppressing the tendency to avoid suffering, the individual tells his fellows, friends, or relatives that he is strong, courageous, devoted, or in grief. Frequently it is not enough to say in words only that one is most unhappy or that one is brave and manly. These attitudes and feelings have to be proved by actual manifestations of stoicism or misery in order to convey the impression of authenticity and sincerity. Thus the pain experience—the sensation as well as the reactions and responses—acquires the significance of a medium of communication in interpersonal relation-

[15] Fison and Howitt, cited in Mead and Calas, 1953, p. 545.

[16] Although this type of behavior is frequent, it is not necessarily universal. For some societies the reverse is true: the initiates cry during the trial but the mourners remain calm and stone-faced.

ships between members of the same social group. Actual behavior during the pain experience, as well as signs indicating the correct conduct, tell people who know how to interpret them that one has lived up to his obligations. Two alumni from the University of Heidelberg will recognize each other as such by the *Schmiss*[17]; in the same manner a member of the Mandan tribe will know how many times his tribesman has mourned his relatives by the absence of his finger joints—amputated as a sign of grief.[18]

The symbolic significance of the pain experience as defined by the cultural traditions, as well as its function in communication between people, makes it expected and acceptable. Self-inflicted or other-inflicted suffering is anticipated in the process of growing up in the community and is closely associated with the life cycle of the individual. From birth to death, pain is part of man's biological and sociocultural life.

An equally important role in the social and cultural life fulfills suffering that is associated not only with rituals and ceremonies but also with illness and injury. Aches, hurts, and twinges that spontaneously accompany many human diseases are well expected but are seldom accepted (unless seen as a Divine punishment). Although they may also be used as an opportunity to show courage and strength of character, in many human societies these pains can be used in a very precise and standardized fashion in relationship to other, nonaffected members of the society. Pain and its incapacitating and crippling effects provoke sympathy, compassion, pity, revulsion, or fear. Whatever the motivation of healthy people—guilt or identification, solidarity or love—they are frequently compelled to offer assistance to the suffering person and, by deed or word, help him to relieve his condition. Members of the same family are expected to succor one another in illness, and the failure to do so causes individual guilt and social disapproval. On the other hand, the patient is frequently allowed to say and do things that under normal circumstances would be inadmissible.

[17] A scar on the face of members of German students' fraternities that was received in a duel.
[18] Henry, cited in Mead and Calas, 1953, p. 443.

42

The Cultural Dimensions of Pain

Moreover, he may use the manifestations of pain and the helpless condition resulting from pain and illness to manipulate his relationships with healthy people, exploiting the prescribed feelings of pity and sympathy. Pain may become a powerful tool to impose one's will upon his social environment and to obtain privileges and favors otherwise denied. A hurt child often gets a toy to dry his tears; in the same spirit, a mother's headaches, actual or imaginary, have stimulated sufficient guilt feelings among children to make them more amenable in situations in which reasoning or parental authority was useless. An example of the powerful pressure that pain might, and is expected to, exercise on society has been given by the forty-one inmates of Rock Quarry State Prison, Georgia, who voluntarily broke their legs in order to obtain better treatment from the prison administration.[19] (It is interesting to note that in this instance self-inflicted pain replaced the usual technique of a hunger strike, thus increasing the impact of the protest.) Naturally, pain as a tool in interpersonal relationships is possible only in a culture that focuses its efforts on avoidance of pain for self and others, for example, the United States. It is doubtful that a similar act among inmates of a concentration camp in a totalitarian society would have any effect on the administration.

These various cultural attitudes toward pain, as well as the different patterns of behavior in pain manifested by members of human societies, are not isolated phenomena in their total cultural life. The anthropological investigations of man's cultures have shown that no cultural manifestation is an isolated, independent occurrence. Each culture forms an integrated whole, in which all elements are closely interrelated and interdependent and in which each element is an expression of the whole. Social, religious, economic, and moral manifestation in the life of a people can be understood only in their relationship to each other.

Rapports between parents and children, citizen and government, worshipers and their deities are expressions of the same values that permeate their moral ideas, economic goals, or family struc-

[19] See *The New York Times,* July 1956; *The New York Post,* Nov. 1956.

ture. The democratic ideas in American culture are manifested in the organization of family life, school system, or industrial corporations. The American emphasis on self-reliance and individual success is equally evident in child rearing, business activities, or the rehabilitation programs of disabled veterans.

Thus, when a social researcher investigates any cultural manifestation in the life of a society, he has to probe and examine its relationships to other cultural and social phenomena; only then can its true meaning and significance be understood and interpreted. Frequently, rituals and religious ideas can be understood in the light of family structure, which in turn can be interpreted through insights into the economic life or historical past of the society. The relationships between these various phenomena is not that of direct cause and effect, but that of different pieces of a gigantic puzzle in which each part has a meaning only in relevance to other pieces and as one element of the total pattern. Of course, each part can be described separately according to its shape or color, but this description will remain incomplete and superficial, for the significance of the shape or color can be understood in terms of their function in the total picture.

The same principle of patterning of cultural manifestations is true for the pain responses. The variety of types of behavior in pain, the special meanings attached to pain in different cultures, and its acceptance or nonacceptance can be comprehended only in the light of the total cultural pattern of the society or its subdivision. Whether a man complains to his wife when he is in pain or tries to withdraw from society in order to hide his sufferings, and whether he is vocal or silent when in pain can be best understood in the light of family structure, general social behavior, or norms regulating forms of communication between members of the society.

Benedict, in her classic anthropological essay *Patterns of Culture* (1946), relates the absence of torture and painful rituals among the Pueblo Indians in New Mexico to the same general spirit of the culture that is expressed in child rearing: "In Zuni whipping is never used as corrective of children. The fact that white

44

parents use it in punishment is a matter for unending amazement."[20] Among Plains Indians, boys are expected to take their pain without complaint during initiation ceremonies; among the Zuni the attitude is quite different: "In the initiation children are supposed to be very frightened and they are not ashamed if they cry aloud." Rejection of violence, which is characteristic of the Pueblo cultural pattern, is also expressed not only in child rearing and initiations but also in the organization of family life and economic activities.

The influence upon attitudes toward pain of such cultural values as acceptance or rejection of violence is rather obvious. There are, however, other values in the culture that seem to be totally unrelated to suffering; nevertheless, a closer scrutiny will reveal even there evidence of strong interdependence. For instance, such a value is the concept of time in the culture. A number of anthropologists have compared ideas about time in various societies and found great differences in attitudes.[21] In Western culture we divide time into past, present, and future. Moreover, we break it up into years, months, weeks, days, hours, minutes, and seconds. All our activities are organized accordingly. We study the past in order to understand the present, and we labor in the present with an eye toward the future. However, this time orientation, which seems to us so obvious and logical, is far from universal. Halowell (1937), in discussing the problem of time orientation, tells us: "In

[20] A similar pattern was observed among the Caingang of South America: "The Caingang show the greatest tenderness to their children, seldom punishing them or using harsh words. . . ." When the initiation ceremonies are taking place, measures are taken to minimize the pain connected with perforation of the lip: "The children are intoxicated with beer and shaken until half unconscious, when their ceremonial fathers pierce their lip with a sharp stick" (Steward, 1946, pp. 463–464).

[21] "Obviously all societies at all times must deal with all three time problems. All have some conception of the past, all have a present, and all give some kind of attention to the future-time dimension. They differ, however, in their emphasis on past, present, or future at a given period, and a great deal can be told about the particular society or part of the society being studied, much about the direction of change within it can be predicted, with a knowledge of where that emphasis is" (Kluckhohn, 1950, p. 380).

some Indian languages the terms for day-before-yesterday and day-after-tomorrow are the same. In the aboriginal cultural pattern, 'days' and 'nights' are not grouped in any temporal unit of higher order. There is no 'week,' nor is there any named 'day,' although there are special terms yesterday, day-before-yesterday, tomorrow, and day-after-tomorrow. Smith (1952) compared the concepts of past, present, and future in Western cultures, among the Hindu, the Chinese, and a group of American Indians from the Pacific coast of Canada. She has discussed the relationship of the individual toward these concepts. She pointed out that, although in Western societies the individual's main interest lies in the future, "the ego expressed in Hindu philosophy, on the other hand, extends infinitely into both past and future." Among the American Indians "the ego extension is hardly concerned with either past or future."

At first glance there seems to be hardly any direct relationship between cultural conceptualization of time and such manifestations as individual responses to pain. However, a closer look will reveal that time orientation has an important bearing on people's attitudes toward pain. As mentioned previously, the significance attributed to pain plays a distinctive role in its acceptance or rejection. The time orientation of the culture may influence the character of the significance given to the experience and, consequently, the emotions associated with it. For instance, individuals reared in cultures that can be qualified as "future oriented" may tend to evaluate the meaning of their pain according to its implications for their future. Such patients will be most concerned with such questions as how their present experience may affect their health, earning capacities, or family life in days or years to come. They will be inclined to think in terms of *effects* of the sensation, rather than in terms of the sensation itself. The future-oriented emphasis of the culture may foster anxieties directed toward the future. On the other hand, in "present-oriented" societies, when people are most concerned with the immediacy of their life experiences, the patients may be more affected by the *actual sensation* of pain rather than by its possible implications for the future. They

46

The Cultural Dimensions of Pain

may be more preoccupied with its relief rather than with the cure of the condition of which the pain is a symptom.

Another cultural trait that may influence people's behavior in pain is the value attributed to expression of emotions by word, sound, or movement. The early explorers of America were impressed not only by the Indians' ability to tolerate pain but also by their general impassivity and ability to sit for hours without uttering a word; so is the "phlegmatic" disposition of the Anglo-Saxons an inexhaustible source of anecdotes all over the world. On the other hand, the volubility of many nations living around the Mediterranean Sea is familiar to anybody who ever visited Italy or the south of France. If some societies disapprove strongly of any public exhibition of emotion, others may emphasize the importance of words and gestures as necessary manifestations of their feelings and will admire those individuals who are able to display their sorrow and grief particularly well, using pathetic speeches and even tears. It is obvious that the importance attributed to the expression or inhibition of emotions will directly influence the sufferer's behavior.

Such cultural values—attitudes toward violence, time orientation, or attitudes toward expressiveness—frequently serve as criteria by which members of different societies judge each other. Future-oriented people consider the present-minded ones childish, immature, or lazy; conversely, individuals who enjoy the present without thinking much about the future will laugh at men who were trained to plan for the "rainy day." The British sees an overt display of emotions as "shocking," whereas the "overemotional" Frenchman seldom misses the opportunity to express his contempt for the Anglo-Saxon "cold-bloodedness." Each considers his attitudes and his behavior as the absolutely correct ones and views them as universal standards and norms of correct behavior.

A logical conclusion of our discussion of cultural and social elements in individual pain experience points toward the important contribution that social sciences can offer to the elucidation of those aspects of people's responses to pain that remain puzzling as long as they are studied only within the neurophysiological frame of

47

reference. Although the physiological study of pain gives us under-standing of the total experience and its biological significance for the preservation of human life, the social and culture superstructure has added so much to the original meaning that the range of hu-man responses cannot be understood without the assistance from sciences studying human society and culture. Individual responses have to be examined not only in the light of the sensory structure and dynamics of pain, not only in the light of specific pathological processes affecting directly its perception and reactions to it, but also as an integral part of man's life as a member of society, with a well-defined pattern of values, norms, customs, and mores.

CHAPTER 2

The Warning Signal

The behavioral response of the patient of Old American background, as described by the patient himself and, often, by people who have been in contact with him during the pain experience, is usually nonexpressive. The patient tends to appear unemotional and calm and is not vocal about his pain. He tries not to show it or to complain, cry, or scream. Only a very small number of patients admit to crying or complaining about pain. The overwhelming majority of patients deny most of the vocal manifestations of pain, and a great number of the patients insist that they tend to hide pain. When he is in pain, the Old American tries to be rational and to control his behavior. He feels that his actions should be directed toward alleviating the con-

49

dition and evaluated according to their effectiveness. Things that help are done; things that do not help are not done. The purposefulness of the activities is the ultimate criterion of behavior.

Screaming, crying, and complaining belong to the category of things that do not help and therefore should be avoided.

> I don't see why I should cry. It won't help any.

> I don't cry for help, I just pull myself together and bite my lip. I like to control my reactions. Crying and screaming can't do you any good.

> It doesn't do any good to complain. Try to bear it—I mean, I got this thing and it's something nobody else can fight for me.

> I don't lay and moan. I mean, that don't get you nothing. It don't get you anywhere moaning about it.

The importance of the practical criterion in behavior while in pain is substantiated by frequent statements to the effect that if crying or complaining would help, the patient would do it.

> If you mean did I ever get down on my knees and cry and yell or yodel—no. I never did. Well, 'cause I just figure it isn't going to help it any. If I thought it would help it I probably would.

> I know I suffered a good deal, but there was no use in making it too loud or anything because I had nobody around me, not even a landlady to come to see whether I was alive or suffering or anything else.

Thus the avoidance of vocal manifestations of pain should be seen primarily in the light of the patient's feelings about the uselessness of these expressions; an aimless, irrational response is strongly disapproved. However, there are also other reasons for the attempts to hide pain, such as the concern for showing a behavior appropriate for an adult male:

The Warning Signal

I never scream—I can take pain like a man.

I don't cry—I want to take my pain like a man—I want to be a real man and not to show my pain.

A major factor in trying to control one's behavior is often the reluctance to be a nuisance to other people; hence the patient will try to suppress the possible tendencies to groan, moan, or cry in order not to trouble others.

I wasn't aware of the fact that I was hiding my pain until night before last when Dr. Z— said, "Well, if you feel miserable, act miserable. Don't be so damned nice." But it just doesn't seem very logical to fuss and complain about it, make everybody else miserable.

The patient tries to be "good," not annoying his roommates or the medical staff. He tends to take into consideration the feelings of others in his environment, and he sees vocal or motor expressions of pain as interfering with their comfort.

It (screaming and yelling) just makes life miserable, not only for themselves but for everybody else. You get a little fed up with somebody yelling and scolding all the time.

When the pain is quite severe, an occasional groan, "ouuh," grimace, or jerk may be an external manifestation of suffering. Even when he is in great pain, the Old American patient tries to express optimism and retain his sense of humor. He may even joke and use humorous language to describe his pain. He likes to be praised for a correct and cooperative behavior and is quite sensitive to expressions of approval and disapproval. He will often tell how doctors were pleased and impressed by his stoicism.

I took it (my pain) patiently and just suffered, that's all. I never complained. They (the doctors) told me I was the best patient they ever had up at the hospital. I smiled and passed it off.

51

'(I had such pain) I could hardly get my breath. And then
I wouldn't complain to the doctors, but just told my youngest
girl, see, and she went and told her mother. The first thing
her mother called up—called up the hospital, and Dr. B—
came around and he said "Gee, if we want to find out anything about you we got to go through Brooklyn to find out
anything about you," he said. "You wouldn't tell us." So—
naturally I wouldn't tell him, see.

A sophisticated patient frankly admitted that he uses pain to provoke admiration.

I would use pain as one of the obstacles which I had successfully overcome. [Would you use it to provoke sympathy?] Oh,
never: to provoke admiration.

Those patients who, under the impact of pain, do not conform to
the correct standards of behavior, and who deviate from the ideal
pattern, are well aware of their fault and express feelings of shame
and guilt.

[Did you show your pain later?] Yes, I think I do show it.
Unfortunately, I do.

When it did happen (that I screamed) more or less I felt
like a baby, screaming. First time it did happen to me like
that . . . and . . . felt bad over . . . there was people there.
That's why I felt bad—people I know and all.

In such instances the patient is apologetic and tries to explain his
incorrect behavior by insisting it was involuntary or that he was
physically unable to control it.

I wouldn't holler. Not unless I didn't know what I was doing.
As long as I knew what I was doing, I wouldn't holler. I'd
clench my teeth.

I used to have certain pains—when they first cut off my leg.
I used to let a yell out every night. And the nurses used to

come in there to me and say "You—you got to keep quiet. You are disturbing the rest of the patients." But—uh—I tried to do the best I could. There was nothing . . . that I could . . . no power I could use to save me from that pain that I had. The pain was terrible.

When the patient admits to screaming or groaning, he often explains his behavior as helpful and as fulfilling a specific function. Thus a number of patients said that they scream in order to help the doctor find the painful area or to help guide injections.

[Did you scream or moan?] No, only when he kept hitting this nerve in the right leg—he hit it a nerve, and it hurt, and I'd grunt, you know. I wanted him to know that he was—uh—off to one side, you see—in other words, the way I understood it there's a right side and a left side and he's got to get in the middle.

Like today, the doctor was pushing something in back there. Well, naturally, the man did the best he could; when he hurt me a little, naturally I wouldn't complain, but I just holler, see. Just to let him know.

These expressions are not considered incorrect; on the contrary, they are seen as a form of cooperation with the doctor and as an active participation in the treatment.

As was mentioned, complaining in a whining or lamenting way, often referred to as making a fuss, is strongly disapproved; but the legitimate complaint, which serves a communicative function and helps the doctor diagnose the case, or which directs the attention of the nurse to a specific need of the patient, is accepted because it has a purpose. The patient sees a difference between making a fuss when he is in pain and complaining when necessary —when the complaint is reasonable and serves the function of informing the right person about his condition in order to get the needed and expected help. It is important to know to whom, how, and when to complain.

People in Pain

> If I think it's something that I—I should tell a doctor about,
> I'd tell him then and see what he says. But I wouldn't . . .
> complain too much about it.

The person to whom the complaint is directed is defined in terms
of his function and role as seen by the patient. For instance, there
is no point in complaining to members of the family because they
cannot help; certain patients feel that it only worries them unnec-
essarily. But one may complain to doctors and, sometimes, nurses,
because it is their function to relieve pain.

> [Would you complain when you are in pain?] That would
> depend upon who I was telling. [Would you tell it to your
> wife?] I don't tell her, no. I mean except when it's obvious.
> I mean if I'm uncomfortable enough I might be a little edgy
> or something and it's obvious, then I tell her. Although she—
> she knows pretty much. What's the sense of reminding her
> about it?

> [Would you hide your pain also in front of the medical
> people?] That doesn't go for nurses. No, a nurse is a—is in a
> class by herself. No—no, I—uh—I—you might say I'm un-
> inhibited in front of doctors and nurses. It's just other people.

> There is no need to complain to them (the nurses); they
> know. Besides, what's the use complaining? If you complain,
> you get less service.

> I might complain to the doctor, but certainly not to the
> nurses. They do their professional job. But they—they can't
> do anything. They can't prescribe; they can't—uh—diagnose.

> Well, see, I'm not the complaining type, you know. I don't
> complain unless it's very serious or something like that. Then
> I tell the doctor.

Complaining when it is uncalled for, crying, moaning, and other
vocal expressions are associated with a defeated condition. Charac-
teristically, the language used in describing such behavior suggests
a helpless and passive position of the body: "lay down and yell,"

"get on the knees and cry," "get down and cry and holler and yell," "lay and moan." On the other hand, the correct behavior is seen as undefeated and resisting the impact of pain; "even the pain could not get her down," said a patient describing the behavior of his old mother in illness.

Unnecessary complaining is also frowned upon because it is seen as looking for sympathy, and is viewed as a selfish tendency to monopolize the attention of the attending people at the expense of other patients who are entitled to their share of care.

> [Why don't you sympathize with these people?] Uh—because —uh—well, basically I think it's selfish. Here they're set up to do a certain type of job; they have only so many nurses for so many patients, and the nurses have got to scamper right around to get their job done. They can't stop and hold somebody's hand. Now, if somebody insists on that, why that deprives someone else of the care which they perhaps need and should get. And I think it's selfish, and I don't sympathize with them.

The Old American patients are quite indignant in describing the behavior of other patients—in most instances from a different ethnic background—who seem to be seeking sympathy.

> This fellow—he gets a lot of pain. He is Italian. He gets very excited. He can bellow that you can hear him from one end of the hospital to the other. He is the fellow you ought to talk to. He ought to be psychoanalyzed. [Why? What's wrong with him?] Well, he's got to have a lot of attention. He's only happy when there are two or three nurses and—uh—an attendant and a doctor around.

The patient does not deny the suffering of a complaining roommate (although he might be somewhat skeptical as to the intensity of his pain), but he disapproves of the behavior because it is useless, selfish, nonsocial, and interferes with the peace of other patients.

People in Pain

Part of it is—is pain. No—no question about that. But beyond that point I think he—he yells before he's hurt. Which is why we don't hear so much of the radio.

Besides the legitimate complaint, there is another form of response to pain that is not only tolerated but even favored by the patients of Old American background: the "griping," which is often expressed in cursing and grumbling. Griping is not complaining of pain or seeking sympathy; rather, it is an expression of annoyance with one's condition, indicating a rebellion against the uncomfortable situation in which the patient finds himself. To the extent that a lamenting complaint shows helplessness and weakness, griping is an expression of fight—of an active response to the situation. It serves the purpose of indicating to the people around and to the patient himself that one is not resigned, that one has preserved his fighting spirit, which is necessary to "lick" the condition.

When I'm in pain, I wouldn't complain, but I would groan and gripe about it; and I would curse.

I would curse. That's all right—that's perfectly manly to cuss. That's all right—yes—that—that is allowed.

[Have you complained about your pain?] I don't think so. Toward the end there. I was telling my wife, "This is getting to be a pain in the—in the ass," as it literally was. I was more annoyed than complaining. Annoyed me. Because I was always so healthy and in such a good condition that—here—I just figured that it was cutting down on my usual, normal activity.

If complaining about pain is wrong, denial of pain when asked about it by competent people is also incorrect. The patient may deny pain before members of his family or before friends in order not to worry them, but he is expected to describe his condition in the greatest detail to the doctor or nurse. In so doing, he cooperates with them, helping the doctor to establish a correct diagnosis and to determine the course of treatment.

> I wouldn't complain to my wife. But if the doctors or other people around here will ask me, of course I'll tell them. If the doctors ask me "Did it hurt you?" well I says, "you hurt me a little."

By the same token, fighting pain is rather infrequent among the Old American patients. Pain is unnecessary and should be eliminated by some means provided by medical science: "What's the sense of having pain when you can stop it?" Fighting pain would be a meaningless waste of energy and effort, as would unnecessary screaming and hollering.

> I don't scream or cry. Just sit there and take it. I don't fight, just sit there. What can you do? No use in hollering or fighting it. The energy that you put out for screaming, and yelling and fighting and exerting yourself—screaming and yelling and twisting and in combating pain is just wasted and makes it only worse.

The rejection of expressive behavior is not absolute and categorical, but it is determined by practical considerations. It is disapproved as a simple manifestation of pain, but it is accepted if expressed at the right time, in the right place, and if it serves a definite purpose as a contribution to the work of the medical people.

In the light of these criteria, crying is always disapproved because it is considered useless. It is viewed as a manifestation of weakness and childishness unbecoming an adult male. However, once in a while, when the pain is unbearable, the patient might show tears. In such cases the patient hastens to add that he was not crying, but that his eyes were wet or he had water in his eyes, meaning that it was not real crying but just tearing, which is seen as a physiological phenomenon associated with intense pain.

[Does pain ever bring tears?] It used to, but hasn't this time . . . It used to—tears would just come out of my eyes. [Did you cry?] Oh no, just a wet eye, that's all. [You mean it wasn't crying?] No, no, no, no, I never cried from pain.

The tears—I don't know—I don't feel I'm crying like people say they cry, but the tears just came, and that's the same whenever I get pain, the tears—the water comes out of my eyes. I don't feel like I'm crying from the heart like a crybaby but the tears just. . . . [So how do you react to pain?] I try to bear it and try to smile.

Yes, I have (cried). But—only a small amount. I mean, in other words, I would never sit down and just cry. I mean, the pain hurt me so much that the tears would come to my eyes from it. But that's very, very seldom that it ever gets that severe. Because that would be a little too much, you know.

Most of the practical criteria that dictate the control of vocal expressions in pain also hold for uncontrolled motor reaction to pain. Not only is it useless, but it can also be harmful. For instance, during an injection a doctor may misguide the needle if the patient moves too vigorously; an intense attack of pain can be made worse because of exerting and wasting energy.

Nevertheless, the patient feels that certain limited motor or even vocal manifestations, like tearing eyes, an exclamation, a grunt, or a jerk of the body, are normal reactions, because he sees them as part of the pain experience. Reactions that everyone makes are normal; therefore they cannot be disapproved because they are involuntary, not emotional.

[Would you jump from pain?] Oh, I suppose, if I'd bump myself in the ribs, I'd flinch. That's—that's normal reaction.

Because expressive behavior is seen as ineffective and is strongly disapproved, the crying and moaning of other patients fail in their communicative intent. For a patient of Old American background, crying and hollering among other patients does not necessarily indicate pain. Because expressive behavior is not a culturally expected response to pain, the onlooker is often confused as to its significance. The patient who cries might receive the benefit of the doubt, but his behavior fails to convey the full intensity of his suffering. However, he is not entirely condemned. There is an admission of the possibility that even the stolid, unemotional patient may break down under very intense pain.

> Well, I've seen people get down and cry and holler and yell—whether—they claim that they was in pain. I don't know whether they were or not—I mean—I'm taking for granted that they were. I felt sorry for them. [Did you approve of their crying or screaming?] Oh well—everybody has the right to do what they want to do, I guess. Personally, I couldn't see that yelling and hollering is going to make it any easier, but maybe it could, maybe I just never had pain that bad, or something. I don't know. [Do you think their pain is worse than yours?] Oh, how—I don't know. I couldn't tell how bad their pain is.

The admission of the possibility that, if the pain gets worse, the patient might cry or scream is quite frequent in the interviews. In describing his behavior in pain, the patient speaks about his past or present experience but avoids committing himself as to any future situation. Because the behavior is not emotional but is dictated by practical and pragmatic considerations, there is always the possibility that, in a different situation, a different behavior might be called for.

> I don't cry from it (pain). Well, maybe I would if it got bad enough, I guess, but—I don't know—I'm not a—I don't know what to say. I just don't cry easy.

A patient may gain reassurance from comparing his own response to pain with the emotional response shown by the crying patient, and from feeling that even he himself might cry if the pain gets very bad. Thus he might bear his pain better knowing that others suffer more.

> I don't lay in bed like one of my roommates up there and yell at the tops of my lungs all day long. And all night. You can always find somebody worse off than you, I don't want to be the low man on the totem pole when it comes to pain.

The tendency to conform to an ideal mode of behavior in pain, which is expressed by almost all the patients of Old American background, does not mean that many of them would not like to behave differently. Many of them would like to be more expressive, more free, and less controlled in the expression of their feelings and emotions. A number of patients admitted frankly that, when they are alone, they cry, moan, and groan if the pain is too severe.

The desire to manifest publicly the correct behavior and the concern for approval by others are so strong among the Old American patients that, only when they are alone can they release the control over their emotions and behave as they would like to behave, rather than as they must. Hence withdrawal from friends, from family, and from people in general becomes a very frequent aspect of their general response to pain. When pain becomes unbearable—when there is a need to cry, to groan, and to feel sorry for oneself—the patient withdraws from his social environment and relaxes the controlling mechanism.

> If I am all by myself I'd groan and moan and sit up and turn on the light and lie down again and turn off the light again.

> '(When there are no people around) then you can relax, because as long as you are with people, you work with the absolute surface. And then you give into it—then you can curse if you want to. I might groan—I might get up and walk around.

The patient withdraws because he does not want anyone to see his pain and because he does not want to appear weak and helpless.

The Warning Signal

I don't want anybody around . . . it would be a case of pride. I—uh—wouldn't want them to see me—uh—in pain and maybe—uh—well, metaphorically speaking burst out crying. And I might say that—that is a matter of great pride with me—uh—that—uh—it—uh—seems to be, looking at it as objectively as I can—it is very, shall we say, effeminate for for a man to cry, and, uh—uh—that, I—don't want to show it. No—that's what it amounts to.

Only when he feels that he can hide his pain well does he say that he would like to have people around him, even if he "has to screech inwardly."

In light of these statements, it seems apparent that the stolid, unemotional, and stoical behavior shown and related by the patients of Old American background is a facade imposed by a cultural code of behavior rather than a spontaneous expression of their attitudes. Social approval and disapproval guide the patient in his behavior in pain, just as they may guide him in other aspects of life.

Other reasons may also account for the withdrawal. Probably one of the most important factors is the reluctance to appear a nuisance and to annoy people with one's own troubles. "The pain is my pain, and not theirs, and I have to keep it to myself" is a frequent explanation for hiding pain. If one is unable to hide it, he has to withdraw.

Concern for public opinion is most characteristic of the Old American patient. In this respect he differs greatly from other groups. The need to follow an ideal "American" pattern of behavior is so strong—and the awareness of "what is allowed" so clear in the mind of the patient—that, regardless of whether he conforms to this pattern, he tends to describe his behavior as following the rules of the game. The direct observation of patients, as well as the impressions of doctors and nurses, points to the fact that the ideal pattern is frequently the actual behavior among the Old American patients.

What general attitudes toward pain in American culture

might account for the behavior of the Old American patient? What is the philosophy of pain held by healthy as well as ill members of this group that may help explain the emphasis on the practical and pragmatic response to suffering? I believe that it is derived from the concept of the purely biological function of pain in the life of a human. Pain is seen as a warning signal that tells the individual something is wrong with his organism. The functions of pain are to alarm the individual and to stimulate his activities in the direction of taking care of or "fixing" the source of pain. Pain, even in the minds of the unsophisticated, plays an important role in the physical survival of the individual. It is unintelligent and harmful to neglect or ignore the warning signal. The activities called for when one is alarmed by the sensation of pain must be rational and efficient and directed toward determining what is wrong, how to eliminate the cause of the pain, and how to alleviate the sensation itself when it has fulfilled its function and become unnecessary. To suffer unnecessary pain is needless and even silly; it is just as silly to ignore pain when it is there or to "kill" pain before its cause is determined. This attitude was clearly expressed by an informant who stated his attitude toward pain in the following words:

> I have a feeling that pain—you have pain for a reason; there is something wrong there, and it is a warning to you. I would—the way I would think about it, and the way I compare it is this: to take pain killer when you have pain that you don't know about—what the source of it is—would be the same thing as the engineer on the railroad. He's coming up for a signal and he's not sure how that signal is going to look, so he fiddles around with his gauge and he doesn't look at it and he goes by. Well, that's all right. That might work for a time, but sometime the signal is going to be red and he might find something in the track and there may be an awful smash. And that is the way I feel about it. Now— uh—this pain I think most I have, I'd put it down as psychogenic origin. But there is a little warning that I'm going down a little too far. I'd better ease up. Now if I go ahead with a pain killer that will kill that, my warning is gone; I

The Warning Signal

will keep tapping my reserve until finally there comes a time
—maybe I will get into some accident or something where I
need my reserve and I don't have any.[1]

As a warning signal, pain acquires a symptomatic significance. In
other words, pain is usually associated with illness.

I think of pain in association with illness. I don't think you
have pain unless it is associated with something that isn't
functioning properly, you see. In that way I associate pain
with illness.

The association of pain with illness usually stimulates anxieties
about the state of health. However, there are instances in life when
pain does not carry a symptomatic significance in terms of illness.
Pain may be an indication of certain normal biological processes
in the organism, and in such cases it is accepted and even welcomed. For instance, consider the following description of the so-
called growing pains of a maturing girl: ". . . pain that you get in
your legs in the spring when you are young when your bones are
growing fast. Nobody knows whether it is that or not, but all Americans believe it. And my daughter certainly complained of it . . .
They're very diffuse pains around the area of your long bones. Now
that seems to be a perfectly valid kind of pain." This pain is not
alarming and is therefore accepted.

Pain may be welcomed by a patient for whom it is an indication of life, as, for instance, with the awareness that a limb,
threatened with complete paralysis and loss of sensation, is still
functioning. In such a case the absence of pain would signify total
or partial death. One patient said he was more worried when he
did not feel any pain than when he did feel it.

There are also pains and aches that are part of certain social
or professional activities, such as pain inflicted on jobs, during
games, or during a prizefight. These pains are unavoidable, but
they do not provoke anxiety because they are socially and culturally accepted.

[1] A similar comparison with a signal is offered by Pfeiffer (1955).

63

However, these valid and accepted pains are not characteristic of hospital patients. Their pain is real, and it indicates illness
—a threat to the well-being, or even life, of the sufferer. When
pain means illness, it also means that appropriate activities are
called for to eliminate the cause of the pain. The individual himself has little knowledge of all the possible causes of pain. As in
many other critical situations in life, he must find an expert who
is specially trained and who has the necessary skill to deal with the
problem. When the sensation of pain suggests that something is
wrong with the body, it is time to call the doctor. Mere complaining and moaning are useless; the right thing to do is to consult the
physician.

> [Were you groaning, moaning, complaining? What would
> you do?] Well, I didn't moan or groan. I just—it just hurt.
> [And what would you do?] Well, I just go to the doctor. And
> the doctor will give me a shot or else give me codeine tablets.
> [Did you complain to your wife?] Well, right after it started
> I just called the doctor.

> [What do you do when something hurts? Do you complain
> about it?] If I think it's something that I should tell the
> doctor about, I'd tell him then and see what he says. But I
> wouldn't complain too much about it. It wouldn't help any.

The doctor, who has the confidence of the patient, is expected to
be able to determine the cause of pain and to mobilize his skill and
knowledge toward its elimination. Conversely, it is foolish and dangerous to ignore the signal and not see the doctor when the sensation of pain calls for it:

> I know a friend of mine—an Irishman—he died because he
> wouldn't go to the doctor. He had a stomachache. He had—
> I think it's called—ulcer, and he died in four or five days.

Not all pains that are seen as symptomatic call for a consultation
with a doctor. A number of ordinary headaches, bellyaches, and
sore throats caused by normal and common illnesses and organic

disturbances can be dealt with by the patient himself without the help of the doctor. They are not ignored but are taken care of by tested remedies known and available to everyone. It is as wrong to run to the doctor with every minor ailment as it is not to consult him when the condition is seen as serious.

> When I have pain, what are you going to do, cry on somebody else's shoulder? I keep it to myself. I subdue it. I hold it. Why, what can anybody do for you? [Would you go to the doctor?] Get a cramp—you going to run to a doctor? Or you have a small cold and no fever, or you have a runny nose, so you got to run to a doctor right away?

> When I have these other pains I go take some aspirin or APC or something and use some Ben Gay. I rub Ben Gay up in this area.

Everyone has a certain knowledge of means to handle these minor discomforts, a knowledge that is acquired in the family, from friends, and, to a great extent, from articles and pamphlets devoted to the hows of home medicine.

Given the possibility of having either an ordinary pain or a pain that is symptomatic of a serious illness, the Old American feels he has the responsibility to decide whether the pain he experiences at a given moment is an ordinary one he expects and accepts or whether it is something calling for the expert knowledge of a doctor. The decision is very difficult. On the one hand, if he decides against the consultation, he may risk the harmful effects of neglecting and ignoring the warning signal, which is plainly stupid: "They [the pains] weren't getting bad enough—uh—to go to the doctor. I must have been too dumb to understand that it was something." On the other hand, if he decides to consult a doctor, he may appear, in the eyes of the physician and in his own eyes, to be a neurotic or a "sissy." "[When I go to the doctor] I'm always afraid that maybe I'm going to be neurotic or borrow trouble."[2]

---

[2] Sometimes the patient tries to shift the responsibility for the consultation onto some member of the family. It is most convenient if some-

People in Pain

The responsibility involved in deciding whether or not to visit the doctor, the conflicts the patient experiences when pain rings the alarm, the tendency to view the sensation of pain as a warning signal with dangerous implications, the fear of underestimating or overestimating the significance of the pain—all these factors provoke a strong state of anxiety among the patients of Old American background.

The anxiety-producing effects of pain are extremely well summarized in the following statement of a sophisticated informant:

> It is anxiety-producing in terms of "Should I do something?" I mean, if it's a pain which means that if I do not do *A, B,* or *C,* something worse will happen: my leg will fall off. All right. Then that's an anxiety-producing event, though you have a theory about it—if action should be taken. It is also anxiety-producing if there is no reason for it. And if you don't know the termination. I mean "Is it something that's going to last forever?" I see a doctor if I think what I've got is the symptom of something that is going to get worse—something that ought to be stopped or is interfering with my doings. That would be if I couldn't classify the pain in any way.

The same feelings were expressed by a less sophisticated patient:

> Well, if I have a symptom that seems to indicate that there was something wrong, I would go to a doctor immediately. It might be pain—something like that I was conscious of— I think occasionally—the pain at night—the next day I felt good, but I thought that this was something that I should know what's happening and then I sought medical advice to see whether or not my own feelings in the matter were good.

---

body will "make you go" to the doctor: [Why didn't you go to the doctor?] Well, you know, if you'd been married, probably your wife would have urged you—urged me to go to check up to—to the doctor. Most wives do. And if I had somebody—like my sister living with me, or some immediate member of the family—probably they would have insisted I go to the doctor. Living alone, you know, you don't bother.

The Warning Signal

The warning-signal function of pain and the conflicts about consulting a doctor are not the only reasons for the strong feelings of anxiety that are provoked by pain. They can also be traced to the more general attitudes the Old American expresses toward health and illness.

Health is seen as the most important asset in the individual's pursuit of his life goals and in his constant struggle for a better job, for more financial security, and for happiness in the family circle. Health is a primary condition for employment, for a normal marriage, and for successful relations with people. If health is poor or impaired, the individual is strongly handicapped in his social and economic activities. It places him in a subordinate and disadvantaged position in relation to the competitive processes of society. Furthermore, he becomes an emotional and financial burden to his community and his family, and he may be avoided or sometimes even isolated from healthy people by the walls of hospitals and sanitariums. Illness deprives the individual of his most valued prerogatives: independence and self-reliance. Illness is often equated and identified with old age, that is, the most undesirable period in human life, when "the body deteriorates, when something keeps one in bed, and makes me a burden for someone for a long time."

Illness and pain, its most frequent symptom, frighten the healthy and sick alike, because to be fully human one has to be healthy:

> I want to get rid of this damn pain. I'd like to get out of here. I want to get rid of this damn pain so I can be a human being again. Not to go around like an old cripple holding my belly and holding my back.

> I suppose I was worrying. I couldn't walk right—I was going around like an old man.

It is no wonder that the thought of health is constantly present in the minds of people and that a great many of their activities are focused on the preservation of health and avoidance of illness. Listening to the healthy as well as to the sick creates the impression

that the Old American likes to see himself as a basically strong and
healthy organism that is constantly threatened by the presence of
hostile elements in the environment. The dangers are often identified, with or without reason, as germs, viruses, or "bugs."

> It makes me angry to think that the body, the wonderful
> human body with this terrific mind—potential mind—can
> become a victim of a nasty, stinking, horrible germ.

This statement formulates pretty well the basic concept of health
and illness common to many Americans. An intestinal disturbance
is seen as the result of "a flu that would get into the stomach and
would knock it out." "Cancer can develop from a neglected cold
or sore throat which you get from a germ." Dust and dirt in the
environment, outside the body, are extremely dangerous because
"the tissues are corroded and caked with this stuff, and one gets
cancer."

The body seems to be extremely vulnerable to dangers from
the outside, whether it is the wrong food, wrong air, wrong living
conditions, or even wrong social environment; and the Old American tends to blame external factors for his illness:

> The next morning I was sick as the deuce, and I went back
> and gave the restaurant keeper a merry razz for giving me a
> bum oyster stew. Later, by the way, I went back to apologize.
> His stew wasn't to blame. It was a virus.

Fear of external danger is reflected in the preoccupation with
healthy, wholesome food and sterile beverages, homes, linen, and
clothing—with the healthy way of life. Hence a great many things
are avoided because of the fear that they might endanger health.

> I felt that if I overate on sweets or things like that, why, I
> might develop it (diabetes).

> The way they (the Italians) do ravioli—it's very doughy.
> And I figure on—if I eat much of it, it wouldn't digest. So
> I avoid things like that.

The Warning Signal

Good health is a major condition for success. Therefore one has to take care of it by leading an orderly and healthy life:

> Oh, I never abused myself in any way, by going around—knocking around. I always had plenty of rest. Because in order to hold a job you have to do that. And when you work from a blueprint you have to have everything accurate.[3]

The preventive activities are the main weapons in the fight against the potential dangers of the environment. However, there is a feeling that, in addition to these conscious and practical activities, the body itself is supplied with an internal, protective force, which is usually referred to as resistance. Resistance is very often mentioned in connection with the patient's struggle against his disease. It seems, however, that, although everybody believes in resistance, nobody is able to define or describe it. In the American health language, which is characterized by rational, pragmatic, and often mechanical vocabulary and concepts, the term *resistance* has acquired an almost mystical connotation.

The human organism is healthy. Health, however, depends to a great extent on the amount of resistance the body is supplied with. This resistance has to be kept on a safe level, by the right kind of food and living. If the resistance is low, the organism becomes vulnerable and health is endangered; the external carriers of disease, which seem to wait for prey, have the opportunity to attack the body. Therefore good health is, to a great extent, a function of resistance. When resistance is poor, the organism is run down and illness may result. Thus resistance, as seen by the patient, can be defined as the capacity of the organism to oppose hostile

[3] These various statements are supported by our own experience. We are all familiar with the extreme emphasis on cleanliness; on personal and social hygiene; and on freshness and sterility of food, shelter, and clothing. This emphasis is also reflected in the great interest we take in the nutritional and health values of the food we consume; we are worried about its content in vitamins, proteins, and calories to the extent that the preparation of a menu might sometimes involve more pharmaceutical than gastronomical considerations. A housewife in her culinary art seems to be competing with the physician composing a prescription (Miner, 1956).

elements; this protective and resistant ability, which is weakened by overwork, age, or undernourishment, should be kept on a high level by supplying it with proper and adequate food, rest, and living conditions. A patient suffering from cancer of the lung attributed his condition to low resistance:

> All right, you got resistance, it works, but over a certain age your resistance is low, you are bound to get some darned thing in there (the lungs).

The concept of resistance in the Old American philosophy of health may also help the individual to feel that he will be fairly well ensured against disease if he keeps his resistance high. In case of an epidemic, for instance, one may escape illness if he builds up his resistance. Finally, the individual can blame his state of resistance if he catches a disease, thus preserving the conviction that his body is basically healthy—a conviction that is very important in dealing with anxieties provoked by pain or other symptoms.

The emphasis on the external causes of illness, as well as the strong tendency to attribute disease to environmental factors, is frequently expressed by the patient in his insistence that he is not really sick but that "something is just wrong" with his stomach, liver, or limb. However, one has the impression that, although the belief is constantly verbalized, he is actually not sure it is really so. In fact, this emphasis on external factors seems to serve the function of reducing the real anxieties with regard to the frailty of the human organism.

A number of indirect clues seem to substantiate this impression. For instance, healthy and sick informants alike often express the notion that an individual may frequently be ill for a long time and not know about it. They tell stories about themselves, about their friends, or about members of the family who died because they were ill for a long time and did not know about it.

> I have no trouble with my throat, but maybe I got tuberculosis without knowing it.

The Warning Signal

I knew a man—he was a terrible drinker. He got sick and couldn't eat and they found out he had cancer for many years and all the whiskey was preserving the cancer in his stomach.

[Were you afraid of an operation?] The only thing I feared was the fact that they might find cancer, and—uh—well—I really didn't expect that they would find cancer but I thought there is a possibility.

[How long was your father sick?] Well, knowingly, about a year. I came home and found Father laying on my davenport, and he'd be all purple. And I'm sure he didn't know about it.

Furthermore, there is quite a common impression among patients that the doctors know a great deal more about the gravity of the patient's illness than they tell him, because they do not want to frighten him with the whole truth about his condition:

They (the doctors) know but won't tell you. You know that. They say, "You have a peptic ulcer." Yet the doctors know they have cancer. If they tell the patients, it would frighten them to death.

The frequent visits to doctors for a checkup that some patients make in order to have peace of mind also indicate their great anxieties about their general state of health.

I have gone for an annual check-over at the cancer clinic. Not that I have any fear whatsoever of cancer, but it's for free. And it gives me a feeling that I'm always all right if I go once a year for this kind of checkup. I plunk down the five bucks for the mental relief that I get from it.

I go over and go through a test—blood pressure and heat and all of that—and—just to find out how I am. [How often?] Oh, maybe once a year.

The fact that the individual feels all right or has no symptoms does not satisfy him. The absence of pain or of symptoms does not give him the assurance that he is healthy. Somewhere in his mind there is a feeling that something might be wrong, and he needs the doctor's statement to regain temporarily his peace of mind. These feelings of anxiety are amply supported by the mass media, which never miss an opportunity to communicate the statistical reality of cancer, heart disease, or insanity.

Another indication of the fears connected with preservation of health is the frequent expectancy of the worst at the onset of a disease:

(When I had the pain) I was afraid I wouldn't be able to walk or something—I did think the worst, you know. Comes natural that people think the worst like that.

I do have—when I have bad pain like I've had the last three —four days—I do consider how long I'm going to have to live. [Live in general or live in pain?] No, live in general.

Sometimes this ever-present expectancy of the worst outcome is not obvious under ordinary circumstances; it is expressed by the patient when he is unable to control his thoughts and emotions:

(When I was hurt) the first thing I said was "I'm paralyzed." Why I plucked that word right out of the air, I don't know. That's the first thing I said.

(Despite extensive probing, the patient denied all knowledge or experience of paralysis before the injury.)

It is not surprising that, with such a predisposition to anxiety about health, a patient's pain, which is seen as a warning signal associated with illness, stimulates him to try to understand the significance of the pain sensation. The interpretation of pain becomes one of the most important aspects of the response to pain. The first thing the patient must decide is whether it is an ordinary pain or a pain that indicates illness.

[(I begin to think) "Why do I have this pain?" "What does

the pain mean?" Either—what did I do—is it a symptom of a disease, or whether it was all because of a dinner or what. Well, now, I work on the explanation as a rule as long as the pain lasts.

[Were you worried about your pain?] The main thing I'd like to know about the thing is—how dangerous is it? [What do you mean by dangerous?] Well, if there is anything wrong with my spine—that I could permanently injure myself.

I think my reaction to pain would depend on how I understood the pain. If—uh—if I understood that I had a pain that is—just there—I could probably stand quite a bit of pain. If I had the same amount of pain and thought that there might be something—then I think I wouldn't be able to stand it so well.

One of the most important functions of the interpretation of the significance of pain is to reduce the anxieties provoked by the sensation. The patient who is attempting to understand the significance of his pain is inclined to interpret it as an ordinary, accepted pain and to minimize the threatening aspect of it.

[So usually you try to find an explanation for your pain?] Yeah. [And what happens when you find an explanation?] I stop worrying. [You stop worrying?] Sure. I'm worrying until I find an explanation. [For instance?] I would go to the doctor if I couldn't classify the pain in any way. This stiff neck for which I had a good reason—a draft.

A patient who had suffered for a long time from an acute circulatory disorder was asked why he had neglected to see a doctor.

I never bothered. Used to pass it off. Say well, I'll get well— just a disturbance, will only last a few days.

A patient with a ruptured disc postponed his visit to the doctor.

I just figured it was a—it was an ordinary muscle sprain and it would go away in a few days.

People in Pain

Another patient with a cancer of the spinal cord reported that, when he had pains in his back:

> I thought I had a little kink in the shoulder, and I used to do this (shrugs his shoulder), and it would go away in a half an hour. Couple of days and I'd get it again.

(Incidentally, this patient had postponed his consultation with the doctor for such a long time that, when he finally did go to see him, it was the last time he stood on his legs.)

Again and again the patients viewed their pain, which was later identified as a symptom of some serious disease, as an ordinary headache, a toothache, the usual stomach trouble, and so on. The Old American patient, in his attempts to fight the anxieties provoked by pain and illness, tries to see his symptom as something everyone else has had or experienced. The ordinary pain is in reality a pain that does not make the patient different from other people, either in sensation or in response to the sensation. When asked about his feelings, he would say that he felt as others would feel in a similar situation.

Repeatedly the patient uses the word *average* in speaking about himself, about the amount of pain he can take, about his illness, or about his behavior. *Average* is normal, correct, accepted, safe, and secure. The patient derives a great deal of reassurance and hope from the statistical change of normality in illness and recovery:

> At the time they told me that I had a spot on my lungs— which floored me. That's the first time I ever knew I had anything like that, and that perturbed me no end. But my father-in-law, who is a doctor, told me that there was nothing to worry about. Statistically they call it T.O.T.B. Almost everybody has it, but a layman when he is first told that is baffled. He thinks he has active T.B. It had me very worried, but as soon as I was told, it didn't bother me. After it was explained to me that—uh—possibly nine-tenths of the city dwellers here in New York have a spot on their lungs.

The Warning Signal

Thus the sensation of pain is heeded, not only because of the discomfort but also because it would be unintelligent and harmful to ignore the warning signal. However, the initial emotional impact is greatly reduced by a euphemistic interpretation—by seeing the pain as of a kind that one does not go to the doctor about.

The Old American goes to the doctor only when he is really sick, when there is something serious, or when all interpretations are of no avail and further postponement of the visit is impossible. Hence the visit to the doctor signifies illness with all its implications. As long as the individual does not go to the doctor, he is not ill—he merely suffers from some kind of temporary discomfort. Frequently the statement "I have never been to a doctor" stands for "I have never been ill."

The tendency of the individual, despite all the anxieties—or, rather, because of the anxieties—is to avoid seeing the doctor when he first feels pain. This avoidance not only reduces the original anxieties and helps minimize the significance of the pain, but also helps the individual show that he is not a sissy or a neurotic.

In his attempt to avoid a consultation with the doctor, and in his attempts not to be classified as sick, the patient uses a number of devices. Again, the most effective way is to follow the principles of preventive measures that are directed toward the general elimination of all possible sources and causes of disease— countless variations on the theme "An apple a day. . . ."

However, when a consultation with a specialist becomes imperative and when longer postponement is impossible, the real doctor is often avoided by consulting various doctor-substitutes, such as druggists, chiropractors, osteopaths, home medical books, and articles in newspapers and popular magazines:

I read a lot of articles, you know, over a number of years. They always put something in the papers, little items pertaining to your health. I read all that stuff.

I woke up with a terrific pain in that left hip region. It was very acute. So I got down to work and a friend of mine had

told me about a physiotherapist who used to work on ball-
players. I figured I'd go down and see if he could fix me.

I have always been chiropractic and osteopathic. When we
go for treatment we feel so much better. And those doctors
are always very cheerful—and there is hope and everything
and I think we worry less.[4]

The reluctance to consult a physician is paradoxically related to
the great confidence in doctors' knowledge. The doctor is seen as
the ultimate expert who knows everything about pain—what it is,
what it signifies, and what to do about it. Only the doctor knows
whether the pain is a symptom of a deadly disease and whether
the patient will die of it. He is the only one who can tell if a person
is really ill:

Well, when you get the doctor to the house, he (examines)
your heart, your chest, your lungs, and all, takes your pulse,
and, if they are all right—you are all right. So I must have
been all right. They said "All that you need—it's the nerves,
and—stomach—you got a nervous stomach or something.
You'll be all right." So in about a week or so, it (the pain)
went away. I was all right. So I said there mustn't have been
nothing the matter.

As already mentioned, the doctor's knowledge is so great that he
can kill a patient by telling him the whole truth about his condition. In his avoidance of consulting the doctor, the patient follows
the familiar "What I don't know won't hurt me!"

On the other hand, even after the patient has consulted the
doctor and heard his opinion, he is often quite dissatisfied and
secretly fearful that the doctor has not actually told him the whole
truth:

[4] One wonders to what extent the popularity of Christian Science,
which had its origin in the United States, is due to the American aversion
to see any doctors: "My father was a Christian Scientist. My uncle was also
a Christian Scientist. That caused him (my father) to go to the doctor at the
very last minute. He didn't go for treatment until—when he was operated
on his cancer was inoperable."

The Warning Signal

I wondered what, what's wrong with me. The majority of them (the doctors) don't give you any—don't tell you anything that you can put your finger on or anything like that. They say you got back trouble there. "We'll fix it up." That's all they tell you.

Often a lack of understanding of the treatment increases the patient's anxieties still more; instead of being reassured by the physician, his worry increases:

When the doctor gives you various medications without telling you what they are for, then you start worrying what is it that he thinks I have or what does he have in mind or anything like that. I mean it does work on your mind.

Another patient gave a rather detailed description of his feelings about his doctor's behavior and its effect on his morale:

Today, they (the doctors) know pretty much about everything and they start telling you, well, you can't do this, you can't do that, and the first thing you start figuring, why can't I do this, and why can't I do that? And in the end you have a pretty good idea, I guess, yourself, and then you start worrying. "Have I got this" or "have I got that?" You're not sure, and it might not be anything, and yet you figure you got some serious disease or anything like that.

Only rarely does an Old American express full confidence in a doctor's words. Such confidence is reflected in the following statement:

The minute I go to a doctor I have the feeling, "Oh, he knows." He gives me the answer. And if he says there's nothing wrong, then I'm sure, and it relieves my mind; I never have to think about it anymore. The minute I talked to him I knew everything was all right so it must have been (slight laugh) indigestion or something.

A distinction should be made between a checkup and a

visit to the doctor when one is ill. When the Old American feels that he is more or less all right, or when he has only vague, general anxieties as to the state of his health, he is much more inclined to go to see a physician to get the necessary reassurance, and he expects the doctor to confirm his feelings that everything is well. However, when the anxieties of the individual are sharply focused on a definite symptom, or when he fears that something is radically wrong with him, then the Old American tends to postpone a consultation with the physician for as long as possible.

The confidence in doctors' skills that is so characteristic of the Old American patient is related to the general confidence in the expert and specialist who has acquired his skills in years of training and experience. Again and again the patients repeat:

> I consider each and every one of them trained in their job to help me.

> The doctor is a fine man. He has definite skill the same way as I have mine.

> They are supposed to know what to do for you if you are sick.

> (I have confidence in them) because that's their chosen field. When a person is sick they are the ones to turn to. You wouldn't turn to a lawyer for healing!

Because of the complete confidence in the physician's knowledge and skill, the patient accepts all aspects of the medical treatment.

> Well, I don't move or anything. You can't move while they are doing that. Just lay there and he puts it in, that's all. I don't say anything to the doctor because I know he has done it so many times, he knows what he is doing and everything.[5]

[5] One patient had such confidence in his dentist that he had accepted the loss of several healthy teeth before he went to a medical doctor, who finally identified his pain as that caused by trigeminal neuralgia!

The Warning Signal

Whatever the doctor does for the patient is for the patient's good; therefore, it must be accepted. "They tell me for my own good—I realize that it's got to be done."

In his relationship to the physician and to the medical treatment, the patient is not a passive subject; on the contrary, he feels that he plays an important, active role by fulfilling the doctor's prescriptions, by being cooperative, and by expressing optimism and a desire to get well:

> I definitely hope I will get the necessary help. They (the doctors) are smarter men than I am and know what they are doing. I am a cooperative patient. I do everything they tell me. I take all the medications they prescribe; I listen to them and I'm sure that I will get well.

A "good" doctor differs from a "bad" one not in terms of his human qualities, but purely in terms of his professional skills. The patient is little concerned with the personality of the doctor; his main concern is the physician's skill and the way in which he handles him:

> [Could you tell me what makes you feel confident about the doctor?] It is just the confidence you have in him—the way he treats you. I mean some doctors—you go in and they rush you in and they stick the finger up your ass and have you stick your tongue out and say "Good-bye, God bless you." Well, a man like that—you ain't got no confidence in him. Another doctor, he takes his time, and looks you over thoroughly and tries to find out what's wrong with you and all. I mean, you just have confidence in him.

When the doctor is called a *good man,* this term refers only to his professional skills. The patient seldom checks the professional and personal background of the physician; the *M.D.* symbol is a sufficient qualification. It tells the patient that the man he is going to visit has been trained in one of the medical schools, was approved by a board of judges, and was found qualified to practice medicine.

Therefore it is good enough to look up a name in the telephone directory or simply to ring the bell on the door with an M.D. plaque on it. Occasionally one may ask a friend or a colleague for the name of a doctor, but it is usually not so much for a recommendation of a skilled doctor as it is to avoid looking up the name in the directory. The problem of finding the "right man" for a special problem is more difficult in a field in which specialization is very great:

> I have a whole series of doctors that I think one of them will be good for this and another will be good for that. So one of the problems whenever anything goes wrong is which doctor is likely to do what I want done at the moment.

But this concern with the selection of the specialist is rather infrequent. As a general rule, the patient never goes to a specialist on his own; he is usually referred to one by the general practitioner or the family doctor.

Obviously, in the presence of such confidence in the physician and in his knowledge, one cannot expect disagreement with his diagnosis. The patient accepts the diagnosis and the prescribed treatment without criticism or discussion. There are almost no instances of checking the doctor's diagnosis against the opinion of a different physician. Only very infrequently does a patient express his opinion about a diagnosis indicating a very grave condition:

> I thought at first I probably had bursitis or something like that and, then the doctors told me—that it might be a tumor on the spine. And *I know, I know* that it's coming from in back or from my shoulders there. It don't affect any other part of my body—my feet or this hand or anything, just this one side. So it's bound to be in the shoulder.

The usual attitude is expressed in: "Well, naturally, your being the specialist, I'm going to take your word for it," or, "They (the doctors)' marked the area of my head, got the picture, (told me)' 'I'll take care of you next week,' and here I am. Still suffering, and

I don't kick. I don't kick or get excited. What I'm going to do won't help anybody."

The general attitude toward health, illness, pain, and doctors is reflected in the way the patient describes his condition to the doctor or to people whom he identifies, to a greater or lesser extent, with the medical profession. If the patient is not quite sure whether he evaluated his pain or other symptoms correctly in terms of the need to consult a medical doctor, he feels that he might be considered by the physician to be a weakling or a neurotic. He does not want to appear childish or effeminate in the doctor's eyes. Nevertheless, because of the worries the symptoms have stimulated, he would like to get a reassuring diagnosis: a qualified opinion that will reestablish his peace of mind and that will make him feel all right. He therefore tends to avoid telling the doctor how he feels emotionally, expecting from the expert an answer that will suggest to him how he *should* feel. He eliminates from the description of his complaints any expressions of emotion, trying to appear rational, calm, and cooperative. He assumes a detached, depersonalized attitude, which is reflected in his manner of speaking and which can best be defined as "reporting" on pain.

Reporting is characterized by a tendency to minimize the expression of the patient's actual feelings about his condition and by a tendency to relate in a most precise and detailed way the qualitative and quantitative aspects of the sensation. In listening to the patient's description of his pain experience, one is impressed by his efforts to be objective, impersonal, and quasi-scientific. He goes into great detail as to the location, duration, and intensity of the pain. He is careful to differentiate between the varying degrees of severity of his pain at different times and in different situations. Sometimes he uses comparisons in order to better communicate the qualitative aspects of the pain: "The pain was sharp like with a knife"; "it was like stabbing with a fork"; "it was a dull pain like hitting with the fist." There is no attempt to play up or exaggerate the pain; on the contrary, the patient somewhat understates its impact on him. Often, instead of telling directly how he felt during an attack of pain, he prefers to speak about the immediate effects of the pain on his usual activities. He communicates the severity of the experience only by implication. To impress upon the physician the extent of his suffering, he would rather say what he had to do to alleviate the pain.

> [How painful was it? How strong was the pain?] Well, pretty bad. They had to give me a shot every so often.

> [How severe were these headaches?] They were severe enough that I went to the medics.

A few examples may help to demonstrate better what is meant by reporting. A migraine patient gave the following description of his headache:

> I can tell you exactly. It starts here (points to the temple) and goes in a circle (encircles temple with finger), and then it crawls around the back of the head to the other side (still following the headline with the finger across the head to the other temple), starts to pain, and forms a circle, and the pain crawls the other way. Then when the two meet, I sort of go out of my mind and can't see anymore.

Another patient remarked:

> [Does your pain change in intensity?] Now this may seem rather silly to you, but to me it seems as if I had three distinct kinds of pain. In the back, as I told you, it is a deep-seated ache. Then—fairly acute ache. In the front, the skin is extremely sensitive and also I have frequently pain in just one spot. I would say that's where the transverse colon meets the descending colon. That's as near as I can figure out the spot. And then my rib—my backbone, right around my sternum— the bone is sore. You just put your finger on the bone—it feels very sore to the touch. Uh—at the moment (the pain) in my side is greater than the pain in my front. And it's— uh—it's a little difficult to say—uh—they all hurt, and which hurts the most I don't know.

The Warning Signal

The description sounds almost as if it were taken from a medical textbook and not as if it were being told by a person who was suffering at the same moment that he was being interviewed! The patient had no medical training—he was a manager of a welfare division in an insurance company.

Thus reporting fulfills an important function of concealing from the doctor—and often from the patient himself—the tensions and emotions provoked by pain. It also gives the patient the opportunity to appear as a "man" and thus win the physician's approval. Moreover, besides the whistling-in-the-dark function, reporting helps the physician to form a better picture of the pain experience and facilitates the diagnosis. In this respect, reporting is seen by the patient as cooperation with the doctor; it gives him a feeling of participation in the doctor's work. The patient and the doctor combine their efforts to determine the source of trouble. This team, which is established at the first examination, will, if necessary, continue as a partnership in fighting whatever is found to be wrong. To this partnership the doctor contributes his professional skill and leadership, and the patient contributes his cooperation and desire to get well. Reporting allows both the patient and the doctor to establish an efficient and businesslike relationship with each other, free from personal and emotional involvement, which is not only unnecessary but often harmful to the possibility of bringing about a successful treatment.

Characteristic of reporting is an attempt to dissociate the self from the pain and illness or from the injured area. The patient will not say "my leg hurts" or "my stomach hurts"; rather he will say *"the* leg hurts," or "I have a bum stomach." In dissociating the affected area from the rest of the body, the patient implies that he is not really sick; the condition is limited to one part, while the rest of him is perfectly all right. In these attempts to dissociate the pain, it is often personified. The patient uses a language that suggests the pain exists outside the body, ready to attack its victim. The verbs and adjectives used by the patients to describe their pain suggest that it is "mean and sneaky," "it comes and goes," and "it grabs you and hurts you." In responding to pain, the patient "fights

83

it," "takes it away," "wears it off," "fools it," "rubs it out," "massages it out," and even "eats it." Finally, he "kills" it with a pain killer.

The personification of pain, besides being an expression of dissociation from the self, helps the patient assume an active role of fighting against a personified enemy—a fight calling for an alliance between the patient with his will and resistance and the doctor with his skill and experience.

Another aspect of the language used in reporting pain is the frequent use of mechanical concepts and vocabulary. The patient sees the functioning of the human organism as the working of a complex machine. Any disfunction is understood in terms of mechanical trouble and therefore can be dealt with by mechanical means. The familiarity of the American patient with machinery and his resourcefulness in dealing with gadgets help a great deal to reduce his anxieties about organic trouble if that trouble is interpreted as a mechanical difficulty. It is not by accident that the patient says the doctor will "fix" his condition; neither is it by accident that a great many health and medical concepts in American society are communicated in the language of mechanics.[6] Perceiving illness as mechanical trouble makes it identifiable and familiar; it can then be considered as a condition that can be successfully treated by a specialist, just like a mechanical disturbance with a car, refrigerator, or television set. Therefore a large number of Old American patients show a tendency to reduce every organic disturbance to a mechanical cause, thus making it identifiable, controllable, and reparable.

This mechanistic image of the body is well illustrated in the following reply of a patient who was asked how he visualized his body:

[6] *Life* magazine (April 21, 1952) published a series of cartoons urging people to go to the right doctors and clinics in case of symptoms that might indicate cancer. These posters used a number of parallel illustrations comparing the correct handling of a car with mechanical troubles: going to a reliable mechanic with adequate equipment with the proper handling of a stomach disorder or going to a reliable doctor with a well-equipped examination room.

The Warning Signal

I'd compare it to a machine. [Why? Do you know anything about machinery?] Well, to an extent. I mean, it—uh—one certain part—uh—there's got to be a certain part that controls all other parts and you have arms and this and that—work different working parts and they all have to function together, to make the machine operate right. The human body is the same thing—all the parts have to function together to make the body operate right.

(Incidentally, this patient's occupation was bookmaking.) With this picture in mind, it is natural to attribute pain to the defective functioning of the body machine: "My pain was caused by a short of two nerves—it's like electricity. If you put two nerves together and they touch each other, it forms a short and that's why I got my pain." This is an explanation for the excruciating pain symptomatic of trigeminal neuralgia. "It seemed to be in the hip joint where the bones are rubbing. And I thought that the muscle is pulling in the wrong way." Thus another patient described his pain, which was caused by a herniated disc.

Similarly, pain is caused by "rust around the nerves," "defective ball bearings," "twisted ligaments," and so on. The mechanistic explanation of pain and illness makes it easier for the patient to accept various aspects of the medical treatment, including the most frightening one: the operation.

In the eyes of the patient, the doctor is provided with excellent tools and equipment, has the necessary skill and experience, and therefore can be trusted when he has to perform an operation.

[And how do you feel about the operation?] Oh, I feel great. I wish they'd do it tomorrow. [Why?] Because—because the doctors know their job. Well, I feel this operation is going to fix me up.

This attitude does not mean that the patient has no anxieties about the operation; it only means that he has an anxiety-reducing device that allows him to accept the operation with less apprehension.

85

Furthermore, he does not accept the suggested operation blindly; he wants to know what "they" will do, why they will do it, and what he himself should expect. Similarly, he will not accept a repair of his car without first having a full description of what is wrong, what is to be fixed, and how the job will be done.

> [Now, would you agree to an operation?] I would if they could show me—you know, in other words, I'd like to see what they're going to do. I wouldn't just say "Go ahead and operate." I want to know what they expect the effects. They know what they're doing, and I think that they can explain it to me clear enough to make me understand. [So you want an explanation about it before?] Yes, before I would agree to operate, because I feel that from what I heard of these doctors up there they're pretty good—they're not just quacks —they're pretty good doctors. And I believe they know what they're doing or I wouldn't have come here. You know? Like I told Dr. B—. He asked me about the same thing. So I told him that—uh—it depends a lot on what you expect. Is it worth what you're going to get?

The more sophisticated and careful informant goes even further than just asking for a detailed estimate of the "fixing job"—he wants to see the blueprint of the operation:

> It is my standard practice, when an operation comes up for either me or my family. I'll go to the library and get *Gray's Surgical Anatomy* and look up the operation. That is standard practice.

He is not checking up on the correctness of the doctor's diagnosis or trying to find out from a different source whether the operation is necessary. His only concern is with *how* and where the operation is performed.

The reluctance to undergo an operation that would eliminate pain was expressed by a disabled patient who felt that it might further impair his motor abilities. He preferred to suffer pain rather than handicap whatever movement was left:

The Warning Signal

> I know there is an operation that can kill the spasms, but
> I'd rather take the pain that goes with them. [Why?] Well,
> the operation—I have movement now, but after the operation
> I may not have no movement.

A patient may also be reluctant to have an operation if it involves
danger to an especially sensitive organ or if the possibility of treating the pain by other means exists:

> [How do you feel about an operation?] That's my last resort.
> [You wouldn't like it?] Not to cut a nerve. [Why?] Aw, just
> that—my mind—I don't want my nerves cut unless I have
> to have them cut. When there's something else will help, why
> cut my nerve?

Incidentally, in discussing his reluctance to undergo an operation,
this patient made use of his mechanistic concept of the body:

> That's—that's my nerve—that's very vital. Nerves is a vital
> thing. I'm not a dummy—I can understand, you know, very
> well. I know how to fix an automobile, and if you know how
> to fix it right you got to be smart, you can't be a dummy.
> I know that nerves are vital. You can cut a nerve—that's the
> end of the nerve. You cut your leg off and you get a wooden
> one. But you can't get a nerve

The operation becomes really threatening when an injured part
cannot be replaced with a "spare part"; conversely, as long as an
organ is replaceable, the operation—even an amputation—becomes
acceptable.

What does the patient expect from the physician in response
to his reporting? Above all, he expects something that will somehow
reduce the anxieties provoked by pain and other symptoms. When
he consults the doctor, the Old American patient has a slight hope
that the medical examination will show that there is nothing basically wrong with him and, as pointed out before, that the pain is
due to some minor, ordinary cause:

Lord knows it may be something else. A man I knew that
had such pain in the back, and after he had gone to all kind
of doctors, they discovered he had flat feet. And he was cured.

If the pain cannot be attributed to some minor cause, however, the patient expects a diagnosis that will *name* the kind of
disturbance that is at the root of his symptom. Having a name for
the disease is most important for the patient, because, if the disease
is known, there is always an assumption that the cure for it is also
known. Or, if it is not yet known, it may be discovered in the
course of medical progress.

It is the unknown disease—the disease that cannot be identified in terms of some namable agent, such as a germ, virus, infection, or allergy—that is most dreaded by the patient.

I'm worried if I think it may mean something that I don't
know about it. This may be worse.

I'm getting worried about it now. I don't know what it is. I
want to get it fixed. I hope the doctors will find out what it is
and eventually will (fix it).

In their fear of the unknown cause of pain, some patients may
even accept the "psychogenic" or "psychosomatic" explanation, so
long as it does not imply that something is basically wrong with
their health. They may also accept such an explanation if it labels
the cause of their pain in terms that, in recent years, have become
quite familiar to readers of the health columns in newspapers and
magazines.

Now—uh—this pain, I think most that I have, I'd put down
as psychogenic origin.

One patient made the following comment about his past pain
experiences: "I think if we had known then what we know about
neurotic behavior, much of it could have been attributed to those
causes." However, this explanation is not the most favored one,
because, for the unsophisticated patient, having pain "in the mind"

88

implies that something is wrong with his mental faculties. Patients have often described how much their anxieties were relieved once they were given a definite and precise identification of their condition. This result is quite understandable because of the great fear of the unknown and because of the fear that something dreadful may be discovered during the medical examination.

The need to know the cause of the pain-provoking condition, as well as the desire to find a name for it in order to label it and classify it, is not an isolated phenomenon in American cultural and social life. Much financial and intellectual effort is being invested in all possible areas of economic, social, and political investigation. Armies of scientists are engaged in searching for causes of market fluctuations, juvenile delinquency, or voting behavior. For the conviction is that, if the cause is known, the control of events is assured. Hence there is a need to watch for every sign of change, every unusual symptom, and every aberration from the normal and predictable, and to fit it into the body of previous experience, thus attenuating the possible threat of the unknown. Security is based on predictability and knowledge of the cause-and-effect relationship. The unknown is often unpredictable, hence dangerous and threatening. The life of the American is frequently focused on look-out-for-warning signals, whether they appear in health, occupation, economics, or political life. Stop-look-listen is a principle that applies not only on the highways, but on the roads toward economic, social, or professional security. The American listens for unusual sounds in his automobile engine; he watches for cracks in the walls of his house; he observes the changes in the mood of his boss. For all these deflections from the normal may be signs indicating the danger of accident, unemployment, or injury. The pragmatic mind of the American does not accept the thought that something may occur without a reason or that some manifestations may be accidental and insignificant. Everything must have a reason and therefore (unless it belongs to such categories as luck, which is supernatural) an effect; moreover, the effects may be harmful.

Something must be wrong if one does not receive an invitation to the luncheon or cocktail party, and it is not an accident that a coworker was selected to handle an important new account. These signs may be indices of social rejection or failure in the competitive efforts for promotion. In a society in which people are sensitive to the significance of signs and social symbols, words become unnecessary and often misleading. Thus social communication is, to a great extent, based on symbols rather than on direct verbal expression.

A great deal of intellectual energy is devoted to decoding various symbols, which are often seen as symptoms—a medical term that has become a part of the everyday language—to denote a threatening manifestation in any area of human life. This preoccupation with symptoms, however, is not necessarily conscious; it has become so internalized and integrated in the communication arsenal that symbolic messages are registered and responded to like traffic signs, without manifest concentration. The wearing effects of the unconscious tension and concentration become apparent only at the end of the journey.

One can speculate about the origin of the "on-guard" phenomenon in American culture. Historically, it can be traced to the unfamiliar and alien environment encountered by the early settlers in the New World, who found strange fruits, animals, and people whose unfamiliar tastes, looks, or comportment could mean destruction and death. For the pioneer and frontiersman the adherence to the stop-look-listen slogan actually meant survival in a setting in which unusual sounds or movements in the forest or prairies could mean a stealthy attack of an enemy or dangerous animal. The skills of the Pathfinder were not a product of the creative imagination of James Fenimore Cooper, but actual tools and weapons of generations of builders of a country in conditions in which overconfidence and insensitivity to environmental manifestations could have had a fatal outcome. In dealing with native tribes, whether in peace or war, much was based on correct interpretation of signs and symbols rather than on verbal communication. Such expressions as *the broken arrow, burying the hatchet,* or *smoking the peace pipe* are familiar examples of this language of symbols and gestures inherited from times when they were not colorful idioms but part of a difficult reality.

The same traditions of the early frontiersmen also give rise to the apprehension with regard to the environment that is expressed in the notion that pain and illness are caused by external agents. People came from countries where every leaf was familiar, where each stream was known, where every insect was intimate—a cultural experience transmitted by generations of English, Dutch, or German farmers. They settled in a land where they had to learn by trial and error the dangers and benefits of their new environment. They had to experience the perils of new plants, waters, and climate. People who were basically strong and healthy became victims of afflictions associated with the new land, be it poison ivy or sumac or fevers of the Rocky Mountains or Texas. In agricultural Europe nature was familiar and beneficial; in the New World it was strange and threatening. In the old country nature was an ally; in the new it was an enemy to be conquered. It is no wonder that the immigrants developed an apprehension and distrust of water, air, and fruits and felt that only a detailed knowledge of the composition and ingredients of the consumed foods could offer an assurance of harmlessness and benefit.

As many other traits of American national character, such as self-reliance, spirit of freedom, or action-mindedness, are traced to the origin of American society in a new setting, so attitudes toward illness and pain could stem from these times. On the one hand were the stern and rigid principles of the Puritans; on the other hand were the absence of medical care, and the failure of the traditional nostrums, potions, and antidotes to respond to new diseases. These factors combined to develop the attitude that there was no use to complain and that, to pull through one had to depend primarily on his physical fitness and his own *resistance* to illness and pain.

Together with other values and attitudes, the early settlers left to future generations of Americans an attitude toward time that was destined to become a most important trait of the American

91

character. All thoughts and activities are concentrated on the future. This future orientation of American culture is one of the major characteristics that differentiates the American from his European ancestors. It was for a better future that the immigrants broke with their past and toiled in the present, and it is for the future that the contemporary American lives, works, and plans. Yesterday is forgotten in the hardships of today for a better tomorrow; for tomorrow means a better job, a bigger car, or a larger house in a nicer neighborhood. The American has little respect for people who live in the past. He considers people immature who live by the day, but he admires those who have the vision of the future for themselves, their children, their community, or the world. The future is not always certain; therefore it requires constant planning, figuring, and watching. All activities thus become oriented toward tomorrow to an extent that, when it arrives, it is only one link in a long chain of anxiety-ridden todays. The present becomes a lifelong pursuit of a future happiness, with the effect that, frequently, there is not time to stop for the enjoyment of the present reality, which was yesterday's goal.

The same preoccupation with the future is manifest in the patient's attitude toward his pain. When he is concerned with the symptomatic meaning of his suffering or worried about the significance and effects of his condition, his thinking is directed toward the future and not toward the immediacy of the sensation. The pain he perceives in the present is disturbing mainly because of its significance for the future. Although the American patient carefully avoids the word *worry* and replaces it with a less emotional *I wonder* or *I think about,* nevertheless his future-oriented anxieties are quite explicit:

> Yes, I wonder about it in a way. The main thing I like to know about this thing—how dangerous is it? What could I do to myself if I went ahead and tried to do something that wasn't just kosher? Could I permanently injure myself? If they could tell me and show me where it is and if there is no danger, it would relieve me very much. [So you are worried

that this type of injury can handicap you in the future?]
That's it. That's what bothers me now.

This concern with the future goes hand in hand with the
planning about "what to do if. . . ."

> Yes, I'm apt to worry. If I have a cold or something like that,
> I'm worried until I feel that I'm over the worst of it. I figure
> if I have a severe illness what would I have to do—when I
> discover it—if I am at home, in bed. I would have to get up,
> dress, get a taxi, and go to the hospital—by myself. I have it
> all planned out. If I feel I have a severe illness, I would do
> just that. I would go to the New York Hospital and tell them
> to notify my doctor that I was there.

The emotional tone of these excerpts reflects the American
ethos with regard to the future: the anxieties, the careful planning,
not leaving anything to chance. The patient plans every detail of a
future situation (which may or may not occur) with the same
thoroughness with which an average American plans his system of
insurance for every possible eventuality, including the college tui-
tion of his children or the indemnity for an injury sustained by a
visitor in his house.

It would be difficult to bear the constant preoccupation with
the future without another gift from the past: the gift of optimism
and faith. No man could survive the hardships of migration and
the struggle for the control of natural forces without a strong belief
in the final success and happiness of the days to come. This optimism and hope, which performed miracles in building the American society and in making it rich and powerful, are also expressed
by the Old American patient, who, although worried about the
painful symptoms of his condition, can still afford a smile when
discussing its final outcome. Frequent comments are: "I'm sure
that I'll get well," "I hope they (the doctors) will fix it," and
"They will find a cure for it." He is always ready to substantiate
his feelings with examples from recent medical discoveries, scien-

tific progress, or personal experiences. Indeed, he refuses to listen to pessimistic and discouraging details:

> I don't like when they go into too many bloody details about how bad they were cut, and what they took out of them, and all that stuff. I like to hear the promising side, the side that they are getting better, well, that they got something to look forward to.

The patient wants to listen to cheerful information and reassuring words from doctors, nurses, and other patients so he can feel that his optimistic smile is supported by his environment.

> [Do you worry about it?] No, I don't think so, because I just feel as though it's something that can be taken care of.

This rationalized optimism finds the necessary support in different life experiences. Everyone can give examples of critical situations in life that were overcome at the end. Fortunes were made, lost, and made again; economic depression was followed by prosperity; diseases were conquered. Besides, there are people who are always worse off than the patient himself, as exemplified by a paraplegic with a great deal of spastic pain:

> Well, in my case I can say I'm lucky. I have my arms and hands whereas I could be a lot more unfortunate. I wouldn't want to be that way, if I could help it, but if I had to be this way I'd rather be a paraplegic than blind and still have my legs.

However, the optimism of the Old American patient is not passive, during which he sits back and waits for a miracle. On the contrary, the first condition of a positive outlook toward the future is incessant activity. The patient can be optimistic only when he knows that something is being done about his pain. Somebody has to do something about the solution of the problem of pain or illness in order to make the patient feel happy and optimistic. The absence of activity provokes discouragement and depression:

The Warning Signal

I'm depressed because nothing is been done. I just keep
laying on a board. A person gets depressed and impatient.
When I asked the doctor whether they are going to give me
some needles or so, or lamp treatment, he said, "No, your
laying on the board is your treatment."

In the mind of the patient, if nothing is being done, it
means nothing *can* be done, which is equivalent to a final con-
demnation:

I can take pain. I always could take it. I didn't complain
about pain. But now everything is gone. I'm depressed. I don't
know what to do. I haven't done anything here. I stay in
bed too much. I would like to walk, to move around, to go
to treatments.

It is no wonder that this action-mindedness of the Old
American patient makes him a most cooperative patient in the hospital setting. He participates actively in his treatment by keeping
busy, that is, by taking medication and going to treatment, by learning to live with his pain or condition, and, most of all, by trying to
get well. Being in the hospital is a full-time job that requires a good
morale and optimism.

Every activity requires its adequate, specialized setting for
best results. The hospital is the most appropriate place for activities
associated with illness. Accordingly, the patient displays a most
positive attitude toward this institution. "Everything is wonderful
here," said a patient when he was asked if he would prefer to be
treated at home. He stated, "No, definitely not. I think that if
something is wrong with you the hospital is the place to do it."
The hospital is the place where the patient can devote himself to
the important task of getting well with the same spirit of initiative
and self-reliance he is expected to show in a shop or office:

Take this hospital—it's so that you come here to help yourself. You try to get yourself well, you know. Not that you
want somebody else trying to do your job for you. You see

that other fellow? He is trying to do things himself—which is right. The same with me. I don't need attention. Because I'm here to help myself.

The Old American patient insists that he does not want sympathy or attention, but merely an opportunity to show his working potentialities. Naturally, the setting must be adequate in terms of staff, equipment, and physical facilities. Thus, when the patient has any complaints to express, they are seldom directed toward people or such hospital traits as lack of warmth or individualized attention (which are often mentioned by patients from other ethnic groups) but against objective shortcomings of the institution, such as staff inefficiency, inadequate plumbing, condition of floors, or poor administration.

The Old American patient is thus the ideal patient, a model used as an example not only by the people who are directly involved in relieving his condition, but also by members of other groups who, although they are also Americans, do not have the adjective *old* included in their national identification.

CHAPTER 3

❀❀❀❀❀❀❀❀❀❀❀❀❀❀❀❀❀❀❀❀❀❀❀❀❀

The Patient
Knows Best

❀❀❀❀❀❀❀❀❀❀❀❀❀❀❀❀❀❀❀❀❀❀❀❀❀

The patient of Jewish origin, when dressed in his hospital pajamas and lying in a bed or sitting in a wheel chair, is indistinguishable from any other patient. Only the elderly World War I veteran can occasionally be identified as a Jew by his speech or by the Yiddish newspaper he may read in bed. Sometimes a conversation in Yiddish between the patient and his visitors can help to identify the Jewish patient. However, these signs are rather infrequent, and even the nurse is not always able to tell whether the patient is Jewish, unless she refers to the chart that carries an *H* (Hebrew) for patients of the Jewish religion. However, an analysis of the background information derived from interviews reveals a number of significant differences between Jewish patients and others.

In terms of socioeconomic status, more than half the Jewish respondents belonged to the lower-middle and middle class, whereas patients of Irish, Italian, and Old American background were predominantly of the lower class. In terms of occupation, more than 50 per cent of the Jews were engaged in nonphysical or intellectual work; the occupations of respondents from other groups were predominantly physical (for example, laborer) or nonphysical with some physical effort (for example, machinist).

The Jewish patients also differed from other groups in terms of educational background: almost half of them had some college education, which is more than twice as many as the Old Americans, who placed second among the four groups interviewed. The Jews were predominantly of the first American-born generation, whereas the Irish were predominantly second generation. However, the Jewish and Italian generational distributions were similar.

In the interview setting the patient of Jewish origin stands out in his role as an informant. The impression of the interviewer is that the Jewish informants are the most verbal, if not the most articulate. Their responses to questions abound in details, which sometimes seem to have only a marginal relationship to the topic. They seem to look forward to the opportunity to talk about their pain, illness, anxieties, intrafamily relationships, and so on. They seem happy to find a listener with whom they can share their feelings, worries, and opinions. A question acts as a stimulus that allows the informant to release a flow of responses, comments, and interpretations. The impression is that they are used to speaking about their troubles and that the interview situation is not their first opportunity to express themselves. Probing is necessary to pinpoint specific information rather than to elicit a fuller answer to a question.

It is not surprising that members of the medical profession

The Patient Knows Best

who expect from the patient a tendency to understate his feelings with reference to his pain experience—an expectation lived up to by the Old American and Irish patients—tend to describe the Jewish patients as overemotional or as exaggerating their pains or illness.

In relating their pain experiences, patients of Jewish origin use a dramatic vocabulary to convey their discomfort and anxieties to the fullest extent. Their way of describing their pain leaves the impression that the patient is afraid that the doctor may not fully grasp the impact of the situation. To define the severity of their pain, the patients use such adjectives as terrific, unbelievable, fantastic, unbearable, excruciating, and agonizing. As if to impress the listener with the intensity of his sufferings, the patient will tell how he was rolling on the floor, jumping around, or hitting his head against the wall:

> Well, I tell you what I think was pain—and to me I think it's a lot of pain. Do you know what a gall bladder attack is? Well, for eight months I took it. I rolled on the floor from this wall to that wall—chewing the carpet. For eight months! Now do you think that's pain?

> I bang my head against the wall, I've shoved my face into boiling water, I've taken heat lamps and gotten so close to it as to where I've seared the skin. I have rolled around where one minute I'm lying prone and the next minute I'm up with my head buried between my legs; the next minute I'm walking around, lying down again, trying all sorts of things that might give me relief.

> I was laying in the house and how many times I used to roll on the floor! Many times I used to feel like jumping through the window—the pain was so severe. Another thing, I used to get relief when I jumped into the bathtub. When I jumped into the bathtub, it stopped. Not entirely, but stopped. So naturally I jumped in and out—in and out—and as soon as you get out you feel a bit chilly, and it pains again. Oh, what I went through!

People in Pain

The patient wants to show that he was actually possessed by his pain, as was suggested by an American-born medical intern who described his own pain experience in no less dramatic terms than the other patients:

> The degree of intensity of pain, when the pain is . . . has reached its maximum, then it's the center of my whole attention. I'm totally incapacitated for any thing. I cannot talk to anybody, because—I—I'm just possessed by the severe pain, and I—I recall thinking or saying to myself that it's fantastic the pain. It's unbelievable. And using these words to myself— unbelievable, fantastic.

Without any inhibition or shame the patient informs the listener that he cannot stand pain, that he cannot tolerate it, and that he has a low threshold of pain. Most of them say that they are very sensitive to pain and can take only a small amount of it when it is associated with a sudden insignificant injury:

> I just couldn't take the pain. I—I'm susceptible to pain, Doctor. No, sir, I can't stand pain. Oh, I don't mean to say that I can't stand any little pain, but the pain I have now . . . I can't.

> Oh, something will drop on my foot; I have kicked my shins, I busted my arm on several different occasions. I've had— on the subject of boils—I've had them cut. And, I think I've taken them normally. Of course, I'll wince with pain and I'll moan a few times, but I've never—outside of these headaches —actually lost control of myself.

With this low tolerance of pain is associated a totally uninhibited, expressive behavior. Groaning, moaning, and complaining are freely reported as part of the pain experience, as are tears. Only a small number of the younger, American-born patients described their reaction to pain in terms of the accepted "American" way:

The Patient Knows Best

I can take pain as well as the average person. I don't think I would groan or moan more than any average person would. I believe I can stand a good amount. I never groaned or moaned about this particular pain. I don't believe I cried from pain.

[Do you complain about your headaches? Do you moan to the nurse or to the doctor?] Well, the doctor asks me how it is. I mean, I'm truthful with him and tell him that it bothers me, yes, but—I mean, I don't go running to the nurse every few minutes and say it bothers me. They have got some really sick people up there; I don't want to bother them.

However, this reserved and inexpressive behavior, although correct according to the hospital expectations, can be considered deviant from the general pattern of the large majority of the Jewish patients. They not only complain freely but consider it wrong not to express their feelings. A patient describing his wife's behavior made the following comments:

She keeps quiet, but I—later on I can notice it—a change in her appearance. She worries inside. Where with me I come right out. If I got something in me, I say it, the hell with it. I want to get out with it. She will not come out with it.

A patient commenting about the inexpressive behavior of his mother disapproved of it quite strongly:

She could be ready to die and she wouldn't open her mouth. I know we took her out one day to show her a good time and, just as we got home, my mother lay down on the couch and passed out. She was sick all day. She didn't tell us. That was a bit meshugga. She wouldn't spoil our fun.

This expressive behavior fulfills a definite function in the pain experience. The Old American is inexpressive because he feels complaining does not help; the Jew complains because he feels it does help.

101

I loosened down—I let out the emotion. Because I knew it's best to let it out than to keep it within yourself. Cry it out and be better off.

I never cry. Except when I get these headaches. It's the only thing I can do—the only outlet I've got.

A patient in the small group of Jews who denied crying commented with regret on his inability to express his feelings with a good cry:

I don't think I've ever cried. I've had tears come to my eyes —tears—but I couldn't—couldn't come out. In fact, sometimes I feel if I could I'd feel much better.

Yet the function of the expressive patterns is not only cathartic. It fulfills also a communicative function in interpersonal relationships. Crying is a message to the social environment, and the expectation is that the message will be responded to by help. After all, how would people know that one is in distress? For thousands of years, words, complaints, and tears have served the Jewish people to mobilize help from parents, neighbors, rulers, and God. In a culture in which kings and prophets have cried when the nation was in grief and in which parents demand Jehovah's help, shedding tears over the prayer book or Friday night candles, the individual is not ashamed to cry when he needs help from a doctor or nurse. Accordingly, the Jewish patient has no qualms about the fact that tears fulfill their function:

Yesterday it hit me like hell. I was crying like a baby. So the nurse came in. I don't know what I would have done if she hadn't helped me. She helped me turn over. She gave me a pill and that relieved me.

When a patient is in pain or discomfort, crying is a natural reaction. However, it is not so much the sensation of pain that makes the patient cry; rather, it is the feeling of helplessness in a situation in which no help is available:

The Patient Knows Best

When I was admitted to the hospital here—I had been sitting in this wheelchair for some time, and sitting doesn't help my back—the doctor had the attendant pull me out of the chair and put me on the table and the pain was so severe that I started to cry. I just couldn't stop myself. I was sobbing and tried to control myself, but I just sobbed on. I felt completely helpless and at a complete loss, and uncontrollably the sobbing and crying took place.

I cried once when I was in severe pain. It was a helpless feeling, more like tears came to my eyes with the light. I felt so helpless.

When the pain was bothering me and bothering me and bothering me, and I couldn't take it. I mean—I—I couldn't take it. It was bothering me and I started to get tears and I —I wanted to put my hands through the wall. I wanted to do something crazy—I mean it was bothering me. Bothered me. Nothing was being done. It was aggravating. I mean, home with my wife when I'd say something, automatically she'd do something. But there I was laying and it was bothering me. I cried because I couldn't do anything about it.

These statements refer to behavior in a hospital, where the patient feels at a loss because of its impersonal atmosphere. At home tears are not necessary to convey the call for help; the Jewish patients know that a complaint will elicit the expected response. When the husband is ill, the wife becomes immediately involved in his condition. However, to adequately live up to her husband's expectation, a mere knowledge of his suffering is insufficient. She is expected to identify herself completely with her husband's pain:

My woman—my wife—she—I drove her almost nuts. You know, she couldn't stand the pains which I had.

She feels them (the pains) as strongly as I do. She's up at the first groan I give. If I sit up in bed, she's up the next second. If it's severe, "What can I get for you—you want the pill now? Do you want the heat pad? Do you want the lamp? You want an ice pack?" Anything that she can possibly do.

103

People in Pain

The normal relationship between husband and wife requires immediate communication as to his condition:

> During the middle of the night I had such pains that I had to wake my wife up, and I couldn't lay down.

Sometimes, in a long-term-illness, constant complaining is unnecessary. The wife is so well trained that a simple word is sufficient to initiate the chain of helping activities:

> [Do you complain to your wife?] No, not generally. No, I tell her I—I don't feel well and she knows the history of this thing pretty much the way I do and I tell her I don't feel well and she generally makes the bed for me, gets the heating pad ready and orange juice, brings the radio into the room, and she makes me comfortable, and from then on she goes about her normal household duties.

The only time the patient does not complain or ask for help is when there is no one around and complaining would be purposeless:

> I fell in my bathtub. Hot bath sometimes relieves the pain. The water was out and I was pushing up and my hands slipped off the sides and I dropped right on the coccyx. Well, that also was one of the great pains that I recall. [Did you scream or call for help?] No, I didn't. I didn't think my wife would help me because I had locked the bathroom door from the inside and she couldn't get in anyway. The pain was so intense that I was thinking I'm going to vomit. But I didn't and finally got back to the bed.

The complaint fulfills its function only when a responsive recipient is around. When a complaint loses its communicative function, tears express the loneliness and helplessness of the sufferer. The patient may cry in the hospital if his complaints are not responded to; he will cry at home if his social environment assumes a similar attitude of unresponsiveness.

The Patient Knows Best

Everyone in the environment of the person in pain is expected to be informed about the discomfort and be ready to offer commiseration, sympathy, and help. The suffering of a member of the family is the suffering of the entire family. Father, mother, wife, or children are supposed to participate in the total pain experience, from its onset to the final relief. Moreover, they are expected to demonstrate their participation by asking questions, showing their worries, expressing their concern, and urging the patient to see the doctor or to take his medicine. The sick member of the family is entitled to "drive nuts" not only his wife but everybody around him. If he becomes irritated or cranky, he does not feel guilty about it, because his annoying behavior is the prerogative of being sick. Regardless of how disagreeable he may be, he cannot stay alone and should not be left alone. Withdrawal from people is inconceivable, because suffering is with people just as the entire process of living is with people. When a patient says that he withdraws in pain or that he wants to be alone, this isolation is relative. There is always a person to share the patient's aloneness and to participate with him in his suffering:

> I can't talk to people, because I have no patience to talk and therefore generally I don't like anybody around because if someone sees me—if one of my friends sees me—he sees I'm obviously in severe pain and will start asking me what's the matter, "Can I help you?" and so forth. I can't stand that. I'd rather be alone. The only other person that I can stand being around is my wife, because she doesn't bother me with silly questions. She leaves me alone. Whatever she does is helpful. That is, if I want anything she'll get it for me without making any fuss. She won't make any undue fuss about it and won't make any comments about it. She might ask me "Is there anything I can do?" and that's all. So I rather like my wife around, because if I need anything she'll get it for me. Otherwise I can't stand anyone around.

The withdrawal pattern is totally absent in the Jewish interviews. Being alone in trouble is contrary to the values of their culture.

People in Pain

The patient's wife, who has to be ready to respond immediately to every sign of discomfort and every verbal complaint, becomes a most attentive nurse of the sick person. Occasionally she accepts this role with some rebellion, and it is not surprising that some wives describe their functions with bitterness. A young American-born wife of a patient made the following comments about the expectations she had to live up to in her husband's family:

> He uses his condition, you know, as an excuse to pamper him a lot. His mother said that he's not supposed to do this, and he's not supposed to do that, and I have—in other words, I have to do the same thing. I have also to pamper him and do things for him, when—and expecting nothing in return too, but I don't feel that's right. No matter what you do for him is not enough. And the more you do the worse it is. Until I feel that I—I do so much, and that—I can't go no more, and it's still not enough.

This attitude toward her husband does not pass unnoticed, and the patient does not hide his resentment against his wife. He feels that she should live up to her role, so much more because "even the government" has recognized the patient's painful condition:

> You might say with those bundles. Now, I know I shouldn't do the bundles, but there, you know, you come up with a problem. "Terry's husband—look at Terry's husband. He washes the bundles every day. Look at that husband; he takes the kids out, this, that, and other things." But what she doesn't realize if she has to be told—in other words I have to say: "Why, you so-and-so. Can't you realize that I'm getting a pension? Is the government paying me because I'm a good boy or something? There must be a reason. Get an understanding person, and it's all right. But where will you find one? Probably after the catastrophe it will be a little better. [What catastrophe?] This. Being in the hospital.

Fortunately for the Jewish patients, most wives are more

understanding and considerate. In most cases the wives, being well informed about their husbands' conditions, do everything that is expected of them.

In general, patients speak of their wives as being sympathetic and well aware of the condition and needs.

> Oh, my wife knows it. She's wonderful. She—I get up in the morning, and she looks at my face and she can see right away.

> I walked around for two weeks with this pain to such extent that I was unbearable and she knew it—because I couldn't lay, I couldn't sit, I couldn't sleep. I couldn't stand. She had to take it.

> She's a sweetheart. Used to bring me a tray up to my bedroom, used to bathe me, alcohol rubs. I mean, I'd keep protesting, but she's wonderful.

The same attitude shown by the wife is expected of every member of the family. Everyone stands ready to take care of the patient, and, regardless of whether it is the father, mother, or child, anyone is entitled to complain when he is sick and is expected to offer help when he is healthy:

> [How did your father take his pain?] Of course, he complains about it. You know, he carries on. Of course, you can't blame him—it's probably very painful. [How does the family feel about it when he complains?] Well, they sympathize with him, of course. It's not new. I mean, he's had a few of these attacks in the last few years.

> And then I called my father and told him about the pain, and he brought me some hot cloths. I don't remember for sure whether I called my father or mother. I know both of them were there and were aware of it. The reason I say my father is because I remember his bringing me some hot, wet washcloths and cold cloths I think—probably both—to apply to my head and to my neck, and it eventually went away.

The participation of everyone in everyone's suffering is so

obvious and self-evident that it takes place automatically, without actual awareness. Often, it is only in the process of discussing family solidarity that the patient realizes its full impact:

> I think you've brought to light something I haven't thought of. We were always very solicitous to sick people—always got the number-one run of the house when I was ill. And got what would heal and T.L.C.—tender loving care.

This family participation in illness is not limited to adult members. Even small children are made aware of the necessity to care for the one who suffers; they get the idea directly, or indirectly, by watching the mother focus her motherliness on the sick father:

> As soon as I have a headache my wife would caution the children. She would shut them out of the house, or "Go upstairs and play. Daddy's got a headache now." She's so much concerned with me that the kids can get away with murder at that particular time.

A patient defined the family atmosphere in case of a person's illness in a short but precise comment:

> When one person is sick in the family, everybody starts worrying. That's the way of it. If there's one guy that doesn't feel good, everybody worries. That's the way it is. Everybody.

Thus the Jewish patient has a very definite and clear concept of complaining. His complaining is just as rational as the noncomplaining of the Old American patient. Complaining fulfills several important functions: it gives relief through its cathartic function; it is an effective medium of communication; it mobilizes the assistance of the environment; and, finally, it reaffirms the kind of family solidarity that is the basis of Jewish family organization.

In the hospital setting the Jewish patient tends to continue to behave according to the same principles. He tries to mobilize the sympathy and attention of the new environment, using the same well-tested means that have proven most effective in his own cultural group: complaining, crying, moaning, and groaning. However, much to his disappointment, he may notice that the hospital environment has a different attitude toward complaining than the one he would expect:

> Sometimes there's a lot of diplomacy that's needed in certain situations. For instance, in a hospital like here complaining didn't help me. It just got me into more difficulty.

Accordingly, a number of patients—especially among the younger ones—tend to control themselves and to behave with the Anglo-Saxon calm and restraint. Some of them even use the same rationale that is so often invoked by the Old American: "I don't complain about it, because it's useless to complain."

However, even when the younger patients verbally express attitudes that are well accepted, the total pattern of their responses lacks the consistency and integration that are characteristic of the Old American behavior. Contradictions and inconsistencies can frequently be detected in their own words and feelings. A patient who denies complaining for himself accepts it as a perfectly normal aspect of his father's behavior. Another young veteran who previously described how bitterly he had cried in the hospital because of his helplessness answered a direct question in words that contradicted his actual behavior:

> I'm not that type of a person. I don't let out any pain. I just hold it in. I would tell the doctor or the nurse, but I wouldn't say to anyone else—I wouldn't complain to my wife. I don't like to bother her, to worry her. I just tell her little things.

The same young man who was most disappointed by his wife's lack of sympathy and who was described by her as a pampered and demanding individual, said the following about his behavior in pain:

I take it inwardly. I'd make faces, but I don't make noise
or nothing. Nothing like that, I don't believe I make noises.

All this testimony points toward a conflict between behavior that is correct according to the traditional patterns of the Jewish
culture and behavior that is expected of members of American society. As in many other cultural and social areas of life, the young
first-generation American Jew is subjected to strong family influences but, at the same time, tends to adopt patterns of behavior
that are prevalent in the larger society and are expected in extra-
family peer groups such as school or the military.

In trying to resolve this conflict, the American-born, first-
generation American Jews tend to follow the standards of American culture; yet, in the process of describing their feelings and emotions, they frequently reveal strong ties with traditional attitudes
transmitted to them by parents and grandparents. It is interesting
to note that, in relating their behavioral responses to pain, they emphasize the American restraint and rationality but seldom mention
two other important traits basic to the American pattern, namely,
independence and self-reliance in pain and illness. The traditions
of dependency and reliance on other people's assistance in times of
stress and affliction seem to be so strong in the Jewish family organization that it is difficult for them to renounce these values even on
a purely verbal level.

Fortunately, the difficulties the American Jewish patients
may encounter in trying to reconcile expressive behavior with the
nonexpressive patterns of the reference group are limited mainly to
the question of how to behave in pain, not to the basic question
with regard to the meaning of the experience.

Concerning the significance of pain, Jewish patients reveal
a striking similarity to the Old Americans, for whom pain is primarily a warning signal, indicating that something is wrong with
their health. The Jews are also preoccupied exclusively with the
symptomatic meaning of pain, that is, with its significance as a
sign of illness.

Jewish preoccupation with health is as old as the history of the Jewish people. The wise teachers of the Talmud said that a person should not settle in a city without a doctor. Some of the famous Jewish scholars and philosophers devoted a great deal of their time to the practice of the art and science of healing. Jewish folklore is extremely rich in sayings and proverbs pertaining to health and illness, and these sayings and proverbs are freely quoted by elderly patients when they speak about their own experiences in pain and illness. Health is one of the most frequent topics of conversation among men, women, friends, and neighbors. The child's health is the greatest worry of a Jewish parent, and the child is constantly warned against the danger of losing it. From speaking to Jewish informants—not necessarily patients—one has the impression that health is perpetually in danger and, consequently, every human is a potential patient. Health is an exception rather than a rule; it is not a permanent state but a temporary lapse between one illness and another; it is a period of convalescence from one disease and preparation for another. In his daily prayers to God, the Jewish man asks for health and livelihood, and every day he is equally worried about losing both. In the light of these ever-present anxieties, it is not surprising that, when a patient is asked about his feelings about health, he answers categorically.

It's only a natural instinct to be concerned with your health.

As long as one is still a *mensh* (human being), he naturally worries about his health.

As a youngster he learns to be concerned with symptoms of illness:

I remember—I must have been about 16—a young girl in the community—about my age—who had got polio. I remember that one of the symptoms apparently was the stiffness of the neck. I remember thinking about my neck at that time and I do remember bending my head down to touch my chin and to my chest to make sure I could move my neck.

According to the old saying that no one is ever secure from

illness, the individual lives in constant expectation that illness will hit him sooner or later:

> We ride along on that premise as long as we can, and, of course, invariably someday it's going to come along. You see it all around you every day. People start suffering from one thing or another.

Hence, following the principle that it is easier to prevent an illness than to cure it, a great deal of thought and activity is devoted to the prevention of disaster. Mothers, fathers, wives, husbands—each one tries to warn and protect the others against the dangers of draft, weather, rain, or food. The system of mutual protection is so strong that no member of the family can leave the house without being reminded to take a warm coat, rubbers, or umbrella. He is cautioned not to eat hamburgers in a restaurant, not to drink cold water when overheated, and to avoid perspiring while playing ball with other children. As a matter of fact, if possible, it is better not to play ball at all:

> As I said before, my mother was a great worrier. She wouldn't let me out in winter without a coat or rubbers. In fact, I was one of these outdoor enthusiasts. I used to make snowballs during the winter and go on hikes, play ball. And my father didn't like it at all. I guess I must have made him very sick.

> Until I was sixteen my mother used to say: "Put on the sweater, don't go with your collar unbuttoned, or put on your scarf." [What about playing ball with kids or any sport?] She wanted them to play nominally, I'd say, rather than extensively. I know she objected to my wanting to play football or if any of us engaged in any sport that she considered hazardous in any respect, she'd frown upon it, and tell us that we shouldn't do it.

Despite all warnings and precautions, the elaborate system of preventive measures against illness is never perfect. Sooner or later some member of the family will show disturbing signs of illness, and, in the atmosphere of preoccupation with health and constant expectation of imminent catastrophe, the signs of disease are bound to be seen more frequently than in a less anxious setting. The reaction to these signs is that of immediate alarm and mobilization of the family in the direction of doing something about it:

> If I see my wife isn't well or if she's got a symptom of illness —or if I see her not acting right on the child—I worry. I'm an alarmist like that. I like my wife to go to a doctor and be checked right away. I don't like her to lay around in the house saying: "I have got a headache" or "I don't feel well" constantly, you know. If it runs for more than a day or two, I like her to make sure she takes her aspirins or if the doctor prescribes her medication. . . .

> When the kids get sick, I'm dying. Just like—like I'm sick. It affects me. I can't do anything—just think about the kids.

The emotional impact of illness on the family is so great that other members of the family readily identify themselves with the affected person to an extent suggesting more than just sympathy. Everyone sees himself in the role of the patient and experiences together with him the ups and downs of the disease. When a patient says that his wife could not stand his pain or that she felt it as strongly as he did, it is not a mere form of speech; it is an accurate expression of his belief. He believes it because, when, in turn, she is the one affected by illness, his response to her discomfort is similar:

> When I went to see her in the hospital I started to get dizzy and nauseous, and I had to leave. I don't know whether it was the hospital or seeing her lay there under anesthesia. But I know I couldn't take it. I remember this: My kid brother discovered he had cancer and when I found out about that I broke down then and cried as if I had it.

Quite often people relating the history of the illnesses of their close relatives say that they were so upset about their condition that doctors assisting the sick person would tell them: "You need a doctor more than the patient." The identification with the illness of a family member is so strong that, traditionally, the healthy members are expected to be affected to the extent that they are unable to care for themselves or attend to their daily needs, such as food, care of children, and even financial problems, all of which have to be handled by neighbors and friends.

In their anxiety about the symptomatic significance of pain, the Jewish patients are not so fortunate as the Old Americans because they do not have anxiety-relieving devices. There is no such thing as attributing a painful symptom to an insignificant cause like an ordinary cold or a simple injury. When the symptom appears, it is immediately associated with a major disease that threatens the future welfare and life of the individual:

> Oh, maybe I'm imaginative. Like the pain I have in my head —that's getting a little bit—that's the reason I came here. It scared me. That's the reason I came to the hospital. I was thinking of all kinds of things—maybe a tumor on the brain —who knows?

> Naturally I got worried, figuring that it was cancer of the back.

> The pain had started subsiding, and I wasn't as panicky as I was before. I was starting to assume that it's only going to last for twenty to twenty-five minutes, these pains. And I tried to restrain myself from carrying on—you know maniacally, in an excited way. I wasn't as fearful of a coronary thrombosis.

> I just wanted to get rid of the pain or whatever it was that was bothering me—in the heart. I was worried then. That was the only time that I can recall of ever really being worried. [What were you worried about?] I thought that I had heart trouble. I mean, I wasn't worried about dying, if that's what you're driving at. I was worried that I had heart trouble.

A patient's wife who was described as "unresponsive" and

"ununderstanding" substantiated her "incorrect" attitude by saying that she did not go along with her husband's fears of cancer:

> I only realized it—recently—that (the thought of cancer) was in his mind. I never knew that it bothered him much. I think that he did say that he was worried that it might have been that. And I never realized that. [Did you ever worry about it?] No. I know that a thing like that—when it does strike—there's always symptoms for it.—But I couldn't see cancer tied in with that.

It is quite possible that the husband's resentment toward her, expressed so freely in the interview, was also caused by her lack of empathy with his basic anxieties, a lack that might indicate insufficient devotion and failure in her wifely role.

The anxieties with which the Jewish patient views any sign or symptom of health impairment are especially strong in association with pain. The patient speaks freely of fear of pain. "I'm afraid of pain," exclaimed one patient, and another offered a dramatic description of his apprehension of a painful attack.

> The pain itself leaves me with a terrible fear. As has often happened, I've gotten up two or three times during the night clutching my head—then realizing I had no pain, and I'd go back to sleep. Or I'll sit around and actually perspire (in anticipation). I'll get the symptomatic pains. And I'll start to perspire profusely—and afraid of when that pain comes, what am I going to do?

The primary factor in the great fear of pain is its significance as a symptom of disease. That pain is a symptom is rarely questioned; the important problem is to know what the disease is that causes the pain. In the mind of the patient there are no easy explanations to alleviate the anxieties. On the contrary, it would be wrong to underestimate the significance of the symptom.

When one of the patients attempted to attribute his aches to a cold, his friends brought him back to reality by pointing out that he might be too careless:

People in Pain

No, no I never thought of any disease. I thought along the lines that possibly it is a cold, and then I was told—I spoke to people, and they said—"Well, you could have arthritis, bursitis." They mentioned different things. Well, of course, it leads to some nervous worry of some sort. It does lead to that.

Pain is too much a matter of life and death. It is much safer to become alarmed and overestimate the condition than to neglect it. The most important thing, therefore, is the diagnosis—the accurate identification of the medical cause. The diagnosis becomes the focus of all worries and anxieties. As long as the patient does not know what causes his pain, he is in constant anguish and despair:

I never really had it diagnosed, and I was worried about it. I didn't know what the diagnosis was. I don't know what's wrong. I wouldn't dare to guess.

Naturally, I worry about it. I thought it might be due to heart. But they say it isn't heart—they took cardiographs. Everybody tells me I haven't got a heart condition. What is it? Why can't I be relieved? Why can't I be normal?

Fear of the unknown is a phrase frequently used by the patients to describe their state of mind before the diagnosis is established; in reality, the "unknown" is a euphemism for a dreadful and deadly disease. The only possible relief from this anxiety is to find out the cause of pain and to identify the illness causing the symptom, because "to know the illness is to know the cure," and "a known illness is only half an illness."

I worry about the pain if I don't know what it is. If I know what it is, no. I don't worry about my pain in the back because I know what it is now. See, I know what's causing it.

[Were you worried about his pain?] No. Because I knew what it was. I say I wasn't worried about it because I knew—I thought I knew what it was. I always imagined in the beginning it was a disc, and I recalled how easily it was remedied when I had it operated on the last time.

The Patient Knows Best

I thought it was appendicitis the same as they did, and I knew appendicitis is nothing: It's almost like having a tooth pulled.

Knowledge of the diagnosis influences not only the degree of anxiety but also the ability to tolerate its severity:

I can stand pain well if the pain has no significance. But if I had a pain that might be related to some serious condition, it would disturb me. That pain would—I'm sure—would disturb me in that I would be concerned about the significance of it.

This pain was driving me crazy. I was aggravated. I asked constantly, "Why is that pain bothering me?" But I never got an answer. It bothered me because I didn't know what it is. It is the fact that it's something unknown. They took X ray's on my feet, my hands, and nothing showed. And I knew that the pain was there. It bothers me.

The patient sees the diagnosis of the disease as a factor that may influence his entire future. When the Jewish patient is concerned with the symptomatic significance of pain, his concern is not limited only to the immediacy of the situation: his anxieties are future oriented. The question "what causes my pain?" embraces a lot more than just the wish to know the disease. In the patient's mind it contains questions pertaining to all possible effects of the disease on his future life, family, and relation to society—questions related to employment, business, support of the family, and the future of the children. As long as the illness is unknown, the patient is prone to imagine his future in the darkest colors. He sees himself incapacitated forever and unable to provide his family with the most necessary means of subsistence. Ignorance of the diagnosis, therefore, is associated with a most acute state of insecurity:

Now, depends on what's going to happen, will I be like this, will I have to wear a brace for my life? Will I have to learn a new trade all over again? I feel insecure to a great extent.

I don't mind if the exploratory operation would prove conclusively that nothing is wrong or prove conclusively that something is there—either way. But just having opinions and pains leave me very insecure in my mind.

My situation worries me a great deal. I don't know what's going to happen. I want to know will I be able to make a living? I have a wife and children—who'll support them if I'm sick? I can't go on the rest of my life taking drugs.

A patient who was interviewed only two hours after he was brought to the hospital with a severe backache exclaimed immediately, "I want to know whether it will last for the duration of my life and whether it can be cured."

It goes without saying that preoccupation with the diagnosis and cure of the illness is true for every patient in the hospital, regardless of his national or cultural background. Every patient wants to know if his condition can be relieved, and everyone is concerned with possible effects of the illness on his employability and role as family provider. However, the patients of Jewish origin seem to stand out as a group: they express their future orientation with the greatest intensity, and their anxieties embrace every possible aspect of social, economic, and family life. Among patients of other groups these anxieties develop at various stages of an illness; very frequently they are broken down according to various areas of life, and—what is most important—they are frequently allayed by an optimistic outlook. Among the Jewish patients the anxieties are triggered off as soon as the symptom appears; they are rarely mitigated by optimistic expectations, and they seem to radiate in every possible direction. The pronounced anxieties refer to self and to the family, to the present and to the future, to business and social life.

The traditional structure of Jewish society does not permit the individual to see himself in any life situation as an isolated individual. The links between the individual and his family are so strong that any event in his life is immediately perceived as meaningful to self and to other members of the family. When the patient

118

speaks about his worries, automatically they are expressed in terms of the individual and his family:

> Oh, yes, I'm worried. I'm worried to the extent that I have certain financial and economic considerations. I have two youngsters to bring along. I'm married and have two children, and it's always a source of consternation for me—as how we'd get along if anything did happen. And that was my principal worry.
>
> I was worrying about my spine. About the cost of fixing it. My worries were that if I leave my business would go down—my home and my family, that they should be provided for. Everything worries me.
>
> In the beginning, as I said, of more concern to me than even the pain is the effect it's having on my home life, my family, children, wife.

The anxieties associated with the appearance of signs of illness very often call for taking steps to ensure oneself and the family against the threatening disaster. The patient and his family have to plan what to do if the expected catastrophe becomes a reality, and this planning is another indication of the future-oriented thinking of the Jewish patient.

> Yes, I was quite worried. But as a matter of fact with all our worrying my wife and I just sat down and decided that we would figure out things we were going to do—just in case certain eventualities took place. We felt if blindness were to be the outcome of my headaches, I would learn Braille and continue my schooling.

An extreme example of planning brought about by anxiety related to illness was shown by a patient who was using up his vacation time for hospitalization, keeping in reserve his sick-leave rights, for, "God forbid, if anything should happen, I may need my sick leave."

119

People in Pain

As suggested, the only possible means to relieve the anxiety is the identification of the cause of pain—the medical diagnosis. The only person capable of defining the disease is the physician. Hence one of the very first responses to pain is a visit to the doctor. Fear of disease, pain, and doctors is strongly linked together in the life of a Jewish family. One brings the other in a causal chain reaction. There is no hesitation about calling the doctor as soon as pain brings to consciousness the ever-present expectation of illness. In the middle of the night the anxiety of the patient will make him grab the telephone and call the physician. Many doctors practicing in Jewish neighborhoods have commented about the impatience of their patients and the number of night calls they receive from them.

If not the patient himself, then some member of the family will suggest calling the doctor in response to complaints of a headache, stomachache, or backache. The patient may wait a day or two before consulting the physician, but the question "maybe we should call the doctor?" was probably expressed as soon as the message of discomfort was received in the family circle. Almost without exception the informants stated that a call to their doctor was their immediate response to pain:

> The pain was so violent that I was sprawling on the floor. I didn't scream, but I was moaning a lot. So my wife grabbed the phone, and she called the doctor.

> When I got the pain in the back, I have been figuring that it is an unhealthy condition to be in. And naturally I did go to the doctor right away. I wanted to find out what it is, get improved, and feel well.

> Of course, when I don't feel well I go to the doctor. We don't wait. And generally "not feeling well" constitutes my back condition.

Frequently the visit to the doctor is not one single consultation in response to the original onset of pain. Sometimes a patient sees the doctor as often as he experiences the painful attacks:

The Patient Knows Best

The only time I go to the doctor is when I really need the doctor. Say with this leg here, the sciatica came. I went to the doctor and it went away, it stopped bothering me. It came back. I went to a doctor again. And so on. Anything I can't stand I want relief, because I cannot stand pain.

Because of the great preoccupation with health and constant expectancy of illness, the Jews tend to visit doctors rather frequently; whenever they suspect something unusual, they see the doctor without losing much time:

I go to the doctor every so often. If I feel that something needs checking. So I go over to the doctor and he looks at me. Here is a hell of a little episode here. About a year ago suddenly I went to the toilet and—no pain—but I noticed a red fluid coming out of my penis—almost like blood. No pain at all. So I went to the doctor, and he said that probably some gravel was in my kidneys and that it worked its way out—which put me at ease.

Unlike the patients of Old American background, the Jewish informants are not afraid of the doctor's diagnosis. The Old Americans avoid doctors in fear of losing their illusions and finding out that they are really sick. The Jewish patient, on the other hand, has no such defenses; on the contrary, the doctor can only reassure him, because most of the time the patient's imagined cause of pain is far more ominous than his actual condition. The Old American patient anticipates that the reality will invalidate his minimization of the cause, whereas the Jewish patient hopes that the doctor will only attenuate his anticipation of the worst.

Thus the doctor is the person who relieves the patient's pain, finds its cause, and brings peace to the worried and apprehensive mind. Unfortunately, the anxieties of the patients are too strong to be appeased by a reassuring statement of one doctor. Who knows whether he was not wrong in his diagnosis? The Jewish patient seems to lack the blind confidence in the medical infallibility of the physician that is characteristic of the Old American. For him the doctor is simply another human, subject to mistakes and limitations. And the same man who said he goes to the doctor every time he is worried made the following comment:

> I have confidence in doctors to the extent that they can't be miracle men; they are not magicians. They try their best. They make mistakes I imagine, the same as any human being would make.
>
> These doctors here are very very conscientious. But I know there's a limit to what they can do.
>
> There is a limit to what they know and to what they can do.

The anxiety-ridden Jewish patient cannot accept these limitations with the resigned equanimity of the Irishman, who, although being skeptical of the doctor's unlimited knowledge and power, nevertheless puts his fate in the very first physician he happens to consult (see Chapter Five). For the Jewish patient the diagnosis of the cause of pain is too much a matter of life and death. Accordingly, he finds a different solution for the problem. One doctor may make a mistake, but several doctors are less likely to err. Hence he visits not one but several physicians to find the answer to his question. Visiting different doctors (specialists in various fields)', comparing notes, and checking up on diagnoses and prescriptions are common events in the medical histories of many patients.

> I went to—let's see—three different doctors. I went to my own doctor, and I went to an orthopedic specialist. And at one time I was up here and someone had recommended me to see Dr. H—. I went to see him, and that's been the extent of my visits with doctors on this back case.
>
> [Who gave you the cortisone?] A doctor. [You went to many doctors before?] Oh, sure. I went to the Crippled and Ruptured Hospital. Over there, naturally, they took X rays, blood test, told me to come next week. Meanwhile, I came

across another doctor, an old gentleman. I say, "Doctor, what's the matter with me?" He says, "You got severe arthritis." So I say, "All right, Doctor, severe arthritis, can you do something for me?" I cannot stand no more the pains; I take all the time aspirins. So he says "What's wrong? It helps you? Take them." So you take them so long until they don't help you neither. So then I went to a private—to a society doctor, and he said the same thing.

I have been to quite a few doctors. I don't stay with one man long enough.

I had pain on the left side of my chest. I thought it might be due to heart. I went to the doctor. He took cardiographs. He said it isn't heart. So I went to St. Albans. They took two cardiographs, and he said, "No it isn't." So I said, "Doctor, I seem very tired." Everybody tells me I haven't got a heart condition so there must be no question about it. Two doctors. I think my own doctor showed me also that there isn't anything wrong with the heart.

Physicians with a large number of Jewish patients generally disapprove of the shopping-around technique. A number of them report rather embarrassing incidents. For example, occasionally a patient went to the doctor with a complaint without mentioning that he had already consulted one or two physicians. When the doctor, after examining the patient, stated his opinion, he was confronted with: "You must be right, Doctor, because Doctor so-and-so told me exactly the same thing." When the physician asked the patient why he did not say he had already been to a doctor, the patient's reply was: "Just to make sure!"

Occasionally, during an examination I have heard patients replying to the doctor's question "What's wrong with you?" with the rather challenging answer "You are the doctor. It's up to you to find out!" Most Jewish patients said that they had previously seen at least one private physician before coming to the veterans hospital.

Members of the patient's family who are strongly involved in their relative's medical experiences frequently contribute valuable data to his inquiries and investigations. They compare information received from the patients with the opinions of friends who might have had a similar illness or with their professional judgment of any doctors or medical students they may have among their friends and relatives.

Frequently the patient is dissatisfied with the way the consulted doctor has presented his diagnosis; he may feel it is too vague or not detailed enough. Despite repeated questioning, he feels that the doctor was not explicit enough or even tended to conceal something. Here again, members of the family fulfill an important role. Mother, father, wife, and other relatives besiege the doctor with questions and inquiries by telephone or in person. Subsequently they report to the patient the received information, compare it with the patient's notes and observations, and draw appropriate conclusions:

> The last time I saw my father, he wanted to bring in a consulting physician—to find out what's the matter. You can't blame him, I mean, after all, he's worried about me—to find out what it is. I told him that the doctors here are good enough, but I guess he's a little worried about how long would it take and what's the matter.

> My father is very worried. He's very close to his children, you know how the Jewish father is. It hurts him but what can he do? He spoke to some lady doctor that looked at me. He ran after her. He called her on the phone, but, of course, she just told him what she told me—that there's nothing to worry about—I'd be O.K.

At times even the information accumulated by the patient and by his family members does not appear to be satisfactory enough for complete peace of mind. Then he himself assumes the role of the doctor by going to the medical literature to find out if the physician's opinion is correct.

> I didn't feel as though an operation would be a complete cure. I have done a little reading on several of these cases—on

related cases—and as far as I can see, they are going to re-
move something and it was going to remain removed and
surely it would become a weak point or a source of constant
thinking about. I had no doubt that it would relieve the pain
and get rid of some of the spasms, but I don't think any
operation is really a cure.

This last quotation suggests two unique elements in Jewish
attitudes in pain and illness. One refers to the problem of relief of
pain and to its relation to the specific cure of illness; the other
deals with attitudes toward the professional qualifications of the
medical profession. It will be more convenient to start with the
latter, as the problem of pain relief will be discussed in relation
to the patients' attitudes toward medications.

The need to check the doctor's diagnosis with several experts and specialists, the tendency to compare notes and information, and the patient's opinion that he can voice a medical judgment on the basis of independent reading seem to indicate that the
skeptical attitude toward a doctor's skill and knowledge is of an
altogether different order from the one expressed by, for instance,
the Irish patient. Moreover, it is not only his great anxiety about
health and illness that makes the patient seek the opinions of several doctors or go to medical literature for information. The activities he displays during his illness seem to be based on a feeling
that he, and only he, is the final judge and authority in matters
pertaining to his health and illness.

The role of the doctor is not that of an indisputable authority or an expert with unique knowledge inaccessible to the layman; his function is consultative and advisory. The final decision
remains with the patient, who, although a layman, feels that he
has sufficient intellectual abilities to establish his own opinion even
in medical matters. After all, where does the doctor acquire his
knowledge? From books, and every literate person can read any
books and form an opinion:

Maybe I may not know the medical terminology of it, true.
But every person should learn something about themselves,

I feel, and even though it can be the biggest of words, I still got a dictionary, a library to go to, to learn what it means, to learn how to help myself. Because just going to a doctor, and the doctor saying, "Well, you have famerosis of the scatterosis." Not knowing what it means in general terms, they say "Well, you can take this medicine and you will be alright." Now I looked into a lot of books on that question of petit mal. I looked into conversion hysteria, which they thought it was. And I have learned to try to distinguish and how to combat. Well, without me asking questions I wouldn't know and I'd be in the dark and I'd be worried and insecure. A person who has no knowledge sometimes can be dangerous, but a person who will utilize knowledge to help himself and others then he is using it right.

There is an old Yiddish proverb that says "Don't ask the doctor, ask the patient." This proverb was paraphrased by a patient as "Every patient knows his own" to support his privilege to interpret his doctor's prescription.

The Jewish patient does not underestimate the doctor's knowledge or lack confidence in his skills. On the contrary, he says, "I wouldn't be here if I didn't have confidence." He appreciates the doctor's conscientiousness, his goodwill, and even his knowledge: "After all, he is a doctor." But his confidence is qualified and conditioned. The mere fact of going to medical school, which is usually the ultimate criterion of expertness, does not impress the patient:

I have that kind of skepticism of doctors and medicine which made me realize that this is just another man. A doctor is just another man who went into that particular specialty. I suppose what impressed me most was some of the boobs that went to school and became doctors. I wouldn't trust my dog to some of them. They may be doctors, but they still look like boobs to me.

It is not the diploma-giving institution or the Medical Board but the patient who decides who is a "real doctor." Therefore, to be sure that the diagnosis of the selected physician is valid, he has to compare it with the opinions of other doctors and with his own independent judgment. Obviously the selection of a doctor is not a simple affair. Before visiting the physician, one has to make sure that he is the best, according to private opinions of friends and relatives and in the light of his hospital affiliations and medical schooling:

> The first doctor I went to happened to be a neighborhood man. He knew his job and I felt—uh—I had a lot of confidence in him. I looked up the medical record. He has there a good record all right, and I said, "He is it." I looked up in a list of doctors—and they have the code alongside of it. I mean—I figured that was enough as far as I was concerned.

> Well, that was the first one. Then when we moved to Jamaica, there I called the hospital in the neighborhood and asked for names of a couple of doctors and they gave them to me, and then my wife told me she heard from the woman next door about a G.P. that as a fellow that he is terrific. Because the woman had a sick child—he stayed all night with that kid. Didn't leave the bedside. That kind of a guy. Whether he is a good doctor or not you don't know until you go and see, but yet you are interested. So next time I had something —I don't know whether it was anything important—I went in and he seemed to know his job. For general purposes— and he knew what he didn't know. And that was important —as important to me as that he did know everything. 'Cause nobody can know everything in this field.

> Because, Dr. S—, he is a neurologist here, told me, and I had confidence in the man. Because I looked up his record—chief of neurology staff—and a man with this qualification is capable in my mind.

However, the excellency of the medical record and the physician's hospital position in themselves still are not sufficient to make the patient completely at ease. An important element in establishing confidence in the doctor's abilities is the extent to which the patient goes along with the diagnosis and proposed therapy. No matter how impressive the physician's titles, if his opinion is not acceptable to the patient, he will not submit himself to the suggested treatment and will continue his search for a "bigger" specialist.

> I was in Medical Center Hospital when I had pneumonia, and four days after I was discharged from the hospital I had terrible pain in the top of my head. And I went back into the hospital, and they admitted me to the neurological clinic, and I was there two days. The doctor examined me and told me that I had a tumor on the brain. So I asked him to discharge me. I somehow or other I had a feeling that he didn't diagnose my case properly. After all, he's a doctor and I'm not, but I just had that feeling, and didn't want to let him operate on me. So I went to Baltimore to a friend of mine who's a doctor, and he took me to see Dr. D——. He was supposed to be the biggest brain specialist in the world at the time, and he had me in Hopkins for seven days. He gave me a thorough examination, and he told me that there were thirty-two different types of pneumonia, and this type just happened to hit my pituitary gland and that's why I had these headaches.

Seeing the doctor as a man and not as a magician allows the Jewish patient to voice freely all kinds of criticisms of his knowledge, personality, or bedside manners. There seldom was a patient in the interviewed group who did not have something to say about doctors. Naturally, they had the highest opinion of the people who were presently treating them at the hospital and of those who had actually helped them in the past. But the opinions expressed of doctors in general suggested a basic feeling of distrust and even hostility, which may, to a certain extent, stem from the conflict between the extreme dependence on doctors and the limited faith in their abilities in general. The most frequently expressed criticism of a doctor dealt with the lack of personalized attention on the part of the attending physician. The impersonal atmosphere of a public or a veterans hospital, in which a patient is one among many and the doctor is not freely selected according to individual judgment, is a difficult experience for the Jewish patient possessed by his pain and anguish. The patients complain bitterly that they are not seen so often as they think they should be seen and that there is insufficient contact between patient and doctor, resulting in the patient's insecurity about the treatment and diagnosis.

A patient comparing a private clinic with the hospital he was in made the following comments:

> In A. and D. they have been more free with the patients. In other words, the patients have been determined in respect to diagnosis. And here I'm somewhat dubious. Somehow I have the feeling that all is not told to me. I realize there are three times the number of patients here than there was in D.

Another patient felt neglected because the doctor did not see him often enough:

> Wednesday I had terrible pains. It just so happened that Tuesday the doctor came to see me and I told him that it felt much better. Wednesday morning he saw me in the chair and asked why I wasn't standing, why I wasn't walking. I told him I couldn't. I said, "Doctor, I'm feeling very bad today." So he said, "I see you later. I have three days' work to do in one." But he didn't come back to see me on Wednesday. And I had such terrible pains.

Another patient compared the treatment given to him by his private physician and that given by the doctors at one of the V.A. clinics:

> When I go to the V.A. clinic, instead of their trying to do something—they are supposed to treat you for certain things. They don't ask me. They said, "How do you feel? Did you get any headaches? Yes? All right, here are some pills." In fact, I have gone to doctors—I have been to my own doctor

and he treated me with diathermy both for my back and for my head, and I felt better.

The most severe criticism, however, is expressed with reference to doctors who are unable to establish a diagnosis or to find an appropriate treatment. For them the patient has only contempt and anger. The patient may be very aware of the fact that "medicine can do so much and no more"; nevertheless, when the doctor does not offer him some kind of opinion or some kind of treatment, then he really becomes angry:

> My whole attitude toward doctors changed an awful lot. I figure they went to school so long, they should know more than they do. I have this pain in the side, and it was really telling on me—it forced me back to bed. See, as soon as I used to lay down it used to be all right. If I sit up, it used to hurt. Now it don't hurt anymore. Just went away by itself. The doctor didn't know what it is. He didn't have any idea what it was. He is a doctor, after all—I mean he should know something.

This critical and skeptical attitude toward doctors allows the patients to feel that they do not have to blindly follow their advice. As the final judge of his condition, the patient feels that, when the doctor's orders are not convenient or convincing enough, he can afford to argue with his physician or even act against his advice:

> I went to a couple of doctors, and they suggested surgery for the disc. Well, I must say it was a quick examination—they didn't even take any X rays. So I asked if there was any harm if I went to a chiropractor, and the doctor answered and said: "Well, of course, he can do you a lot of damage. He can make your other leg pain too. And then you wouldn't be able to walk at all." So I took the attitude that, if the chiropractor does me any great damage, then the surgeon, once he has me open, can fix both of them. So I was very fortunate or lucky—the chiropractor did the trick.

The Patient Knows Best

The patient's attitude toward medication is a logical outcome of his believing that he knows best what is good for him, he is the final judge of the doctor's medical knowledge and skill, and he is the one who decides whether to accept or reject the diagnosis. Usually, when the patient accepts his doctor's opinion, he also accepts the prescribed treatment. He feels that, to get well, he has to cooperate with all therapeutic measures. He religiously takes his drugs, submits himself to injections, and even accepts the dreaded operation—usually after having consulted a number of specialists:

I'm a funny fellow. If I believe in a man, I'll have confidence in that man. For instance, I had confidence in Dr. G—. He told me I had what is called a cyst. He said, "It isn't too bad, but it should be operated on." And I'm the type of fellow who says, "Doc, when do you want me to go in?" See what I mean? If I got confidence in a man, I like to take a man's word.

Having made up your mind that you're going to let someone make decisions for you—of a certain order—then for heaven's sake do as you are told. You have got to make the preliminary decision as to which one you're going to listen to, but if you do that, stick to him and listen to him.

Having accepted the course of treatment, the patient is ready even to suffer pain if the treatment requires it:

When they work on me here, once in a while the tears would come down, but it is just because I want to hold on to the pain. My idea is I'm trying to help the man that's trying to help me. It's got to do me some good, or he wouldn't do it. I don't understand what's he doing, but I feel that's his job. He's supposed to know that. So I try to take as much pain as possible while he does it.

Yet, in accepting the treatment, the patient is as cautious as in the selection of the physician who prescribes it. He likes the individualized attention of the doctor, and, in the same vein, he prefers a medicine especially prescribed for him. The patient feels that his illness is special and requires an individual treatment suited to his own medical problems. To be effective, a drug has to be prescribed individually; therefore, he is not too enthusiastic about patented medicines:

> I don't like patent medicines. I mean, if the doctor tells me to take medicine, I take it. I never go in a drugstore to ask for anything like that. I don't feel that they are any good. Seems that for it to be prescribed for the general public doesn't make much sense to me.

Medication has to be individualized, for illness is an individual experience. The patient resents being seen as an average case; being average means lack of individual attention, indifference, and being lost in the faceless crowd.

Neither does the patient accept ignorance as to the type of medicine prescribed for him. He has to know the name of the drug, what it is for, and the expected effects. The Jewish patient is rarely satisfied with the statement so frequently offered by doctors or nurses to their patients: "It's good for you." This information is more readily accepted by the majority of patients, who do not feel qualified to understand the mysteries of medicine and drugs. Whereas another patient will identify the drug by size or color, the Jewish patient will use the professional trade name:

> Till I came to this hospital, I was taking various kinds of dope—demerol, ambutol, some barbiturates. I tried amoirins. I took them only on prescription and only when I would get the headaches. Now I have been prescribed caffrigin and nergit. I had been prescribed pyrobenzinine, but there I took them according to prescription every three hours. [You seem to know very well the medication they used to give you?] Well, yes, I'd always ask, "what am I taking now?"

Again, the mere knowledge of the drug and of its expected effect does not satisfy the patient. Being the ultimate judge of his own condition, he carefully observes how the drug affects him, interprets its action in the light of his individual experience, and applies the results of his observation and interpretation to the prescribed schedule. He may change the time of taking the drug, he may sometimes increase or decrease the number of pills to be taken, and he may even reject them completely if he comes to the conclusion that they are not helpful or that the drug is harmful. Frequently in this process of modification of the prescribed treatment, he avoids consulting the doctor, who might not always agree with the introduced changes.

"Every patient knows best what's good for him," said a patient who worked out his individual schedule of taking an analgesic:

> I got to go every three hours—to take two Empirins, and it takes about 15–20 minutes until it takes effect. But I don't take them always like that—I tell you why. You see, for instance, when I get the pain at eight o'clock, eight thirty, I try my best not to take, because if I take them at eight, by ten or ten thirty I'll be up. Therefore, *Yeder Kranker weisst zayns* (Every patient knows his own), so, therefore I wait to take them at ten o'clock so I can sleep till twelve, twelve thirty.

Because of low tolerance of pain, the patient is very eager to get something to relieve his discomfort. Unfortunately, the most effective pain killers are classified as "dope" and are known to be habit forming. For the future-oriented Jewish patient who views every aspect of his experience in the light of its future implications, taking analgesics is the least desirable means for relieving pain. Moreover, because of his great concern with the symptomatic meaning of pain, the patient feels that the mere relief of the symptom contributes little toward the final cure, which is his primary concern:

> At one time I would say that taking a pill for pain is all right because makes you feel better. But I feel that that is not getting rid of the cause.

I always felt that something like that might be habit forming, and I didn't want any such habits. Besides, I consider them artificial panaceas—you might call them that.

In view of this conflict between the pain-relieving effects of "dope" and their habit-forming properties, the patient assumes the same attitude he manifests throughout his entire medical experience. He is the one who shall decide when and if the drug should be taken. As in any other area, he depends on his own intelligence, which helps him determine when he should take the harmful drug:

The only time I take them is when I can't stand it anymore, but I don't want to take it every day or stuff like that. You see, you know damned well, it's habit forming and getting you in enough trouble. Thank God, you still got your brain, so you can have your judgment.

It depends. If it's severe pain, I'd probably ask for one. I try not to if I could. I don't believe in them because they get to be a habit.

At home the patient is free to use his own better judgment as to when, if, and how to take the prescribed medication. He knows that, whatever he decides, he will have the full cooperation of those concerned with his illness. In the hospital the situation is different. Upon admission the patient loses his rights to independence, and the physician and nurses become his masters in charge of the treatment. Hence the patient, as long as he is physically and mentally able, must use different devices and techniques to preserve some control over medication. Nurses described long, frustrating arguments and discussions regarding medication offered to patients who questioned suspiciously the dosage, size, or color of the pill or injection. Nurses found pills hidden under pillows, and patients reported avoiding taking barbiturates or analgesics by hiding them under the tongue and getting rid of them when the medication nurse left the room.

If illness is a major crisis for every patient, for the Jewish patient the crisis is compounded by the necessity to solve a long list of conflicts and dilemmas. Which doctor should he choose? Should he be treated at home or in the hospital? Should he accept the doctor's diagnosis or consult the opinion of a "bigger" specialist? Should he accept the prescribed treatment or modify it according to his own judgment? Unlike patients of other ethnic groups, he cannot accept freely the opinion of the expert, for he himself is the ultimate authority—only partly helped by consultations with friends and family members. They feel with him, they suffer with him, but still they are not him: only the patient knows what is best for him, and only he knows when and to whom he can relinquish the responsibility for his health and well-being.

Thus in pain and illness the behavior of the Jewish patient reflects a value system that has developed throughout the ages and has been transmitted from parents to children, reinforced at times by tragic interactions with a hostile world in which one could depend only upon himself and his family in matters of life and death.

❀❀❀❀❀❀❀❀❀❀❀❀|❀❀❀❀❀❀❀❀❀❀❀❀

Fa Malo!

❀❀❀❀❀❀❀❀❀❀❀❀❀❀❀❀❀❀❀❀❀❀❀❀

W hen hospital personnel speak about patients who are overemotional or who exaggerate their pain, they usually mention in one breath the Jewish and Italian patients. Both groups of patients are seen in contrast to the Irish or Nordic behavior. Like the Jewish patient, the Italian patient is often described as a person who makes no effort to control his emotional reactions to pain, who demands attention, and who freely expresses his pain by sound and gesture. On the whole, the behavior of the Italian patients is seen as nonconforming to the standards of the hospital, which emphasizes restraint and self-control. However, in speaking about the Italian patients, members of the hospital staff frequently mention a number of their positive character traits, such as personal warmth, congeniality, and good humor. From conversations with doctors and nurses one obtains the impression that the usual resentment against complaining patients who are described as nuisances or pests is toned down with reference to the Italians,

136

against whom the complaints become more tolerant and indulgent. "They are like children," said a nurse. "When they are in pain, they cry, call for attention, and are *so* unhappy; but when the pain is over, they are sweet."

In terms of their background, the Italians differ very little from other patients in the hospital. Like the Jewish patients, they are predominantly of the first American-born generation. Like the Irish, they are mainly of lower or lower-middle class. Their education is that of a grammar school or high school, with a few individuals who have attended college. Their occupations are usually of a type that requires physical effort, although sometimes to a lesser extent than those of the Irish patients. Like the patients of Irish origin, they are Catholic; and like the Jews, they frequently speak their native language, because the older immigrant patients have some difficulties with English.

The impressions of people who are in constant contact with the patients and who get to know their habits and behavior are confirmed not only from direct observation but also by the statements of the patients themselves.

With an uninhibited frankness they state that they cannot "take" or "stand" pain, and these statements confirm the frequent observations about the low tolerance, or low threshold, of pain among Italian patients.

They readily speak about their tendency to be quite expressive, and, although a few of them seem to try to control their behavior, most of them feel that it is only natural to cry, moan, and complain under the impact of pain. There is no shame or guilt associated with these types of behavior.

> While I was sleeping at nighttime, the pain came down so hard—right down my wrist. That's when I was screaming hard, you know. I couldn't—oh, the pain—it was just somebody pulled a knife on me. And I was hollering, "ouch, ouch, ouch, ouch." Then I said, "What's the devil I got in my arm? What is it?"
>
> [What do you do when you are in pain?] I moan—I yell to a

certain extent. [Do you cry?] Well, if it is necessary, I mean, but I've not cried from this pain, no. I've cried from pain before, but not for this. Oh, sure, pain would make me cry. A needle—any kind of needles or—depends how it's will make me cry. Sure.

The pain is very severe, Doctor. I—I broke down and cried many times with severe pain, and I'm a pretty tough man to break down. And I'd break down constantly.

[Do you complain to the doctor about your pain?] Yeah, when I get the chance to grab him. [Do you complain to the nurses?] Oh, yeah. Well, they should know all about it for the pills. I certainly do. After all, I do want to come down to the point so I get well and go back to work.

In speaking about their tears and complaints, the patients often realize that it does not help or perform any useful function in relieving pain. Nevertheless, they cry because they feel that crying is a natural part of the pain experience. Pain and tears are inseparable. The body needs an outlet when a person is in pain; therefore, one should not stop tears when they are coming out of the eyes.

Cry don't going to help me over. Sometimes it does bring the little wet on the side of my eye. So I figured maybe the body wants. I don't know how to say it in America—there's something that wants to coming out, you know what I mean? So tears sometimes coming in on the side, but I mean—what can I do? I mean, what's the use in me scream? There is nothing to help.

One night, I was in such terrific pain—I just couldn't hold out—I cried a little bit. I said, "What the hell am I crying for? That ain't going to stop the pain." But when the body wants to cry—can't stop it.

A patient who admitted that he groaned, moaned, and cursed while in pain also added that it did not do any good.

It is inconceivable for an Italian patient to hide pain when he has it:

Fa Malo

[Don't you try to hide your pain when you have it?] No, no, no, you can't hide it. It's too tough. Yeah, you can't hide it. You know you have got it, because you got to moan or scream or do something.

Besides the feeling that one cannot and should not hide pain, the Italian also feels that "it's not nice to keep quiet about it." An Italian "deviant" who tried to control his pain was somehow embarrassed about it:

Well, I don't know—I'm funny that way. I feel—well, it's going to hurt, and I don't want to be a crybaby about it, see. It just—I control it. It's painful, but I've learned to control pain. It sounds funny, but—uh—.

The younger Italian veteran knows very well that expressive behavior such as crying or screaming is viewed in American culture as childish and unmanly conduct. Thus a few of them try to restrain themselves from being too emotional: "I don't moan, I don't groan—I like to be the real he-man type, you know." Yet few are successful in these attempts. A young Korean veteran, in describing his failing efforts to control his reactions, echoed indirectly the basic American values with reference to pain:

First I try hard to keep it for myself, I try to muffle my pain I like to keep things for myself. I don't like to talk about my trouble. I don't want to burden anybody with my worries. But pain takes the upper hand. Then sometimes I start to moan and even to cry. All the times I was in service I had those pains in the back. Nobody knew about it. I didn't want to be like those guys who whenever there is a hike or exercise run to the doctor with complaints.

Tears and pain are so inseparable that even in a most embarrassing social situation the patient cannot control his urge to cry in response to the pain attack:

Oh, when the pain come in, I—I—I mean, I just can't stand

139

the pain. It's—it brings tears to my eyes, and—as a rule now
—a fellow—grown man like me—I'm thirty-nine years old—
that I would actually cry in front of a bunch of men that
I'm the foreman of. So the pain must have been terrific for
me to cry, because I wouldn't cry like that—bunch of men
that I'm in charge of, see?

Some Italian patients who are aware of the annoying effects
of their expressiveness on the environment either try to control it
or express some guilt feelings about it:

I try not to groan to attract attention. I feel the pain, and
I—occasionally I give vent to such phrases as "O God!" or
"How long will this last?" and so forth. But not too often,
because I've seen too many people annoyed by the people
who were in pain giving vent to remarks that affect other
people.

People don't bother me; I think I bother them by moaning
and screaming.

The overall impression is that the Italian patient is quite
concerned with the effects of his behavior on his environment. It
is especially noticeable when the patient speaks about complaining.
Although, as already quoted, they complain freely to doctors and
nurses, they deny complaining to members of their family. In this
respect they are unlike Jewish patients. Whereas the Jewish patient
complains a great deal at home, especially to his wife, trying to
provoke her anxieties and to motivate her to take care of him, the
Italian patient assumes a totally different attitude. He does not
complain to his wife because he does not want to worry her. He
seems to take for granted that his wife sympathizes with his suffering to such an extent that it is unnecessary to complain to get the
required attention. Moreover, he expresses great concern for his
wife's peace of mind and happiness; even in his most agonizing
moments, he tries to refrain from the natural expressions of pain,
such as crying, moaning, or complaining.

In situations in which the Jewish patient would say that he

"drives his wife nuts" until she feels his pain as much as he does, the Italian patient remarked:

> I don't shout. I don't shout to my wife. She's a good woman. She's sympathetic to me.
>
> I didn't want to scream. My wife was alongside me.
>
> I don't like to aggravate somebody else for my pain. I'll try to keep them happy as much as I can. Because why she's got to worry about me more. This way you only put somebody else to worry. Have trouble myself and make you worry too?
>
> No, I try not to complain. I prefer not to. She's a very very hearty girl, and she tries very hard to keep me well and happy, and I feel I would demoralize her if I continually complained.

A wife or mother does not have to be told about the patient's suffering: "Just by looking at me they know how I feel." The patient knows that they are concerned with his condition and are ready to do anything to help him:

> Oh, I wouldn't complain to my wife—she could see it. I don't like to tell too much. She could see the condition, and the less she knows the better it is for her mind.
>
> And like my mother would come over and say, "How do you feel today?" "Oh, I feel fine." And my wife would say, "He does not, Mom. He didn't sleep all night." Well, I'd go into the bathroom once in a while—it's an awful thing to say, but I could just stand so much and then—and then I'd go to the bathroom, and I'd fall. But I didn't want anybody to know about it. Maybe two or three o'clock in the morning. I'd close the door, but my wife told my mother. She says, "I hear him in there."

On the other hand, the patient who does complain to his wife feels quite guilty about it:

> I do complain to my wife, and it's not nice. It upsets her too. She has to go to work and worries.

By this attitude toward his family members, the Italian expresses on the one hand a great deal of concern for their happiness and on the other hand a strong confidence in their feelings toward him and their unconditional readiness to help when help is needed.

The avoidance of complaining within the family circle is a pattern that can be traced to early childhood.

> We don't complain too much in the family. We have learned it when we were kids.

As a small child, he is taught not to run to mother with complaints about pain. But at the same time he is aware of his mother's devotion to him and feels that she, without being told, knows of her child's trouble and is ready to help when necessary. Her function is to comfort the members of her household—the children or their father—and she does not have to complain to get assistance:

> She'd find out in the long run, but I never went home and told her that I was hurt. But, I mean, she'd find out, because she knows—she knows her children.

> If the children were sick, she didn't let you know you were sick, she just instilled a lot of confidence in you. My father is the same way. He broke his collarbone and his arm here a few years ago, but he wouldn't complain to mother. It seems to run in the family.

The same motherly care is given to the patient in his adulthood by his wife, and he is deeply appreciative of her sympathy:

> She's been very nice. She's been dressing my back physically for four months. She's had to undress me every night and rub me down in bed, feed me in bed. All of the things that I'm getting here in the hospital she used to give me at home,

142

in addition to taking care of the children and of the business. She's my secretary as well as my wife.

It is only outside the family circle, where the patient is not sure of the sympathy that is part of the family atmosphere, that he is inclined to complain to get relief and assistance. Despite his desire not to disturb his fellow man, he will ask for help, especially in the presence of a doctor or nurse whose business is to relieve his pain:

> If it is severe enough, I'd tell people. Oh, yes, I have had enough pain to moan since I have been hurt. While I got those headaches I sort of get hysterical, you might say. I moan and groan and call out even though there is no one around. I just call out for someone to help me. The fellows were telling me that I was calling out for the nurse, and the nurse wasn't in the room. I was telling her to get me something— to get me a doctor because the doctor wasn't present at the time. He came down and gave me a nerve block.

> I came down and I met people, and people see me walk like that so they asked, "What happened?" So I told them, I said, "I have pain over here. I don't know what it is." So they called the doctor.

The American or Irish idea of self-reliance and independence is quite alien to the Italian patient. When one is in need of help, he is entitled to ask for it and also expects to get it:

> I had a cast on my arm and I took help. I mean, I was not ashamed. It didn't bother me at all. I knew I couldn't help myself, so what's the sense of shying away from it? When I need help, I used to ask for it. That's all there was to it. I'll call for it. Now I ask my friends to tie my shoes and I don't feel ashamed when I do it, because I know I can't do it myself. So I might as well ask somebody else who's in a position to help me. He might need help some other way, so I'll help him.

People in Pain

People who rely on other people's help in case of distress obviously would not withdraw from society in case of pain. Unlike the Old Americans and Irish, who try to avoid their friends when they are subject to suffering, the Italians never speak about being alone in pain. They never mention it spontaneously, but, when asked directly, they say that they like to have people around and that they enjoy their presence. However, they do not like to be reminded of their pains and aches by unnecessary questions:

> I don't mind people around, provided they don't ask too many questions. Because then it gets repetitious after a while. Nobody likes to be reminded of his troubles. They are perfectly welcome. They can stay and talk about different things and then I enjoy it. It takes my mind off the pain.

Tears are physiological and emotional expressions of pain. They are seen as an outlet for the suffering body. But tears are more than just a manifestation of pain. By crying, the patients express self-pity and grief about their sad condition. Tears are an expression of helplessness and frustration:

> Sometimes I cry from pain but also because I'm "hard luck." I see the situation in which I am.

> Well, I don't think I cried from pain, but I cried to think of the condition I was in.

Frequently during an interview a patient would begin to cry when asked to describe his condition. A tall, strong laborer related with tears in his eyes his immediate reaction to the incapacitating effects of pain:

> I cried like a God-damned baby. I cried early in the morning. The first day I couldn't go to work in the morning. I got up, I told my wife, I says, "I can't go to work." And I started to cry. Yeah, and I told my wife, I says, "I can't go no more."

There is no shame associated with such tears. How could

Fa Malo

there be when even the patient's father, the strict Italian patriarch, used to cry when he was in pain?

> Father was constantly aching, and I saw him moan and cry from pain. I wished I could do something about it. Mother was around the house all the time. She's been very sympathetic to him.

Tears, complaints, groaning, and moaning are not the only manifestations of suffering; some patients speak of feelings of deep depression or of loss of energy and vitality under the impact of pain. Only the Italians mention depression to describe the effects of pain on their state of mind, and only they seem to speak about lack of energy in describing their condition.

They view their pain as an evil, unnatural force that takes away from them the benefits of life, deprives them of the opportunity to enjoy the good things in life, and interferes with their participation in the normal process of living. Remarked one patient, "It isn't normal for a person to go around with pain; there is no sense in suffering."

Thus almost every Italian patient emphasizes his inability to relish such things as food or the pleasures of family life when he is in pain:

> I got cramps and I can't stand them. I can't stand this pain. Who wants to have a bum stomach? I'm Italian and you know you have raviolis, and that other dish with a lot of cheese—lasagna. See, when we go to my mother's to eat, she —that's one of the dishes she likes to make, you know, and all of the family is gathered, so for me she has to make a little plate of spaghetti on the side. And that isn't right, you know.

> Before at home, I used to sit down, I did make it to the kitchen, and I'd eat my meat and then the pain started coming back, and I'd eat half of the food, and I'd run back to bed. And I'd say, "No, I know I can't eat that way." I don't like to eat that way. I like to eat like a human being—sitting, you know.

145

It's too much for me. It's going on five weeks now. I have
to eat fast—do everything fast. It doesn't pay. I mean, there's
no life there. I look at the eats, I eat a little, the pain comes,
I got to stop 'cause I can't eat it. And, you know, when I
eat I gotta eat fast and then I got to rest. That's no life.

With this I can't work, I can't sit on a chair, I can't take a
rest, I cannot sleep, I can't eat. The appetite has been good.
Want to eat, but cannot eat. Every time I sit down to eat
I got to jump and turn around and jump and turn around.
I got the pain and got to stop to eat.

It affects my appetite. I can't work properly and I can't enjoy
myself.

I always like a beautiful girl and I always like beautiful things
—nice clothes, nice colors—and I always like to go to the
movies. And now!

It is no wonder that the reaction to the inability to take
advantage of life is as intense as the pleasure derived from it. The
patient becomes depressed and discouraged. The young veteran
who said that he did not show his pain because he wanted to be a
"he-man" said sadly:

I get depressed and sort of mope around. Not much energy.
Don't feel like doing much of anything. That's about it, as
far as it goes.

The strong laborer who complained of not being able to
enjoy his food because of his pain had lost his original vitality:

I couldn't stand it no more. You don't feel like doing nothing
no more. You got no energy to pick up nothing. You just feel
like dropping everything.

The feeling of depression associated with the pain experience is not only expressed in direct answer to questions; it perme-
ates the entire interview. It is manifested in the patient's facial ex-

pression, in his gestures, and in his tone of voice. The only time when the sadness and melancholy disappear is when the informant speaks about his family, about his life before the illness, and about food.

When the patient is alone, or at nighttime, he feels the depressing effects of pain the strongest, and he cannot rest or sleep. When the Irish patient was "taking" his pain, one of his techniques in handling the experience was relaxing. For the Italian patient relaxing in pain is inconceivable. It not only does not relieve his condition, but it aggravates it. The way to alleviate agony is by motion, activity, or conversation—anything to keep the mind off the present discomfort. Being still or trying to relax only makes things worse:

> Seems like I get more pain when I relax. That's when I seem to get it—when I relax.

> I don't get it too often, during the day, but at night I can't lay down. When I'm lying down I can't stop the pain; I gotta jump out of bed, and sit like that, and go like that. I gotta get up—I gotta get up. I can't lay in bed with that pain in my jaw—I can't relax.

It is a well-known phenomenon that physical or mental occupation helps in bearing pain. Patients of all ethnic backgrounds have often commented about it. However, the impression is that the Italian patient is much more sensitive to the impact of pain when he is unoccupied than are the patients of the other ethnic groups studied. This fact was expressed indirectly by a patient who felt that, when he was in pain, it was much better for him not to be at home but to go out among people or work:

> Staying at home only thing is making me worse. If I stay in the house you're thinking more. You worry more. You are better off to stay outside. Stay in the house there looking at the four walls all the time. Because you figure you got a pain there and you worry. When you are outside you got a little

pain you don't think about it. You forget it—because I come out—"Good morning" to you and I forget that pain at the same time. When you stay home, you start to say, "Oh, oh, oh."

The depression the patient expresses is not of a long duration. As soon as the pain is relieved, or when he forgets it, he becomes his old self—happy, joyful, and optimistic. The pain-relieving pill or injection seems to perform miracles with Italian patients.

With the relief of pain the mood changes from somber despair to gaiety and good humor. The patient himself admits that, with the elimination of the sensation of pain, he is a changed man:

> The nurse gave me a pill. And the pain went away. I said, "Gee, I feel wonderful." The fellow had the radio down, and I said, "Gee, I want to sit over here with you," because that's very seldom that I can sit like I'm sitting now. I sit a little while, and I got to jump back into bed again. So I says, "I'm going to sit up with you." So I sit up, and I looked at the whole program. So this morning I said, "Gee, I feel pretty good." I didn't use the wheelchair or nothing; I walked in and shaved myself.

> When the pain is relieved I—oh—I'm terrifically happy. As long as I'm well and happy, I'd pack the family in the car and we'd go out for a drive. One day I was feeling very good and I did all my bookkeeping for a month and a half in four or five days.

The patient's mood is a direct function of presence or absence of pain; it oscillates from deep depression to cheerfulness:

> When I get these headaches I think they are unbearable. I mean at the moment I just don't want to do anything but die. I want something for the pain, and that's all there is to it. I can't stand it. And—after the headaches go I'm completely at ease again. I don't bother for anything. But when I get them I sort of get hysterical.

This emotional polarity can be attributed to the absence of

a concern for the symptomatic significance of pain on the one hand and to a strong apprehension with regard to the sensation itself on the other hand. When the patient perceives pain, he responds to the immediacy of the experience, thinking about its implications for his health and possible future effects. During the experience the patient is mainly present oriented. He worries neither about his pain as a symptom of illness nor about what its consequences will be. He is mainly disturbed with what he lives through while he perceives pain; he is depressed because at that moment he is deprived of the pleasures of life. However, as soon as the pain disappears, it becomes part of an unpleasant past. The patient can enjoy the painless present, even if it is of a short duration, without worrying about the significance of the uncomfortable event.

This present orientation with reference to pain seems to be an efficient defense against the apprehension the patient experiences with great intensity in association with pain. It allows him to enjoy every period of time that is free of pain and to assume a happy-go-lucky attitude with regard to his immediate future:

> The pain that's past is always forgotten, and the one that you have now is the one that hurts the most. The pain I have now, that's the one that hurts most. The ones that are past you always forget.

> Sometimes when you have a lot of pain always comes a little worry. But after a little while you forget about it when the pain goes away. It'll stay today, and tomorrow you forget about it. What's the use worrying? If I worry, I'll be worse. Only puts myself in sickness or it puts myself in bed. Life— always take it like it comes—that's all.

A patient with a long history of a painful back compared his present pain with previous attacks:

> It was pain, but I say this is the worst one. *It is,* Doctor. I tell you the truth. The other pains went away and this one I got. . . .

The present orientation allows the patient to be optimistic every time he feels better:

> When you feel good, you sort of hope that it will go away completely, and when it comes back, it's a big disappointment. You get disgusted.

A patient suffering from a severe chronic disease remarked rather definitively:

> As soon as pain goes away, I don't worry about it any more. I don't need to worry.

The Italian is so deeply impressed by his pain that, for him, it is not a symptom of illness but the disease itself; accordingly, when pain is relieved, he feels that the condition has been cured:

> I worry about that pain. Because I'm thinking that if the pain goes away, then I am cured. See, that's what I'm worried about. I don't know what to do to get the pain away.

A similar attitude was expressed by a patient who related the pattern of his visits to the physician:

> Well, the doctor gave me three treatments. He claims that— that I didn't keep going back to him enough for that treatment. I only came back when I had severe pain. [Didn't you go regularly for your treatments?] No. See, when I didn't have pain, I didn't go to him. Figured, what the hell, I'm all right. I'll stay home. Why should I go to the doctor? And then when I used to get pain, I used to go to him for the morphine. He used to say to me, "I told you once before." Finally, when I went to him the last time, he says to me, "You better go out yourself in the hospital," he said. "If you don't watch that, God knows what will happen."

The identification of pain with illness and of absence of pain with its cure eliminates the symptomatic significance of pain.

Fa Malo

That attitude is frequently expressed by the patients who, like the Irish, deny any relationship between the pain and any possible pathological condition. The Italians are disturbed by the sensation and by its immediate effects on their life habits, and they are concerned with prompt relief; but they do not express any worries about being ill:

[Does the pain worry you?] To the extent that naturally it's painful. I'm young. It hampers my movements. I like to do a lot of things which I'm unable to do because of this pain, and, then, of course, there is always involved my job. [Were you ever thinking about your pains in terms of a disease?] Disease, no. I've always thought that with the proper care the pain can be taken care of, so it doesn't worry me.

[When you had this pain, were you worried about it?] No, not seriously worried. You are trying to drive at the point that I might be considering this to be a serious illness like a cancer or something like it—no. I never associated those thoughts with this pain. I was troubled only by the pain. That's the only thing that bothered me.

To tell you the truth, I never worried about the pain. I only think something has to be done about it. I didn't think I had any disease. Naturally, you get nervous, depressed. I can't do what I want to.

In almost every interview the emphasis was on immediate relief of pain, with little or no concern for its medical implications. The Italian patient does not seem to be preoccupied with his health and the possibilities of losing it. The few statements pertaining to general health problems confirm this impression. A patient with a sad history of contradictory diagnosis of multiple sclerosis said that he never used to worry about his health until he became a patient in the hospital:

I don't like the word *multiple sclerosis* either—which I don't believe I have. The first doctor I went to with my pain—a diagnostician—he was very hasty—young fellow. And he diagnosed it as multiple sclerosis. And I had another doctor come in. He said that I didn't have it. I just don't like to worry. I mean, I never really had the impact of what it was until I got here. Well, I don't like to worry, and I don't like to have even a semblance of doubt. It's what's natural, don't you believe?

When a patient was asked whether he worried about his health, he said:

I don't give it too much thought—up until I get sick. Then I start thinking about it.

Another patient was rather surprised when he was asked the same question because "I always was in good condition and liked exercise."

In general, the patients do not like the idea of worrying with regard to their condition. The Italian is not a worrier. He may think about his condition, he may wonder about it, and he will be nervous and depressed; but he will not agree with the idea that he is worried:

No, I never was worried, because I have been at work all the time and nothing to worry about. I don't feel worried about nothing—I never did worry nothing. [Didn't you worry about the pain?] Well, I think about the pain, because I figure, how this thing it can come over.

[Tell me, are you worried about your pain?] No. I'm not worried about it, but it gets annoying as hell at times.

I think of it just as pain. I—I seek relief for it, but I'm not worried—like some of the patients up there.

On a few occasions some patients mentioned worrying, but those were extreme cases in which the condition had an immediate and real bearing on their livelihood. For instance, a patient suffering from Berger's disease who had already lost one leg, spoke about his concerns without admitting that he was really worried:

And the thing that's bothering me now is what I'm going to do for a living. I mean, after all, I have got to make a living. That's the thing which is uppermost in my mind. And how I'm going to make it—how long this right leg is going to hold out. I mean, I don't worry about it. I know that I'm going to lose it. But just how long it's going to take, that's the thing—that's. Certain amount of worry to it. Naturally, I can't sit here and say that I'm not worried about it. I know that when they take that off then I'm going to be that much farther from making a good living. With one good leg I can hop around, but when they take both of them, well. . . .

A badly disabled patient who had lost the power to move his legs told about his worries at the onset of the condition and how he gave up worrying when it became chronic:

Yes, I was quite scared—not for myself, but for the family, because my wife told me I kept hollering, "What am I going to do now for work to support the children?" I was worried about—most for the kids and the family than for myself. I didn't care for myself, I guess, according to my wife. I was sort of worried, but I figured it happened now, let its course take its chance. What could I do? I couldn't worry any more. I had enough worries as it was about paying the rent and everything else.

The Italian patient thinks in terms of the immediacy and the reality of the situation. He meets it with apprehension and despair, but he refuses to direct his thinking toward its future implication. He is neither pessimistic like the Jewish patient nor optimistic like the Old American. He is merely present oriented, and the quality of his present-oriented response is in direct and immediate relation to the intensity of the condition as it is being experienced at any given moment. When he is asked point-blank about the future, he refuses to consider it:

[So, I was asking you if you were worried about your pain. You are not worried. Now, do you think it can affect in any way your future?] I can't say now. I won't be able to say until I get the leg straightened out.

I don't know if I'll be able to go back to my same work—the way the doctors told me. [What are you going to do when you leave the hospital?] That means I can't go back to my original work. Well, if I can't, I can't. I was always a hustler, making a dollar. So I guess something else will do. When I leave, I'll see.

Quite consistent with the present-oriented attitude with regard to pain is a relatively infrequent concern with the cause and interpretation of pain. The tendency to explain the cause of pain often serves an anxiety-allaying function. The patient attributes his pain to some normal, culturally accepted causes and in this manner minimizes its significance. Regardless of whether the patient is worried about the symptomatic significance of pain (the Old American) or about its crippling implications (the Irish), the process of reducing the causes of pain to nonthreatening factors indicates future-oriented anxieties. The Italian patient does not seem to be too concerned with the future, and he is equally unconcerned about finding out the reasons for his pain. His primary preoccupations are the immediate consequences of the experience and instant relief.

In the few instances in which the patient did express some interest about the cause of pain, he either left the task of determining it to the doctor or attributed it to some vague cause within his anatomy, such as muscles or nerves:

I told the doctors downstairs—if it's any possibility—whatever the cause is, I want to know. I says whatever you find I want to know what's wrong.

I don't know. I'm not a doctor, but I believe that it's the muscles in my leg, because they get tired.

I have pains. They seem like in my legs. They're nerve pains.

One patient expressed more of a curiosity than real concern about the cause of his pain:

It sort of gets me wondering just what could be the cause. Wish I was more smarter so I would know what would the cause be.

Another patient, a plumber, offered an explanation for his pain in the leg, borrowed from his occupational model:

Whenever I seem to have some gas in my stomach, it bubbles now near the rectum and it won't come through, and it seems to affect the leg. I seem to get that bubbling feeling going down the leg.

One patient attributed his pain to draft and sweat, and another to "bones working against each other."

Along with extreme apprehension of pain, the Italian patients seem to have an idea of expected and accepted pain, that is, a pain that does not provoke tears or complaints but that is normal. As among the Irish patients, this pain is associated with physical activities, mainly with athletic performance. About this type of pain a patient spoke with complete indifference:

Sure, I've been hit hard, but the next day it was gone. I wouldn't get excited about it, because I knew what was causing it.

I'm sensitive to pain, but in sports I don't mind it too much. When we were kids we used to have a game—"being tough." We used to flex the muscle in the stomach and hit as hard as possible. I could take it.

A couple of patients who took their training as prizefighters commented with pride on their ability to take pain as part of their training. It is the unexpected, spontaneous pain that is much feared by the patient. However, unlike patients of other groups, the Italian hardly ever uses the anxiety-allaying mechanism of reducing this dreaded pain to one that is accepted.

The present orientation with regard to pain and illness that is so explicit in various statements of the Italian patient is an attitude manifested not only in this particular life experience. A number of general statements with reference to the past, present, and future suggest that it is an expression of a general time value essential to the culture of the informants. The echo of the ancient Roman slogan *carpe diem* is heard whenever the patient refers to time. It is the present that counts in life, and one will have time to consider the future when it becomes the present. Nobody knows what tomorrow will look like; therefore, one had better wait until it becomes today. There is no need to worry about the future because it would not help anyway and would only spoil the enjoyment of the present. When one relishes today's meal, he cannot cry about tomorrow's pain, which may or may not happen. The intensity of an emotional response is directed only toward the immediate experience, regardless of whether it is pleasant or unpleasant:

I like to get the thing that I'm doing over with—present things which have to be done. I don't look far into the future. I have no idea what the future will be like.

No, I never bother. I never think about the future. No. I don't think of what is going to come. I live by the day, you know. Why should I worry the few more years I got to live? To worry what's going to happen? Oh, no.

This carpe diem attitude is most fully expressed in the way an Italian patient, paralyzed from the waist down and deprived of his bowel and sex functions, described his feelings toward his disability:

Well, I get pain, but I'm the type of a fellow who ain't going to worry about it. I don't—in other words, I'm just like I was before I got hurt. This type of injury ain't going to worry me, because so what I'm going to do about it? I'm paralyzed; I get around the best I can. I get a check from the government, and I got a car to ride around with; what I'm going to worry about? Gray hair? I can meet girls; I can go out with them; I can go out to a show. Million guys worse off

than me here in the hospital. What am I kicking about? I
am happy. I am lucky.

This time value, which seems to be an integral part of the
Italian ethos, is directly applied toward any manifestation of physical stress, whether it is pain, illness, or disability. Hence it is no
wonder that the patient who thinks little or not at all about the
future implications and effects of his pain concentrates on the discomfort and unpleasant aspects of the sensation itself. He is concerned mainly with the immediate relief of the sensation. He will
accept anything to get rid of the pain, feeling that, once the sensation is relieved, everything is alright. This viewpoint is expressed
directly with regard to pain-relieving drugs.

Most of the interviewed patients, regardless of their ethnic
background, expressed their awareness of a real or imaginary harm-
fulness of analgesics. They indicated their concern with the habit-
forming dangers of "dope" and revealed their reluctance to take
any. Usually they accepted the analgesics when there was no other
choice or when their pain was beyond all control. A number of
patients refused to take the pain-relieving drugs for fear of future
effects. The Italian patient did not differ from other patients in
his awareness of the dangers of the pain killer, but his impatience
with the immediate experience of pain was so great and his concern
with future so insignificant that he was ready to take anything to be
relieved from a sensation that caused despair and depression. Moreover, he would not wait until such a drug was given to him; he
went and asked for it from anyone who was in a position to hand
it to him, be it a doctor or a nurse. Asking for relief of pain—for
pills or injections—is characteristic of Italian patients and is frequently seen by the hospital staff as an exaggerated complaining of
pain. In some cases this actual need for pain relief was interpreted
by doctors and nurses as the malingering of an addict complaining
of pain in order to obtain a dose of Demerol or morphine.

Without any inhibition patients told the interviewer how
eager they were to get the pill or powder in order to get some relief
and sleep.

I told the doctor this morning, I said, "Hey, Doc, you better give me something to make me sleep tonight." You see I don't sleep—for four weeks I ain't slept a night. He said, "Well, tell the nurse to give you a sleeping powder." Well, I said: "Well that's something I don't know. Every time I go to the nurse, they—they—eat you up—they don't want to give it to you unless you get an O.K." So I told the doctor, I says, "Now, I'm suffering with this pain too much. I gotta get a sleeping tablet—make me sleep. I have to get some sleep." I can't—I don't sleep all night.

Well, two nights this week I asked the nurse to please give me something—that I couldn't tolerate the pain.

I don't like them, but what else can I do to relieve that pain?

Furthermore, the patient not only feels that he should ask for relief as soon as he gets pain; he is also of the opinion that the doctors themselves should suggest a similar attitude to those patients who might be inhibited and self-conscious about asking for relief.

Like, many a time I was in pain, and I couldn't sleep, and I just used to go ask for a sedative. I mean, I didn't die waiting for the nurse to come all night long. What's the sense? There's no sense in that. You know what I mean? If you need something, ask for it. That's how I feel. Like, some fellows are bashful. Like some—when I first come in here, I was bashful to ask for some—for sedatives for something. You know what I mean? But I found out that if you don't ask for it, you don't get it. But they should make—I think they should stress—like the doctor should stress to the patient: "If you're in pain, don't be bashful. Ask for it. Ask the nurse or ask someone." But they never tell you that. You know what I mean?

The doctor may explain to the patient the ill effects of the drugs and advise him to keep away from them as much as possible; the patient, however, is too concerned with the sensation to be able to accept the professional suggestion.

158

Well, the doctor told me—he believed you become accustomed to it and all that stuff. And I told him, "Listen, if you are in pain it is very hard to sleep," and I wasn't getting any sleep at all. He says, "Yeah, I understand all that," he says. "But try—try and," he said, "you'll have to get your body accustomed to the pain." But it is not very easy to get accustomed to the pain. I mean, when you're hurting, you're— you can feel it. I mean, there is no sense in kidding anybody. And sometimes I ask the nurse for a sleeping pill. "What? What do you want it for?" I can't see that nonsense. A person knows. If he needs something, he needs it. Like they hand you this nonsense of becoming a dope addict. I can't see that, because I think it's very foolish. A dope addict will want it all day long, you know what I mean? He will want it—he'd be crazy for it. But a guy that just wants it at night to relax and go to sleep—you know what I mean? They shouldn't have any trouble.

It is interesting to note that some patients, in their tendency to attribute more importance to pain relief than to the possibility of drug addiction, seem to develop a rationale that such danger is actually exaggerated. They feel that, as soon as the pain is relieved, they will be able to discontinue the taking of the drug. The following episode was related to me by a patient who insisted that he had no difficulty putting an end to "hypos" after the amputation of his painful leg:

When I was admitted the second time, they looked at my record. "Why," they said, "I see you have been on Demerol." I says, "That's right." He asks me how long, and I told him, and I explained to him that I'd have to have a big dose of it —that's when I'd go to sleep. He asked me why, and I told him that I'd been on it so long that my body had built up a resistance to it. So, I told him, I says, "You just take this leg off and I'll cut that out like that." I said, "You get rid of that pain for me and I'll cut it out." He says, "I heard that before." I says, "Well, you haven't heard from me." So he couldn't believe it. But anyhow they took my leg off, and from then on, why, I asked him for one hypo at nighttime, and then only, I think it was once. Just enough to—a little edge—take a little pain away from the fresh cut. When they just took the leg off. So then I didn't ask for any more. And the doctor called me in the room one day; he says, "I want to speak to you," he says. "Close the door." I was in the wheelchair, and I pulled in the room and closed the door. He says, "You have a problem," he says, "and I want to help you. And that's what I'm here for. I'm a doctor, and I want to help you, but I want you to lay your cards on the table and I'll lay mine." I says, "Well, anything I can do just ask." He says, "Well, what I want to know is where are you getting your hypos?" So, I mean, I thought as a statement where was I getting them? And I says, "Why, here, on the floor— off the nurse." He says, "No—what I mean, where are you getting your extra hypos?" I says, "Why, I'm not. I don't. Any time you want me you know where to find me. I'm not getting any hypos—only the one that I got at twelve o'clock in order to go to sleep." And he says, "Are you sure?" And I said, "Well, for God's sake, what made you think?" He says, "Well, the nurse tells me that—I sign an order for hypos for you and you are not asking for them. Anybody that has taken as many hypos and as much Demerol as you have—they can't just cut it off like that." I says, "Well, you remember what I told you, doctor, when you cut the source of pain away, that I'd get off it myself?" And he says, "Well, I have heard it told many times, but I've never seen it happen." And I says, "Well, might be I'm one of the flukes, but that's the way I feel, and I didn't want it. There's no sense in taking it if I didn't have to have it. On the other hand, this thing started to bother me tomorrow and caused me enough pain—where I couldn't stand it any more—then I ask you for a hypo. And that's just the way it is. I wouldn't ask for it unless I really have it.[1]

---

[1] This story is quoted in full because it reflects the attitude toward narcotics that has been expressed by many other Italian patients, that is, their lack of belief in chronic addiction, as well as a strong conviction that, with the removal of source of pain or of the pain itself, they will also eliminate the need for the drug. I was not able to check the accuracy of the

Fa Malo

The desire to "get rid" of pain seems to be so strong among these patients that they assert their readiness to accept even more radical means of pain relief than the use of narcotics.

Like so many other patients, the Italian is very much afraid of the "knife," and he speaks with great apprehension about the eventuality of surgery. He would accept an operation only when it is absolutely required:

> When you have to have an operation, because the illness is a direct threat to your life, well, you can't help it—you do it. But when a choice is given to you, you are afraid of it.

> Well, if the thing has got to be done and you tell me the truth, yes, I'll accept it. But at the same time you realize it's taking a chance, and everybody makes mistakes. Sometimes maybe the doctor makes a mistake too. Because sometime maybe he go with a knife—slip or something. Maybe he cut one thing for another?

Despite this fear, a number of Italian patients said that they would rather accept the amputation of a leg or arm than suffer chronic pain. The fear of pain appears to be more intense than the fear of the loss of a limb. When the patient suffers from pain, he does not think much of the possibility of becoming a cripple as a consequence of the amputation. Unlike the Irish patient, he associates surgery only with the elimination of the source of pain.

Occasionally this attitude was qualified as immature by those members of the hospital staff who, in the tradition of the American culture, were thinking of the future implications of an operation. Disability is probably one of the greatest evils for a person reared in a culture in which independence and self-reliance are of paramount value in achieving social and economic success. The surgeon will think twice before suggesting an amputation to a pa-

---

story as it was given to me. Nevertheless, I had an opportunity to observe at a later date two Italian patients who were considered by the hospital staff as Demerol addicts. Yet after their condition had been improved, they completely abandoned their former habits.

tient and will do it only when no other choice is available and when death might be the result of acute infection. The Italian patient, however, is disturbed to such an extent by the immediate pain caused by the condition of the leg and its direct effects upon his present life that he cannot understand the hesitation of the doctors:

> I'm sick of being laid up. I want them to get over with it— get to the point of it so I can get out. If they have to cut— like I told them two or three weeks ago—do it.

Time and again the patients speak about their desire to be operated on and to "get rid of the pain":

> [How would you feel about an operation?] That's what I want. [You want an operation?] Yes, sir. I'd feel I'd have a better chance with an operation. This will only happen again, and I can't stand it. I'm not fooling anybody. It will happen again. Give me an operation and send me home and it would be 100 per cent.

> I wanted the amputation. I requested the amputation because I was in such pain that I begged them to take it off. I begged them to take it off here and put a wooden one, but they wouldn't listen. They said, "Now it will be all right."

> It gets to a point where I want the operation. I want it, and I want to get over with it, and I want to be sound and healthy and be able to do all the normal things I used to do before this darned condition came along.

A laborer, whose entire livelihood depended on the wholeness of his body and who worked most of the time outdoors and loved it, said:

> I wouldn't be worried about an operation, no sir. As long as they cure this—get the pain out of there, that's all. 'Cause the pain is too strong. It's too much for me.

Fa Malo

The readiness for a radical operation is, like everything else, strictly present oriented. As soon as the pain is over, the patient changes his attitude and is opposed to surgery, being influenced by his original fears:

In the beginning I was ready for an operation—for anything —it was like torture. Now I wouldn't like an operation. I keep thinking that I'm better.

So, in considering an operation, the main criterion is the relief of pain. But it is not the only criterion. Life and its enjoyment are the yardsticks of Italian attitudes. After all, the patient wants relief of pain because pain interferes with pleasure. There is no point in relieving pain by an operation if surgery will also eliminate the possibility of enjoyment. In choosing between pain and pleasure, the pleasure principle defeats the fear of pain:

I don't like to think about this operation (cordotomy). I don't think I'll agree to it. You know what I mean? It's— uh—well—I guess that's one of your pleasures—sex. You know what I mean?

This statement was made by a patient suffering from intractable pain due to a spinal injury. Cordotomy was suggested as the only possible measure to stop his agonizing spasms, but it would also affect his sex functions.

These changes in mood are frequently misunderstood by the hospital staff, doctors, and nurses, who, using their own standards of correct behavior, expect a rational and realistic attitude toward pain and its relief. To the great dismay of the patient, they are likely to qualify him as unstable, overemotional, or hypochondriac. At times these opinions are even entered into a patient's medical chart and subsequently become labels transmitted from one shift to another or from one doctor to his successor. They may even become part of the thinking of his fellow patients:

At the time I was in the hospital, one of the boys had access to the records, and, if I recall properly, it annoyed me at the time. But then in my annoyance I was amused to think that a doctor would misconstruct my complaints. He had written me up as a "hypochondriac Italian male." And I laughed, because I thought, "By golly, I wasn't that stupid." I had had bona fide surgery done on me. There was a definite reason for it. I hadn't gone in with a—uh—psychosomatic pain, so to speak, or anything else like that.

As a matter of fact, the "hypochondriac Italian male" who at times may be annoying to doctors and nurses because of his intense emotionality in seeking relief from dreaded pain is actually a rather good patient. He complies with orders, he accepts whatever is told to him, and he has the proper attitude toward doctors and medication. The only time when he might transgress some doctor's order is in the matter of diet. The hospital food is not always tasty to the patient who loves spicy and starchy Italian cooking. Most of the time he is condemned to consume the wholesome but frequently bland combinations of lettuce, tomatoes, peas, and string beans, which are prized by many other patients who were reared on similar diets. When an Italian patient speaks about his distaste for the hospital food, he sounds as dramatic as when he speaks about his painful condition:

> [Why would you prefer to go home?] I got enough to be here, and for the food—for the food I gotta be home. The food they give me downstairs! I was 160 pounds, and look what I am now. I lost all that since I left home. I cannot eat cereal, I cannot eat cornflakes, I cannot eat beef steaks, and I cannot eat cabbage. Anything fine I cannot eat. I cannot eat spaghetti with sauce because the doctor says if I lose it's better for me. But after that I lost so much and I was weak, weak, weak. So the doctor gave me iron in the bottle instead of food—one bottle, two bottles, three bottles. Home I got one daughter, she comes, another daughter comes, my son— everybody comes. You know what I mean? One cooks one

164

thing; the other brings other cooking. You know what I
mean?[2]

Frequently, to the horror of the nurse, the hospital tray is
supplemented by a piece of hot salami or a sip of red wine smug-
gled into the hospital by understanding relatives.[3]

Diet is one part of the hospital routine that the patient has
a hard time understanding and complying with. He was brought
up in a culture in which the enjoyment of food is one of the great
pleasures of life. There cannot be any evil in food. "Food is good
for you," especially food you get in the family, prepared by mother
or wife. Even foreign, unfamiliar food is "good for you," as long
as it is being served by Mother:

Home we have Italian food. But I can eat German cooking,
Jewish cooking, Hungarian cooking—makes no difference. As
long as it is home cooked. I can eat anything. I figure if your
mother cooks it, it's good for you. It's got to be good for me.
See? Of course, you've got to get used to the dishes.

It is no wonder that one of the most unpleasant features of
hospital life is the meal, which not only is unfamiliar but also is not
home cooked. Hospital food, despite the dietetic and medicinal

[2] A patient who did not want to appear tactless about the hospital
food expressed his opinion in a rather discreet fashion: [Do you like the
food here?] "Well, sometimes. You know, we eat different, but I'm not particular."

[3] Many times, after having established cordial relationships with the
patient during the interview, I had the privilege of being invited to share
home delicacies kept in the drawer of the night table, together with home
souvenirs and religious objects known for their therapeutic value. For the
patients, I was not a "Doc" or a nurse who watched carefully the exact
proportions of proteins and vitamins in the patient's meal. Neither was
the patient afraid that I would betray his "secret." I guess he also felt that,
because of my European background, which he quickly detected during the
interview, I would be able to appreciate the familiar taste of his native
cuisine.

qualities, has an effect on some of the Italian patients that is totally unpredicted by the doctors and dieticians:

> My bowls have been off for the last week. I don't know—change of climate or food. At home I get richer food. So it—that hasn't helped me, you know, being off. I have taken laxatives since I've come here. Do I like the food here? It's edible, I guess. But I'm used to very, very good food. Because I come from a family of good cooks—spicy Italian foods and stuff like that.

The ill effects of hospital food on the digestive system of the patients probably also stem from other factors not necessarily of a gastronomic nature. In the Italian family, food appears to play an important role in promoting the feeling of belongingness and security:

> In my family we eat Italian, and everything is Italian cooking, although we do have American dishes like mashed potatoes or roast beef now and then—but not as often as spaghetti. Uh—like I told my mother just the other day—she said, "Gee, some Sunday I want to have something besides spaghetti." And I said, "No, don't, because it just doesn't seem like home without spaghetti." And every Sunday I have spaghetti. Whether I have something else besides, it is of secondary nature. But I just don't feel like it's Sunday unless I have spaghetti. And I think that makes me primarily in the Italian line and makes me feel good.

This home atmosphere induced by Mother's spaghetti and tomato sauce is lost in the sterile and hygienic hospital kitchen and, with it, the security of the patient. Fortunately, it is partially regained during visiting hours, when the patient and his female relatives enjoy their home delicacies (making sure, however, that their little feast remains unnoticed by the nurse on duty).

The attitude that food is good for you as long as it is given by a well-wishing person is carried over to medication prescribed by a doctor who enjoys the patient's confidence. In general, the

Italian patient has some misgivings about drugs and medication. The primary reason for his skepticism is the fact that drugs are not natural:

> I would take it, but I wouldn't particularly care for it. It is not what you call natural. It's not a natural thing. I don't think drugs are a natural thing.

Whenever a patient has the opportunity, he would rather rely on "natural" remedies, which are, by the way, closely related to foods:

> I get headaches—probably—a logginess. I try not to take laxatives. I try to take natural foods. I think stuff like orange juices or prune juices or apricot are good for you.

Moreover, the patient feels that, although medication is sometimes helpful in one way, it might be harmful in another because of its effect upon his stomach—a vital part of his body: "I figure I might ruin the stomach, and what is an Italian with a bum stomach?"

Nevertheless, despite the original skepticism, the patient takes the prescribed medication. After all, the doctor has prescribed it, he knows what he is doing, he wishes you well, and, therefore, "it's good for you":

> Well, that's a common trend—that a person doesn't care for needles. I mean, it makes you feel funny, but if it's for my benefit, it's going to help me. I did go right ahead with them. I've never objected to anything. The doctors—I'm 100 per cent for what the doctors say.

> If they want to give it to me, it must be good for me.

> No matter what it is, you got to take it, because that's your own benefit. Then, in other words, what it is, it's good for you. If you don't take—so what the doctor going to do? He can't open your mouth and give it to you, right? And force you. If he forces you, it makes it worse. So, in other words, take it nice. They know it's not going to kill me. It's good

for me. Maybe it's sour in my mouth, but after going in it's all over. I mean, I realize that.

In their attitude toward medication, characterized on the one hand by skepticism and slight apprehension and on the other hand by the feeling that it is beneficial, some patients introduce another element—so far encountered only among those of Italian origin. They speak about the psychological function of the drug. They might be skeptical as to the actual efficiency of the drug, because it is not natural; nevertheless, they accept the fact that they have been relieved by it and attribute the beneficial result to its psychological impact:

> I think it's all in the head. You take an aspirin, you'll feel better. I don't think the aspirin does anything for you.

> Last time I'd taken some aspirin. It seemed to relieve it slightly, but I don't know whether that's psychological or whether the aspirin actually took effect. Still and all, it did relieve it—the aspirin.

This emphasis on the psychological effects of the drug seems to be related to a tendency to see the medication not only as a drug but as a medium in doctor-patient relationships. It is not *what* is being prescribed to the patient that counts, but *who* prescribes it. The personality of the doctor and his relationship toward the patient seem to play a most important role in the therapeutic effect of the medication.

From the point of view of medical philosophy, the above statement is a truism. The medical literature is rich in essays devoted to this same subject, and probably every medical student is able to comment on this topic by referring to his school lectures. However, this concept was seldom mentioned by patients in the hospital—a population that was not very sophisticated in medical matters. Yet the patients of Italian origin, regardless of their education or socioeconomic status, were the only ones who stressed the primary importance of the interpersonal-relationship factor in medical treatment.

Fa Malo

Unquestionably, the Italian patient has great confidence in the physician. His trust in the doctor's abilities is almost of a mystical nature. The doctor is frequently seen as a miracle man. However, the magical powers of the physician are less attributed to his factual knowledge than to his personality. Again and again the Italian patient emphasized that, in his confidence in doctors, their medical skill was of secondary importance, the primary significance being ascribed to his character and humanitarian attitude. The relationship the patient establishes with his doctor is not formed along professional lines but along friendship patterns, based on empathy and human warmth:

> In some doctors, frankly, I have confidence, and some, of course, no—depending on their personality. You get certain doctors. I can't quite explain it, but it's just—I guess it's just a natural thing among most people. I guess it is just like friendship. You take to certain people, and to certain people you just don't take. Same thing with doctors. First of all, he's got to make me feel relaxed. If I feel relaxed, I have confidence in him. If he makes me feel as if I want to run out of the room, then I lost confidence in him. That's—that's the important thing. [And do you have confidence in their knowledge—in their skill?] In their knowledge, and in their skill. I assume that they are doctors. They've got to have a certain amount of knowledge and skill, but—even though—that still doesn't carry too much weight with me. Still, personality has a lot to do with it: the way he speaks to me, the way he treats me.

Being a doctor is a trade like any other trade. Hence the special skill does not make much difference; it is the human relationship that matters for the Italian patient. The initial approach to the doctor is that of trust and faith. In this respect it is similar to an attitude toward any human who cares for a person's welfare:

> I think that whatever he says, he's out to see my welfare, and that's—that's all that matters. I mean, I have no—so far I

169

have had no distrust in any of the doctors that I have come across. I have had all the faith I need in them.

However, the final criterion is the behavior of the doctor and the human character of his rapport:

Like the doctor I had at that hospital there—no. I had no confidence in him, because he never came to me and tried to treat me like a human being. He never talked to me—never told me what was wrong and how long would take me to get better.

Once the human rapport with the doctor is established, the patient is ready to put himself into his hands. He will follow all his advice and suggestions and remain loyal to him:

Certainly I have confidence in him. I wouldn't let him treat me this time if I didn't. He was nice to me. He fixed me up five or six years ago. I figured, well, he might do it again.[4]

Even with regard to hospitalization the Italian patients use different criteria than patients of other groups. They do not seem to pay much attention to the medical aspects of the hospital setting or to the efficiency of medical care. Rather, they think in terms of the staff's attitude toward them, of the general emotional atmosphere of the hospital, and, naturally, of food. Given a choice, the patient would rather be ill at home than in the hospital, because:

---

[4] In the process of my study, I had ample opportunity to observe the importance of the human element in professional relationships with Italian patients. Their response to the interview situation was that of trust, warmth, and sincerity. As soon as they became aware of the objectives of my questions and realized that, by answering them, in some indirect way they might contribute to the welfare of other patients, they reacted with admirable grace and charm. After a very short period the interview lost its formal character and became a friendly conversation between two people interested in their mutual opinions and feelings. Neither they nor I ever forgot the two hours of our meeting together, and many of them who years later were readmitted to the hospital greeted me again with the same expressions of friendliness and cordiality.

Fa Malo

Nobody likes to be in the hospital. Being in the hospital is another thing that's not natural.

Moreover, a sensitive person is likely to become quite depressed seeing the helplessness of many patients, especially those suffering from a disease similar to his:

> They told me not to worry about MS. But I don't care what you say, you come to a place like this and you are going to see the effects of something like that, and you are certainly going to think. Don't you think I am right?

But, if hospitalization is necessary, one has to accept it and make the best of it:

> Who wants to be in a hospital? Who wants to be in a hospital unless you got to be in? If you got to come, you got to come —that's all.

However, the patient's feelings about the hospital are primarily influenced by the way he is treated there. If the nurses and doctors show a personal interest in his sufferings and respond with sympathy to his complaints, the patient is happy and contented. He is appreciative and thankful for every sign of attention and regard shown to him by the hospital staff:

> Oh, very nice here! I feel like in my own home. I didn't think it will be so good. Everybody is nice to me. The doctors, the nurses, everybody. Imagine, today they came to give me a bath. Even the food isn't bad.

In their rapports with the hospital staff and fellow patients on the ward, most of the Italian patients display a great deal of human dignity and personal security. These security feelings are quite noticeable, despite tears and complaints and despite the fluctuations of mood from despair to insouciance. Their attitudes toward medication, doctors, life, and people in general suggest a basic ease and assurance. This feeling is reflected in the absence of future-oriented anxieties, in the uninhibited expressions of their emotions, and in the great emphasis on interpersonal relationships. The ability to respond with an uninhibited spontaneity and directness to the immediate experience, pleasant or unpleasant, is indicative of a secure person. A person who cries because he suffers and not because his pain may be a symptom of some dreadful disease, who can relish his food without worrying about the ill effects of overeating, and who is able to enjoy the pleasure of today without anxious thoughts about tomorrow is a person who feels basically safe and not threatened.

In the American culture this kind of behavior is often associated with immaturity and an unrealistic approach to life. As a matter of fact, patients of Italian origin were at times described as childish by members of the hospital staff. More than once, people concerned with the patients' social and economic problems reported on their unrealistic attitude toward the planning of the future. This evaluation of the patient's attitudes is nothing else but a consequence of a conflict between two cultural value systems, the American (or Jewish) and the Italian, and between a future-oriented and a present-oriented culture. Without going into a discussion of objective criteria of maturity and immaturity, I would like to point out that, judging from the interviews, the "immature" Italian patients were able to lead a life that was socially and economically as sound and successful as that of members of other, more "realistic" groups.

The feeling of basic security, which appears to be an important clue for an understanding of the Italian pattern of responses to pain and stress, can be traced to two major factors: family structure and strong group identification.[5]

When the Italian patient relates his family life, as a child

[5] I do not mean that these two factors are the only ones that foster the shaping of security feelings of the Italian patient; it so happens that the interview material is exceptionally rich in data pertaining to the role of the family and group belongingness, and these two areas could be adequately exploited for the analysis.

or as an adult, there is no doubt in his mind that he has always been loved by his parents, siblings, and wife. Mutual love and respect within the family are frequently mentioned. Even when he speaks about punishments he received as a child, he adds the same comment that is so often applied to doctors' care and medication: "It was good for me." When he talks about the spankings and lashings he received from his father, there is no hostility in his voice. On the contrary, he feels that they were well deserved and that they did not affect the love relationship between him and his parents.

This love relationship between family members fosters a strong feeling of solidarity and mutual dependence. Every member of the family feels that, when one is in need, there will always be a helping hand. Parents support their children with the conviction that, when they will be unable to work, the children will support them. The children feel the same way. Siblings support one another in school or business. Frictions and tensions that may occur between individual members of the family do not seem to affect the basic ties of solidarity.

The patriarchal structure of the Italian family is reflected in many interviews, but the father is always seen as a good man and as a loving person:

When my father would say "Bring something," he didn't have to repeat it twice. Otherwise, he would grab anything —a strap, a stick—and would beat me. He was a good man. He was a good father, and I'm thankful to him for what he has done for me.

He was a little on the discipline side. I remember a good spanking I got when I was not home for supper. See, we had to be home for supper. I was playing with another boy. I got it good. But he was a good provider and he was a home fellow —a good family man.

My father was one of the best men in the world. He's all for the family. He's taught us right from wrong. He cares for one child as he does the other. He divides them equal. His love for us is equal, yes sir. He's punished us for not doing the right things. I mean, what the father should do to a child.

The image of the mother is that of a loving, wonderful person who, although dominated by the father, is always ready to defend her children. She devotes her entire life to the welfare of her husband and children, and in case of need she will sacrifice her own pleasures for the good of her children.

My mother would never punish me. She was always very good to me. When my father would beat me, she would tell my father, "Don't forget it's your son." When my father would beat me, I would cry, but I knew I deserved it. I wouldn't complain to Mother.

When my father died, we were all crying—everybody was crying. My mother had a pretty tough time keeping us together, and she didn't remarry. She used to sew, wash dishes and floors to keep us together. She would punish us, but she didn't mean it. It hurt her more than it hurt us.

She was sweet. Nonchalant—nothing bothered her. Hard working woman. A real Italian mother. Very sweet person. But as sweet as she was, she knew her place.

She is wonderful. She is the best mother a son could ever have. She's understanding. She's very kind—that's all.

The motherly love is intense without being demonstrative. She does not have to show her feelings toward the children by being overprotective or by undue solicitude. The child *feels* his mother's sentiments in the atmosphere she creates at home.

Naturally, she worries whenever we're sick. But no matter how much she worries, that doesn't mean that she won't perform her duties. In other words, when we are sick, she takes good care of us and all that. She is not squeamish—let's put it that way. As far as feeding goes, we ate the basic Italian food. She wouldn't stuff us. She'd make sure that we ate something. Eating was never her problem, anyway, because we all ate like horses.

The only way she babied me—I've noticed—is looking in at me at nights. I've noticed it every once in a while—and make sure I was covered. She's never got that into her head that I was grown up. But she wouldn't show it to me. Father, he more or less talks to me as a grownup, an adult. As children we thought that he was strict, but it wasn't—it was for our own good.

The echo of this inconspicuous but ever-present protection is heard in a comment offered by an Italian informant who was not a hospital patient:

We want someone who will be sympathetic toward you— sort of understanding when you are not feeling well, and probably maybe wait on you a little bit to make you feel comfortable, and do it in such a way that you feel they're not doing it just out of pity or sympathy. They are doing it because they really want to. It gives you a sense of security. When you are sick there is someone who really cares—who will take care of you.

The general tone of family relationships is summarized in the following short statements:

Oh, our family—our family is very close, very close. Now understand, I mean, we have our spats amongst ourselves and all, but still, we're very close.

I've been brought up by Father and Mother—by brothers and sisters. We were always happy together. We lived together, and we always get along well.

In this atmosphere of love and closeness, strong ties of solidarity are developed. Children are grateful to their father and mother for the love and security they received in their childhood and feel that it is their duty to repay it when their parents become ill or old and are unable to support themselves:

> My father not working for twenty years. We are supporting my father. Sure. My brother die—the one that was in the family—he die a few years ago. Now we have to support my father and mother. We are children, yes. Anything he need. One time I give him a pair of shoes and my brother a shirt. We are in business. It is nice to give him. Anything my father wants—ten dollars. He can say to the children give him. It is my duty to my father.

> My mother worked very hard for us children, and we cannot do enough to satisfy her, to make her life as easy as possible now.

When children have this understanding of their obligations toward parents, the parents have no reason to worry about their old-age problems. They are not afraid of becoming a burden to their children, because it is only normal to expect that the children will help them.

When the old people are laid up or ill in the hospital, they can afford to concentrate only on their pain, without worrying too much about their future. They know that, if they are unable to work, they will be well taken care of:

> I never think about the future. I got my son. I brought him up right, and he can help me. If I were mean with my son, he could tell me, "My father was so mean to me, I don't care for him." But when I treat him right, the boy, he thinks about me too. Oh, he'd take care of me. That's what they say— "Pop and Mama, don't worry, because anything happen to one or the other, then I'll take care of."

This feeling of security is fostered not only by the solidarity and devotion between parents and children but also among siblings. The life histories of the Italian patients are rich in examples of sacrifice of one sibling for the benefit of the other. Usually the older ones do their utmost to secure a better life for the younger ones:

> I didn't have much education. I wanted to get out to work. We needed money in the house. I'm not sorry I did it. I put my kid brother—we sent him to high school, and now he's taking a course in college. He had the opportunity, being the last one in the family—the youngest one. We all helped out, sure. I went into the service before my time. In fact, I left my mother and kid brother alone. That's when I felt very bad—when I was in boot camp. Every dollar I had I used to send home.

> I went to high school three years, but I had to quit because it was around Depression time, and I had to go out to work to allow my brothers to get a good education.

> All of us did went to work at an early age with the exception of my younger brother and sister. We tried to keep them in school as long as possible. My brother went through college. He's an accountant.

The same solidarity is displayed when one of the siblings is ill:

> I always do my brothers favors. They do favors to me. They give my wife their pay and buy milk. They all chip in to help 'cause they know we have no money. They pay my milkman; they pay my insurance—try to keep it going.

The role of family life in shaping the security feelings of an Italian is something that he himself is well aware of. He knows that, to feel safe and happy in health and in illness, he needs a home, a wife, and children. An Italian patient who had a most unhappy life—he had lost his parents at an early age and was brought up by an uncle and aunt who were "always wonderful" to him— became most depressed in the hospital. One reason for his mood was the hesitation of doctors in diagnosing his illness. His reaction to the situation at the time seemed to be that of constant worry and depression. This patient made the following comment about his state of mind:

> I told you, I miss a real, natural, you know, family life. I do miss it. I'm twenty-nine, but I miss it. I know that it could have a change in my life. It wouldn't have made me so high strung. I know that if I ever get married, I'll feel sure of myself. I always wanted a natural home life. I see people around me that have it—friends of mine that live next door. And I can see if the pattern is worked out right, there is a pretty good life. Nice and secure. I can see that. And I know that if I ever get married, I'm going to have it that way.

As suggested, Italian behavior patterns in pain are characterized by a feeling of security, and this feeling of security can be traced to a great extent to the family structure and emotional atmosphere within the family. The same point can be illustrated by a case of an Italian patient who manifested a number of deviant traits. The behavior of this patient was typified by anxiety and insecurity. His first comment about himself was, "I worry about a lot of things in life." He worried about his wife, his work, and his health. One of his major concerns was his inability to succeed in planning for the future:

> Have a lot of things to worry about, don't pan out right. You try to build and plan—try to get a dollar. Right away something happens. And then on the job there's a lot of aggravation.

Like many other Italian patients, he could not stand pain and cried and complained about it. But he was different because he stressed his worries about the significance of pain and about its effects on his future:

> I was getting worried about this. I don't know what's turning out with this leg. How do I know if I'll become a cripple? Maybe I've got—I have always figured maybe I hurt a vessel

178

in there. Maybe I hurt a muscle in there. I would like to know, and every doctor I go to—they tell me nothing. I'm worried about it. Sure. 'Cause it never lasted me so long. It's beginning to prey on my mind. Since January. What would it be? My brother says, "Don't worry!" "What kind of don't worry?" I says. I can't help worry.

His anxieties were constantly on his mind, and he could not enjoy anything in life. He was tense and scared:

[Are you tense, scared?] Probably you would call it that. One doctor said that I'm a little high tense, but he said that I should learn to enjoy myself in life. Yeah, but how do you do that? I don't know how to do it. It's easy to tell a person here you got to go and sit down and enjoy yourself. How could you do it when you have no desire? "Go ahead, sit down and eat that there turkey. Enjoy it!" You've got to be in a mood to do it. I'm never in the mood to do these things.

He was afraid of the treatment he was getting, especially the injections:

I'm afraid if you give me a needle. I'm thinking about that. I'm scared of the dentist. The first day I got to him I was very nervous. I'm scared of blood tests.

He also worried about what the next day would bring:

As I told my wife yesterday, I said, "Gee, I don't know what's going to bring tomorrow."

He was in constant fear of testing and experiments. He made the following comment after watching with apprehension other patients who went through certain uncomfortable aspects of treatment:

The only thing I have on my mind—who's going to call me next? What kind of an experiment are they going to try on me next? That's the next that is always on my mind. You see, this fellow over there, he got a needle in his spine. They took pictures. I figured they're going to try all that stuff on me. Sure, I'm nervous about it. I can't help it.

Despite his apprehensions, the hospital was the only place where he felt secure. And, contrary to the usual feelings of Italian patients about the hospital kitchen, he said with great enthusiasm:

> This is a wonderful hospital—I mean, the meals are wonderful. I eat three good meals a day. I'm enjoying the food very much. I eat them heartily. Lots of time at home I had no desire—I don't know why. But here I seem to eat three good meals a day. I move my bowels. They don't bother you. I mean, you relax. Nobody annoys you too much. I think it's wonderful.

All these attitudes are systematically different from what could be expected from an Italian patient and certainly deserve some consideration from the point of view of his deviancy. The interview material is insufficient for a thorough analysis. Unquestionably, an intensive psychological study could reveal a mental and emotional pattern that would explain the patient's difficulties and anxieties. Such a study is, regretfully, outside the limits of this research. Yet the information he offered about his family experience throws some light on the understanding of the problem if it is viewed within the framework of the suggested hypothesis of the relationship between the Italian feeling of security and family structure. It seems that this patient's reported family experience was as different from other patients' experiences as his attitudes toward pain and illness:

> [How long ago did your father die?] I was in California— three years ago. I never seen him. He was separated from the home for a good many years. I seen him on and off, when I was younger, but then when I got married I never seen him no more. He lived with us until I was about twelve years old. Then he left home. He used to fight with Mother an awful lot. He used to break up a lot of things in the house.

One time, I remember, he broke the whole bedroom set. He wasn't a good father.

Although his mother was a "wonderful person" who took good care of him, he always felt sorry for her "because she was unhappy alone. She used to say that she was blue." When his father took him to court for support, he refused to pay by saying to the judge: "This man has never been home to support us. I don't think I should support him." After he got married (to a Hungarian woman), he lived with his wife for a while until they separated. The patient gave the following reason for the separation: "I don't know how to explain it. Maybe it was me. She claims I'm a very hard person to get along with and please." After a period of separation he returned to his wife, but the relationship remained rather distant: "The wife tells me, 'You never like to talk to me.' What am I going to talk about? Her kind of things? Her kind of things I am not interested in. My wife says, 'That's your whole trouble. You don't laugh, you don't talk.' I can't sit around in a chair and hold a conversation with her. I have no patience, no desire."

From all this material it is clear that the family life of this patient was very much unlike the usual experiences of other patients of a similar ethnic background.[6] It seems safe to infer that his case history is a good illustration of the influence of a culturally deviant family structure on the shaping of deviant cultural attitudes and behavior.

Another patient who also differed in many areas of behavior from other Italian patients similarly reported a great many problems related to his family life. His difficulties were mainly in the area of interpersonal relationships. In the beginning of the interview he was most suspicious and hostile. He refused to speak about himself, his emotions, or his experiences. Most of his answers were limited to "yes" or "no," which were uttered in a bored or indifferent tone of voice. He disliked the doctors, the nurses, and the

[6] I cannot resist the temptation to draw a parallel between the life history of this patient and the data derived from the interviews with patients of Irish origin.

other patients. He did not care much about his pain. He felt he could stand it as well as the other patients. He never cried or complained. When his pain got annoying, he asked for something to relieve it but never got excited about it.

In the course of the interview he revealed a most disturbing life history: an early separation between his father and mother and life in three different foster homes. "My father had my mother locked up when I was six years old as an unsuitable mother. The state took us six kids away from them. I lived in foster homes all my life."

His ambition was to become an embalmer: "I like this profession. I don't mind working with corpses because they are dead." He liked to hide his feelings from other people because he felt it was nobody's business if he had a problem. He did not like people to feel sorry for him.

He did not feel any love for his brothers and sisters:

> I haven't a thing in common with them. I'm trying to make a living for myself, and, as far as I'm concerned, the ties of the family are broken. And they are going to stay that way if I can help it.

It is worth adding that this patient's name was purely Anglo-Saxon. According to his own comments, he had nothing in common with Italian life. Obviously he not only missed the family influence on the shaping of his attitudes, but also did not feel any sense of ethnic group belongingness.

Almost every Italian patient emphasized his feelings of belongingness to, and identification with, the Italian society and culture. Not only the older immigrant patients but even the American-born Italians expressed enthusiastic feelings about their heritage. Although members of other ethnic groups frequently identified themselves as Americans or "hyphenated" Americans, patients of Italian origin spoke of themselves mainly as Italians. In this respect they were approximated only by the Irish, who also stated proudly that they were Irish. They spoke frequently about their love for

Italian food, they defined their parents as an Italian father and mother, and they often introduced their comments by "we Italians. . . ."

No member of any other ethnic group expressed himself with such love and pride about his background as this American-born disabled veteran:

> Well, if anybody ever asks me my nationality, I'm always proud to say I'm Italian instead of—like so many people say—they're Americans. I don't see myself superior to anyone—don't get me wrong. But I think deep down inside that Italian is the best. Why? Maybe it's something inside of me which I can't identify just yet. My parents were Italian, all my friends—my real close friends. Before I got hurt I would say 90 per cent of my friends were Italians. In my family we eat Italian and everything is Italian. We still at home listen to an Italian opera, and if I don't know what it means, I can always ask my father and he can always explain it to me. And if my father doesn't know, maybe my mother knows or maybe my brother knows. The relatives were always around. We had a lot of Italian friends we visited too. We usually had one of the aunts or uncles on both sides more or less.

A healthy Italian informant interviewed about his feelings concerning pain and illness made the following comment:

> I've always been so proud of my heritage because of my love for Italian opera and for painting. I feel that I've inherited many of the talents. Of course, it comes of my Italian heritage.

Another young patient tied closely together his emotions for the family and his national background:

> I love Italian families. I don't know whether you've met many Italian families. They are very happy people—very jubilant people. That's why I like my own people very much, for that reason.

This strong ethnic-group identification is formed in the

family. The home language, at least partially, is Italian: "You know, there are certain idiomatic expressions that are better understood with Italian phrases. Occasionally to make a joke we use them." The cooking, which is one of the most persistent cultural traits, is predominantly Italian. The intrafamily relationships follow traditional patterns: "Like I say, you're brought up to respect your parents, no matter what the case might be, no matter what he might have done—not like American children. I respected my father and my brother, because he was the oldest." Marriages tend to be concluded within the group: "My wife is Italian too. Not from the same town where my folks came, but from the same province."

In case of a radical breaking away from national traditions, the family can apply unpleasant sanctions, which, again, are based on the idea of family solidarity. A patient who described himself as the "wild one of the family," who married twice, first a Jewish girl whom he divorced and then a German woman, spoke with great bitterness of his family's attitude toward him and his wife:

> They called me the wild one because I got divorced and have two children. I got married again to a German woman. Well, we had an argument. I don't talk to them—my mother and two brothers. That's nothing. That don't bother me. No. No, sir. I'm sore at them. I'll tell you why: When my father-in-law died, no one came up and paid their respect. If they don't pay respect to my wife, I don't want no part of them.

The strength of this ethnic and familial tradition is still so powerful that even a very Americanized Italian individual made the following comments on the principles of child rearing that he would like to apply in his family:

> They are pure Americans today. The generation that has been brought up today, they think like Americans, they act like Americans, and—notice the modern Italian parents: they are very liberal in their ways and thoughts. [So, you are against the late spankings of children?] Huh-uh? No, sir!

Fa Malo

Sorry to say so. All I know is that if I can't control my child by speaking to him, there is only one thing—you have to use a little physical violence on him. If my child, when I get married, of course, does anything wrong, I'll speak to him first, but after that, if he continues to violate, that's where I set down my law. He's got to be spanked.

Another young Italian father who was bringing up his son in the American way spoke with nostalgia about the "old ways":

I guess Italians, like all the European people, have great respect for the mother and father. Like now today—the children of today are very, very fast. You know what I mean? Like in those days I never dared answer my mother or father or my brother—my oldest brother, you know. I'd get the pants beat off me. But nowadays my son fights with me. My little three-year-old son tells me to shut up.

It is interesting to note that in the described case of the anxiety-ridden patient, the feelings of Italian identification were as weak as the family ties:

I don't speak Italian. I don't like Italian food. I have a distaste for it. I don't know—I just don't have a taste for it. I like Hungarian food better than Italian. I live in a Jewish neighborhood I never familiar with my own race of people. I don't dislike them, but I never been raised with them.

Again, as in the discussion of the role of family structure, an example of deviance may help illustrate the function of group identification. An Italian patient was referred to the study as one who manifested non-Italian behavior. He was very unemotional and nonexpressive about his pains, despite a very severe case of a herniated disc. Although he was polite and cooperative, he lacked the usual warmth in his relationships with the staff.

When interviewed, one of his first comments was that he did not like to smile and enjoy himself. He denied all knowledge of Italian, despite his upbringing in an Italian immigrant family and

185

neighborhood. He disliked Italian food and opera. He objected to all old-country customs, which he found ridiculous.

In the course of the interview it was revealed that, at the age of fourteen, he was told by his parents that he had been adopted. Subsequently he developed a fantasy that he was in reality of Anglo-Saxon origin. This fantasy was supported by his physical appearance (he was very tall and blond). "I don't look like an Italian fellow," he said with great pride. The implication of his fantasy was a consistent and conscious shedding of Italian behavior and feelings to the extent that he did everything in direct opposition to what he thought an Italian would do. He refused to smile and joke, he became inexpressive and silent, and, finally, in his responses to his pain experience, he assumed a caricature of the Anglo-Saxon attitude.

From all the data collected on Italian patients, conforming as well as deviant, the conclusion is that the strength of group ties —both family and ethnic—provides the patient with a security that is reflected in the way he reacts to critical situations, such as pain, disability, or illness. The awareness of love, solidarity, and acceptance that the Italian patient brings into the hospital allows him to view this experience without much fear and anxiety about its significance and to react mainly to its emotional quality.

Chapter 5

They Suffer Alone

As a group the Irish patients differ little from patients of Old American stock. Only after a close acquaintance is it possible to identify the Irishman by name; by his religion, which is predominantly Roman Catholic; and, sometimes, by the colorful brogue that is characteristic of the speech of the elderly immigrant. Most of them are of the second and third generations, and, according to the analysis of the background information collected in the interviews, there was hardly any difference between the Irish and the Old American groups as to age, occupation, or socioeconomic status. Only in their educational background did there seem to be a slight difference: somewhat more Old American patients had a college education, while more Irishmen went only to high school. A careful examination of the life histories of the informants confirmed the observations made by a number of students of Irish sociology, to the effect that there seemed to exist a characteristic attitude toward marriage manifested in a relatively high number of bachelors and people who married late in their lives. There was also a relatively high proportion of individuals who had been separated from their wives or who had deserted them once or twice in their life. In this respect they differed significantly from the Old Americans of marriageable age, who were usually married and living with their wives and children.

The similarity between the Irish and Old American patients is also apparent in their behavior as patients and in their observable response to pain associated with illness. The tendency to appear calm and unemotional seems to characterize the Irish patients. Their reactions to pain tend to be nonexpressive, nonvocal, and noncomplaining. They also belong to the group described by the hospital personnel as patients who take their pain well, who are not too emotional about it, and who do not make too much fuss. They are not singled out as Irishmen or as a special group of patients, because they live up to the pattern of behavior expected in the hospital; they behave as the average, good patient should behave. Some of the interviewed physicians made the observation that the Irish patients seemed to take their pain exceptionally well and that they did not pay enough attention to their pain, sometimes coming to the doctor too late. However, this incorrect behavior from the point of view of an American physician was attributed to the lower social and educational level of the Irish patient, not to his Irishness.

The researcher devoting his time to the observation of patients' behavior on the ward might have noticed certain almost intangible differences between the Irish and the Old American patients in pain. For example, the Irishman is much more reluctant to speak about his pain experience than the Old American patient, who is ready to share with the interviewer his feelings and opinions. However, this difference acquired a meaning only in the light of long and tedious interviewing of the Irish patients, and the feeling of similarity with the Old Americans was still the predominant result of observation.

They Suffer Alone

In the initial stage of the interview, answers to questions dealing with the patient's reaction to pain, his ability to tolerate it, and his preference for nonexpressive behavior sounded very much like answers familiar from interviews with Old Americans:

Oh, I can stand it pretty good. Yes, I can stand it. I don't get excited over anything like that. No, no. I wouldn't groan or moan. I usually keep pretty calm.

Oh, no, I wouldn't complain. I'd just wait till it went away, that's all. I'm not that bad about it.

I wouldn't complain about it. I'd say it hurt, but that's about as far as it would go.

Although he may utter an "ouch" or an "oh," if the pain gets really bad, he would not go around moaning and groaning. Screaming is considered definitely extreme, and he would not go that far. Even if he felt like screaming, he would do everything to control himself:

I don't want to scream. Sometimes I felt like it, but I'd just grab onto something. I try to do something—get up, sit down, press on it.

A patient with an extremely painful arm, which suggested a diagnosis of causalgia, felt that his pain was not "killing" and therefore would not make him scream:

No, I never scream—not that I know of. I mean, I've had an instant—a few of them—somebody would come over and grab my hand, and I couldn't do much. I just grabbed them. I mean—it—it hurt me. But it's not enough to—uh—it isn't a pain that makes me die—scream.

It seems, however, that, with old age, the control of expressive behavior becomes relaxed, and the patient readily admits a behavior that is unacceptable for a person who considers himself young (regardless of the chronological age). For instance, an Irish-

189

man who described himself as an old man made the following comment when asked whether he complained:

> Oh, yes, oh yes. I groan and moan and try to stretch and do everything.

Denial of crying from pain is as frequent and as general among the Irish patients as among the Old Americans. Uniformly they answer "no" to the question of whether they cried from pain. Even a patient whose pain brought tears to his eyes refused to admit that he was crying:

> The first day, yes—it did bring tears to my eyes. I don't know what it was. It just come out like—it wasn't crying.

The denial of crying in pain is much more significant among the Irish patients as they freely admit tears caused by emotion:

> Oh, I guess I cry for any reason. I'm easy to cry, in other words. [Would pain make you cry?] No, no, not that kind of —a different thing. It's not emotion.

When the Old American patient described his calm and uncomplaining behavior in pain, his explanation was that complaining or crying does not help. Occasionally an Irish patient would also speak about the uselessness of tears or complaints:

> I wouldn't complain much. Complaining, cursing, that's— isn't going to do you any good. I'd say, "Oh, I got a pain— hurt" or something like that, but I can never see much sense to laying here and moan and groan. It doesn't help.

However, this type of comment is rather rare; it is as infrequent as other Old American rationalizations of controlled behavior, such as that complaining behavior is unmanly, typical of a sissy, or inconsiderate of other people:

They Suffer Alone

I don't believe it's a man's place to complain.

I don't want to complain. Complaining is just like a little boy—running to his mother—like a child does complain of.

There is no use bothering—making a pest out of yourself.

The relative infrequency of such reasons for nonexpressive behavior is the first noticeable difference between the Irish and Old American responses.

Occasionally informants express the same tolerant contempt expressed by the Old American for the fussing patient who is a nuisance on the ward.

Yeah, we have a buddy down there that suffers very loud. Doesn't bother me. He—well, I felt for him, but I can't quite reach him. Well, it doesn't bother me—bothers other people —tell him to shut up, or something like that. Yeah, he moans and groans. He can't help it. Well, I'll tell you, if it gives him—probably affords him a measure of relief to do a little groaning, so I don't see any wrong in it.

I'll never say "My God, it's killing me" or something like that. I know some of the boys—always complaining. I know, I've seen them myself, right here in the hospital.

Thus the first impressions gained from initial observations and verbal responses were that Irish patients do not differ much from patients of Old American background. However, after intensive probing, a closer scrutiny revealed that behind this apparent similarity there is a pattern of attitudes that indicates a quality specific only to patients of Irish origin. In other words, although the behavioral response to pain among the Irish and Old American seems to be similar, the attitudes behind this behavior are different.

The nature of the responses to questions pertaining to the pain experience suggested that the Irish feel differently about it. The answers of the Old American are spontaneous, full, and clear; the Irish answers are often laconic, almost abrupt, and frequently

191

limited to a mere "yes" or "no." Frequent hesitations and a certain vagueness and even confusion in phrasing seem to indicate a reluctance—almost an inability—to speak about pain. To elicit sufficient information, the interviewer had to resort to repeated questioning and intensive probing. The phenomenon is much more striking because, in other areas of the interview, the informant was free, articulate, and even verbose. The proverbial Irish eloquency that is exemplified in answers pertaining to life memories or to the cultural background disappears when the patient is talking about pain.

Another distinctive feature of the interview is the use of the word *suffering* in speaking about pain. This word, which appeared rarely in the interviews with Old Americans, is used by almost every Irish informant. Moreover, when the patient speaks about suffering he emphasizes the need to suffer *alone and by himself*. The Irishman seems to view his pain experience as *suffering* that he refuses to *share* with anybody else:

> I can take it pretty well. Sometimes I might have pain and nobody will know it. I'll suffer myself.
>
> [You don't seem to tell people that you are in pain?] That's it—I want to suffer by myself.
>
> I like to be quiet—just quiet. Don't be disturbed. I'd rather be—you know—away by myself. I like to suffer in silence, I guess.

This wish to suffer alone seems to be of a different nature than the tendency to withdraw, which is expressed by the Old Americans refusing to be seen as weak and helpless. The Irish patient is not ashamed of being seen in pain. He likes people and visitors to cheer him up when he is in the hospital, but he does not want to be disturbed because he wants to suffer by himself. He would not mind telling his friends to leave him when he is in pain, and he would tell them frankly the reason why he wants to be alone:

They Suffer Alone

Oh, I like to be alone then. When I am in pain, I like to be away from people. I tell them to get out. "I'm in pain—you better go."

If I have an awful pain in my leg and if somebody is asking me like—too many questions—why, I walk away. And if he wonders why I walk away from them, so I tell them the next day, "I had such a pain in my leg that I just couldn't stand it, you know, so I walked away." When I got a pain like that, I like just to be left alone, that's all.

A sophisticated schoolteacher, who had endured a great deal of pain associated with a metastatic process, which caused his death a few days after the interview, suggested an almost masochistic delight in prolonging his suffering alone:

[Do you complain about your pain?] Not until it gets well along. Not until I've had it about two and a half hours—something like that. [How do you complain about it? Do you call the nurse?] Well, I call the attendant *if he's handy,* and *he'll speak* to the nurse, and the nurse will give me a hypo. With the hypo I can doze and sleep—an hour and three quarters at most.

The primary feature of lonely suffering is enduring pain without doing anything to relieve it. The Irishman is proud when he can say, "I can stand it pretty good. Yeah, I can stand it," because when he had pain he *had* to take it, as part of the total experience:

[What do you do for it?] Well, what can you do? Have to take it.

Just have to take it, that's all.

I don't mind taking it. I can take it if I had to.

"Taking" and "standing" pain require special techniques that depend on the individual and on the intensity of the sensation.

193

The informants relate two such techniques in taking pain: relaxing and fighting. Relaxing is sitting quietly and moving only when it gets bad. Relaxing in pain seems to be a passive process during which the patient is subjected to pain and concentrates on absorbing it without action, sound, or complaint. The most important aspects of relaxing are quiet and not being disturbed by people.

Fighting pain, which is a technique used more frequently, calls for a mobilization of all moral and physical resources when there is a danger of defeat. The patient who is trying to fight pain describes this process very vividly:

> You just hang on—grit your teeth and hang on, that's all. Try to fight it—bear under it. Just grit your teeth and hang on.

It is not a passive attitude. On the contrary, it implies a struggle involving the participation of the entire body:

> I stiffen up. Everything is tense—yeah. In fact, the first night in there I had such pain in the back I—I got false teeth—and bit down and split the plate.

In relaxing and in fighting, the patient tries to avoid anything that might suggest a defeat. An Irishman suffering from excruciating stomach pains due to an advanced carcinoma (the nurse insisted upon giving him an injection during the interview) described his experience of fighting pain as follows:

> Well, I stand quite a lot. Now I have to stand a lot. I got used to have to stand it all night. Well, you just suffer and suffer. So, now they give me a hypo and that's all there is to it. But I try to fight it. I try to keep away from pills, you know. I don't want no pills. Not if I can help it. But that's the only thing that gives me relief—that kills the pain.

Another patient expressed a feeling of guilt for not being able to fight his pain successfully:

194

They Suffer Alone

Oh, I can't help it. Gee—I feel like a sissy when I scream, but it's terrific. It just—it just comes. You can't fight it—can't fight it at all. Ordinarily, yes, I can. I can stand pain, but I've never had a pain like that before.

Avoidance of relief of pain is associated with the tendency to get used to pain. The patient feels that if he gets accustomed to relieving pain, he will lose the ability of taking it successfully; therefore he tries to get used to the experience:

My own doctor gave me some kind of capsule—said when the pain got pretty bad to take one or two of them. But I didn't like to take too much of that stuff, because I figured if I'm going to have pain maybe I'd better get used to it, rather than try to deaden it all the time.

The taking and fighting of pain are viewed by the patient as processes in which he stands alone and in which he alone is responsible for being able to succeed without external relief.

From the point of view of the Old American, such an attitude is, of course, considered irrational. We have heard them say that pain is unnecessary and that fighting pain is only a useless waste of energy if one can do something to relieve it. Occasionally an Irishman also may admit that his attitude might be wrong:

[Is it a kind of pride not to give in?] I guess maybe it was stupid—I don't know.

He might try to explain his irrational behavior:

[Would you be able to tell me why, do you think, you do repress your pain?] Oh, I suppose it may produce admiration in others. Which I think is—is—damned stupid now. But —uh—I suppose, in the long run, that's the only reason. You may feel that you are an inconvenience to others by complaining, when actually there is no need for it. That's about the only two things I can think of.

195

People in Pain

One patient attributed his taking of pain to a complex of shame, and another expressed a clearly other-oriented, American attitude:

> I try to fight it. I don't like to yell to annoy the nurse or doctors. There are more patients here than me. I figure there are more—much more ill than I am.

The majority of the informants, however, were unable to offer a reason for their behavior and were slightly annoyed by the question. They would say, "I don't know," or "When you are in pain, you have to take it."

Looking back to the statements about taking and fighting pain in silence and solitude, for long, agonizing hours, for days and nights, without help and relief, it becomes understandable why an Irishman prefers to speak about *suffering* and not about pain. The pain experience becomes an extremely complex process in terms of quality, intensity, duration, and emotional and physical anguish. The patient has to call upon all his resources to respond to pain in the expected way. He does not simply perceive or feel pain; he *suffers*. Thus the stoic behavior, which is in many respects similar to the Old American's, acquires a deeper and more dramatic character, for which the only adequate word is *suffering*—a word that implies time and anguish.

Why do they suffer? Why do they not respond to their agony in a rational, American way? As mentioned, a direct question addressed to the informant is of little help. The isolated, Americanized rationalizations lack the consistency and homogeneity expressed in interviews with Old American patients. The Irish convey a slightly apologetic tone, which does not seem to reflect an authentic, well-integrated pattern of values of the group as a whole. Thus the answer to the question of why they suffer seemed to be as complex as the suffering itself and had to be reconstructed from a number of elements scattered throughout the interviews.

A clue to the understanding of the answer to the question was offered by a patient a few days before his death. Speaking about his tendency to fight pain and to "push it down," he analyzed a certain change in his attitude:

> I felt that there was a certain amount of honor, I suppose, attached to it in refusing to admit that you had pain. And occasionally I would do that, and try to force it all down and go ahead. And I'm beginning to realize that it (admitting pain) is *one of the ways of expressing yourself*—so that actually you shouldn't push it down too much—you *should give it an expression.* Yes, but there is still the degree—in there—that I haven't broken completely.

This statement confirmed an earlier impression suggested by the interviews: that the Irishman has difficulties in communicating about pain, and the need for a free self-expression is strongly controlled. Moreover, it is not only with regard to pain that he cannot communicate; it is also true of all kinds of trouble. Not even the closest members of the family can be informed of a "guy's trouble":

> [Why don't you complain about it?] Well, I don't want to tell the other guy all my trouble. [Would you tell your wife?] No. She'll ask me what's the matter when I bend down I can't put my shoes on. I don't tell her, you know. I don't say, "It hurts." [Why wouldn't you say that to her?] No, no I wouldn't be ashamed of it—it's—how would you put it?—I don't know. I don't believe it's . . . [What?] I don't know.

Everybody has his own troubles and has to deal with them individually without communicating them, regardless of whether they entail pain, worry, illness, or hospitalization:

> [Do your sisters come to see you in the hospital?] They don't know I'm in the hospital. [Why?] I didn't tell them. [How come?] I didn't think it was necessary. People have enough troubles of their own, you know, without worrying about somebody else. I have my own.

The lack of communication in stress situations between

197

members of the same family is suggested not only by the fact that the patient would not tell his troubles to his wife or sister, but also by his ignorance as to how other members of his family would feel about his difficulties if they noticed them without being directly informed:

[Did you tell your wife about it?] No, but she knew. [Did you complain to her?] Oh, no, no. [Was she worried about it?] I don't know. She doesn't tell me.

[Does your sickness worry your wife?] Well, I imagine she does. [Does she tell you she worries?] No—we don't talk too much.

[Was she worried about it?] Well, I wouldn't say yes—I wouldn't say no. Because—uh—my wife is a person who doesn't show her feelings too much.

Thus the patterns of communication with regard to stress within the Irish family foster the feeling that one is alone with his trouble and that one is not expected to share it with anybody, just as nobody will share it with him, regardless of whether it is a parent, a wife, or a sibling. Where people do not talk about their difficulties, they also develop the feeling that there is no point in speaking about it because nobody will understand it anyway. Accordingly, when an Irishman was asked to describe his pain, he said:

When you got the pain, you know how it feels, and when you haven't got it, the pain, you can't explain it.

When the patient is pressed to explain his feeling of pain, he might become completely confused and does not find adequate words to describe it:

Pain is funny. It's funny. Sometimes I feel like—if a man is in pain—if he is in pain, he is out of his mind from pain. I couldn't explain that.

The inability to communicate about pain is reflected through the interviews. A great deal of probing is required to elicit information about pain from the Irish patient, who tries to avoid answering the question as to the quality or intensity of his pain with such noncommittal understatements as: "I have quite a bit of pain," "It was pretty bad," or "After working six hours with this pain, I'm a little tired." In extreme cases the patient denies pain completely. Thus one patient who was referred for an interview as having severe pain requiring codeine treatment denied his pain throughout the interview, although he admitted that he had been getting treatment for his pain "because the doctor says so." The following excerpt from an interview demonstrates the difficulties the patient encountered in trying to describe his experience:

[Do you have pain?] No. Never have inclination to it. [No pain at all?] No pain at all. [Doesn't your condition cause pain?] Only the arthritis does. [Severe pain?] Well, I can't walk. [Can't walk?] No. I'm only on my feet now two days. Knocks me right out. [So, your legs hurt you?] Oh. And the pain when I touch them in different spots. Bottom of my feet and this time it was my knee. It ain't always in the joints, though. It's always traveling around. Wrists and elbow. It's around—around the joints. [Is it a sharp pain?] Well, I wouldn't know what to say, sharp or not. It's just pain. [How often do you have these pains?] Oh, I wouldn't be able to say, [Do you know when they started?] Five years ago. [When you come to the hospital, did you come because of the urine difficulties?] Well—I—wouldn't be able to tell you.

These and similar responses, which are quite usual in the interviews with the Irish patients, are especially striking when compared with the precision and clarity of the Old American reporting on pain.

The inability to communicate about pain, which makes the patient suffer alone and in silence, sometimes creates a feeling of an individual uniqueness in responding to the pain experience. Although the Old American patients emphasize the averageness of their experience and derive a great deal of security from the feeling

199

that they are not different from other people in similar conditions, the Irish patients emphasize that they are a type who feel and react in their own, individual way to the situation:

> I am the type. Other fellows up there would probably say, "Oh, I have a headache and want an aspirin." I don't bother. It's got to get me down before I really give up.

When people do not talk about their pain, they have little opportunity to find out the extent of other people's suffering. The hospital provides, for some patients, the first chance to learn about it—if not verbally, at least through observation:

> I learned a lot in this hospital. I never knew anything like that was going on. You see all this suffering—it's terrible. I never knew it went on like that. Never knew of people like that. I am much better off. I am alive. Gosh, it's terrible.

Like the Old American, the Irish patient also preferred to describe the intensity of his pain indirectly, by implication. However, here as in many other areas the difference between the two groups is quite apparent. The Old American patient, who feels that pain is unnecessary and that something should be done about relieving it, implies the severity of his sensation by telling *what he had to do* to relieve the pain. The Irishman who would not do anything to relieve it, who handled it by relaxing or fighting, implies the severity of the pain by describing the *physical effects* of the experience. (Not one Irish patient ever mentioned spontaneously doing something about his pain while telling how bad it was.)

> It was so painful that I didn't get much sleep. I can tell you that.

> I was getting disgusted (with the pain)—no eating and no sleep.

> [Is it a severe pain?] Yeah. [Very severe?] Yeah. [How severe would you say?] Well, I can't walk. I have to lean. [Do they

do anything to relieve the pain?] Well, I get them needles to
kill the pain. [How often do you get a needle?] Every six hours.

This emphasis on the physical effects of pain not only reflects the fact that the Irish patient would not do anything to relieve it, but also offers an important clue for the understanding of
the basic anxieties associated with pain. These anxieties seemed to
be linked to the image of masculinity and manhood. Physical fitness, able-bodiedness, and ability to work are seen as the main assets
of a man. It is not health in itself that is emphasized as desirable,
but the physical implications of health, that is, physical strength
and activity. Ability to work is the measure of physical and moral
fitness, which are also associated with health and youth; inability
to work is associated with deterioration and old age.

In describing anxieties and worries associated with the condition that caused the hospitalization, the Irish patient stresses fears
about his physical appearance or performance in direct relationship to his ability to work. Conversely, in relating their premor-
bid condition, the patients emphasize mobility, activity, and work.
Again and again the Irishman would say that he "just likes to
work" and mention how unhappy he was because of the hospital
immobility and idleness:

I must—I got to get to work. I want out. I want out. I want
to get back to work. I'm not cut out for this kind of life. I
have been active all my life, and when I come to a letdown
like this, I just don't like it, that's all.

I'd like to get out again, and get back to work and get going.
I like it—I always like it.

In commenting about their temperament, the patients speak
about their love for action and mobility:

I don't like a sitting job. I like to be on the go. I like fights,
sports, baseball television programs. I got all enthused—
I'm right in the game. [Do you always have to do something

201

—always be active?] Oh, yes, I'd go crazy otherwise. I can't stay alone. At home, on a day off, I go back and forth, from one room to another, put on the coffeepot, have a cup of coffee, run down, get the newspaper, get another cup of coffee, go down, get the next edition of the newspaper. [For how long can you sit and read?] Until I get impatient—maybe an hour. Then I have to do something.

I have had a desk job, but I don't like it. I had a tax job—bonds and stocks—and I felt I was too confined. I have been that way in here. I—laying in bed, I get up, out of bed, I'll have to go one place and the other—keep moving.

The importance of work is singled out in connection with another stressful condition that seems to cause a conflict in the Irish group, that is, in connection with drinking. The patients seem to take it for granted that every man drinks a great deal; however, as long as drinking does not interfere with work, it is not disapproved. Only when alcohol interferes with working does it become a sign of a physical and moral deterioration; only then is it stigmatized. Thus a number of statements suggest that the influence of drinking on working capacities is seen as the only significant criterion to evaluate the effects of alcohol:

I drink, yes, but I never lost a day's work in my life through drinking.

Yes, sir, I still like a good drink. But I never miss a day's work for anything. My father drank. He did come home and smell like he'd fallen in a brewery someplace, but he never was home from work from drinking. I mean he wasn't—he didn't lay around the house and drink.

My father drank, but, well, he always manages to get up and everything—go to work.

Declining age is associated with loss of masculine strength and with inability to work. "Everything happens after you are fifty." After one reaches a certain age, it is the beginning of the

202

end, and one has nothing to expect but loss of vigor, of masculinity, and of health:

> Just when I'm sick I start thinking. I don't like it. I'm nervous now, I imagine. I know I'm getting old.

The Irishman fears the physical *symptoms* of old age, the loss of the most valued attributes of manhood—strength and work:

> I saw the doctor. And then he gives me some thoughts. He told me point blank that I'm through. "You're through. You can't do that no more. Swinging about kegs and that stuff." He said, "Now at your age anything can happen." He said, "You are no chicken and of course like the young fellows." He said, "From now on you'll have to take it easy. There will be no more of this laborious work." And I lost thirteen pounds since I went up there. What would—would become of me? To be truthful, I said, "Where the devil will I go?" I'm getting older every year.

As in their attitude toward alcohol, the Irish feel that, as long as they can work, there is no reason to worry about pain. However, when pain interferes with work, the anxieties began to increase:

> I have quite a bit of pain that's annoying me to no end. It interferes with my work to an extent where it really aggravates me.

> I can't live like that. I can't live with it anymore. I can't work—can't sleep.

> Well, until last Monday I wasn't worried. Then I became worried because I couldn't hardly work anymore.

> I just worried about the pain. I knew there was something wrong with my back. My work and all—when the back goes, everything goes.

The anxiety reached its peak when the physical effects of

pain with which the patient was concerned from the onset of the sensation became a reality:

> [Monday, when you had this bad pain, were you worried about it?] Yeah, I thought my legs were gone on me. I thought they were gone on me. It did worry me. Yeah, I have to admit that. After I got up to work, I started worrying about it. [Were you worried before?] It confused me so much. When I did get down in the morning to put my socks on, I couldn't do it. It would start to worry me. I figured there was something wrong.

Because the visible indication of youthfulness and strength is a healthy, fit body, the Irish patient in pain is greatly concerned with the effects of pain on his physical appearance. When a deformity caused by pain becomes a reality, he tries to hide it as much as possible, trying "not to look awkward." However, at the onset of pain, many patients express their concern for its crippling effects on their physique:

> Yeah, I'm very much worried. I don't want to become a cripple. Can't help but think about it.

> Well, the general thing I had in my mind would be—well, if it gets worse now, and pretty soon, maybe in three or four years—what's it going to be? What am I going to be—a cripple?

Along the same lines, a patient whose illness was associated with very severe headaches and backaches made a distinction between his pains, referring to the crippling effects of the backache:

> [Was the pain severe?] It was very severe. I couldn't straighten up. [Was it as bad as the headache?] That's altogether different. [What do you mean different?] 'Cause I couldn't straighten up.

Thus the Irish patient seems to be concerned less with the

discomfort associated with the sensation of pain than with its crippling and immobilizing effects. One could take pain; one could fight it; but when it downs the individual and makes him stop working, then one begins to worry. Hence the logical implication is to fight these evil effects of pain by continuing to work, do things, and be active. Activity is seen as the best remedy against pain:

I used to be alright when I was working, but I couldn't work.

Continuing to work while in pain is seen as a means to deny its effects. For a while the patient may have the impression that the pain goes away and he is alright again, until it is beyond his ability to take it:

I can stand it. I don't mind working with it because I figure it's going to go away. I don't let it bother me too much.

See, it never dawned on me. Maybe it would come on me over a period of years, and I go to work and it would work out.

When there's intense pain, I can't sit or stand. I've got to keep in action. Like when I was home I used to—well— I'd go to work and stand at the lathe all day. See, I wake up in the morning, I'm stiff, and it aches terrible. I can't hardly walk. But as soon as I start to get into motion. But I force myself to go to work. I mean, I could give in to it and —just go to bed. But I was working at that time. So I kept it until I couldn't take it anymore. The pain was terrific.

It is not difficult to imagine how much the effort to continue to work and deny pain added to the suffering and anguish of the patient.

In all these worries and anxieties about pain, there is a striking absence of a concern for the pathology that provoked the pain. The concept of pain as a warning signal, which dominates the attitude of Old Americans, is never mentioned. Pain is not seen as a symptom of a disease; it is seen as an independent experience that is only loosely associated with illness.

The Irish patient freely admits his anxieties about the physical effects of pain and its influence on his working capacities, but he flatly denies all concern about the illness or the disease in association with pain:

[Now, while you had this pain, were you worried about it?] "Oh, yes, I guess I was. I knew there is something wrong with my back. My work is all—when my back goes, everything goes. You are out of business. [Were you worried about having any disease, of being sick?] No, no, I don't think so. [You weren't thinking of any disease?] Just worried about the pain. I—no, I don't think it was any disease or anything like that. [You were just thinking about the pain, which makes you uncomfortable and doesn't let you work?] Yes.

[When you had this backache, did you think of having some kind of disease?] No, no. [You say you were worried?] Yes, when it came to walking, why I started worrying. But I never thought of a disease or anything. [You say you never thought of any illness?] No, I didn't.

A patient who had lost one lung because of cancer and developed metastatic pain a few months later remarked:

Well, guess I was worried, you know. But I wasn't worried too much. [Did you worry about being sick or anything like that?] Gee, I wasn't.

Often it is only in the hospital, where everything is focused on illness and treatment, that the patient develops some ideas about being ill. Again, when he thought about the disease, he became concerned about its crippling effects:

That's the only thing I was worrying, because I don't like to be crippled up or something like that. [Were you concerned with any kind of disease?] Well—uh—in the last couple of weeks I was—uh—kind of worried about it in case it would be polio or something.

[Do you worry now about your health?] Yes, I'm very much

worried. I don't want to be a cripple. I don't know, I listen to these armchair guys in the ward, you know. I mean, they get me all upset, too, you know. I say I don't mind but I think about it, anyway. Can't help but think about it. [Did you think about it before you came to the hospital?] No, but now I know how serious it was because I have seen other people having it.

The lack of concern for a pathological condition that provokes pain is reflected also in the inability to think about the disease independently. The patients tended to define their condition by what "people say":

[How do you know you have arthritis?] I don't know. That's what people say: "You got arthritis." You hear that all the time. [Who told you this?] People you talk to when you are out. "You got arthritis."

Thus the image of an Irishman as it emerges from the interviews seems to be that of a patient who suffers a great deal from his pain, who is greatly worried about the effects of his experience on his body and working abilities, and who is unable to relate his condition to a pathological cause. However, although he is unable to see his pain as associated with a disease, he is nevertheless greatly concerned about the cause of the pain. Unable to accept the explanation of pain as due to illness or old age, the patient tends to find an explanation that is plausible enough to allay his anxieties and is realistic in terms of his cultural experience. When pain becomes a reality that interferes with his movements and work, and when a simple denial is no longer possible, the Irishman begins to search for causes that he could accept without too much anguish. One way of explaining pain is to minimize its significance by attributing it to futile causes that are common and not considered dangerous. In this respect the process is similar to the one used by the Old American patients:

When it started, it felt like a cramp—muscle cramp in my

shoulder. Well, I just shook it off. I figured it was a cramp and it would go away.

It might be a cold, now, because I—I still have a little effect here right now. Right now, like the muscle of the neck or whatever it is. I figure that might be sleeping wrong or something. I don't know. I don't bother with every little pain and ache until I have to. It's got to get me down before I really give up. Not trying to cure myself, but thinking of the idea that it will pass away.

I started getting pain in the back. Didn't think nothing of it, you know. I thought it was a plain backache.

Figured at first it was a cold in the back, and I would go to work and it would work out.

However, minimizing pain or attributing it to insignificant or accepted causes, such as a cold, a cramp, or the weather, is not always satisfactory, especially when pain is persistent and intense. When the pain does not go away, despite efforts not to give in or to ignore it, one has to find a better, more convincing explanation. In such a case the Irishman tends to look for another familiar cause of pain that could be equally accepted and therefore would not provoke anxiety feelings. Such a cause would be an external injury received in the process of some physical activity, be it work, sport, or a fight.

We have seen how highly the Irishman values youth, physical abilities, and performance. Often these attitudes are associated with violent sports and occasional fights with resulting injuries to the body. These injuries are part of the total experience and therefore are expected and accepted. The pain inflicted by these injuries has to be taken without complaint. Moreover, taking pain becomes part of the training to become a man according to the masculine standards of the Irishman.

Whenever an Irishman speaks about his past pain experiences, he takes the opportunity to emphasize how often he suffered pain from injuries in sports and how well he took it. This attitude toward pain inflicted in sports, as well as the attitude toward pain in general, which he has developed since childhood, is exemplified in the following statement:

> [Do you remember any pain experience from your childhood?] Well, quite a few. Mostly cuts, bruises, and sprains. I was confined to bed one summer as far as I can remember since I was ten. I felt that there was a certain amount of honor, I suppose, attached to it—in refusing to admit that you had pain. And occasionally I would do just that, and try to force it all down and go ahead. I dislocated my left knee playing football. The first time it was kind of a shock—quite painful. But after two or three times it became routine. [You kind of expected to get hurt?] Yes. [Would you be afraid of getting hurt?] I'd be conscious of it. Not afraid of the actual pain I would get. [You would say—you would enjoy the game and that you wouldn't mind the pain?] That's pretty close to it.

A similar attitude of expectancy and acceptance of pain inflicted in a fight was expressed by an Irishman who "liked a good fight" and who never carried a knife "because some time I might harm people when I get real mad":

> No, I don't mind pain. No—being beat up—I never felt it. It still hurt, you know, I mean like, you get hit in the nose, your nose is pushed up this way—that's a bad shock. But it goes away. This I would not mind.

An analogous lack of anxiety is shown with reference to pain associated with accident injuries. These injuries seem to fall in the category of expected and accepted pain. Therefore, the patient could speak about it with a casual equanimity:

> Well, I was hit by an automobile in 1947. I was pretty well banged up at that time. I had ten stitches in the head; I had a broken nose, two stitches in the mouth, and I had a broken pelvis and a dislocated knee. But it never bothered me. Never. [Were you in pain?] Not too much, not too much. I just laid

209

flat on the board for thirty days. Nothing to speak of. When
I'd go to move my legs—you'd get a little pain once in a
while. Nothing to amount to anything.

The general feeling seems to be that pain caused by an external injury will somehow go away without leaving any permanent
effect to impair the physical and working abilities of the individual.
Accordingly, in searching for the cause of pain, the patient, to relieve his anxieties, will try to reduce it to an external injury. Hence
many patients suffering from cancer, spinal disease, or any other
acute illness try to figure out how they were hurt:

I tried to trace it back as what—if I had done anything to
offset it. The only thing I could see that the night previous
I had slipped off a swivel chair, but I didn't hit anything to
my knowledge. In fact, I don't believe I hurt myself there.
But I tried—I tried to think back as to—as to what I done
that would bring on some sort of condition of this sort. [Now
you say you tried to trace back your pain. You say you weren't
worried about it. Didn't you think about any disease?] No, no
I didn't have. I just wondered how could anybody get sick
without doing anything to themselves? Well, when it hurt
me—I feel I must have banged it or hit it or something like
that, and from that angle I—I try to look back to see if I did
it or in any way hurt it that would cause trouble in my back.

I didn't worry about it. I just took it as a matter of course.
Thought maybe I just got hurt, you know, or something.
I pulled a muscle—and just work it out, that's all.

The fact that the Irish patient accepts without anxiety pain
produced by an injury is substantiated by statements that external
flesh wounds are less dangerous. They feel a great deal of apprehension about internal pain, especially pain that originates in the
stomach:

I got hit on the foot once. But it didn't—it was only a flesh
wound—nothing serious. The spike, it just went through the
boot and into the flesh, and stopped. So they cleaned it out

210

and it was all set. Never had a bit of trouble. [Can you take pain?] Well, not in the stomach like I have to.

[Is the pain in the stomach worse than the pain in the back?] No, I wouldn't say, no. Absolutely not. But, you see, I am always afraid of the stomach.

Looking for expected and accepted causes of pain seems to be a general tendency among the Irish patients as well as among the Old American. However, they differ as to what kind of pain is accepted and expected. Whereas the Old American would find a germ or virus to fit his general preoccupation with health and his confidence in medical treatment, the Irishman would try to find an external injury that would correspond to his cultural interest in fights and sports.[1]

Only very infrequently does an Irishman try to find a mechanical explanation for his pain—an explanation that is quite common among the Old American. One patient devised an elaborate mechanical theory to relieve his anxieties:

Well, I was figuring out—well, I used to figure out for myself that when they took out the lung, that must have left a vacancy in there, and it was growing in—to fill the empty space. No, sir, I didn't worry. Used to have a—the gas used to form around there, and I—I didn't worry about it either because I used to figure, well, there was a vacancy there.

The patient is not always able to trace his pain to a cold or injury. Despite a great deal of thinking and remembering, his efforts in this direction may not always be successful. At times he might become confused to such an extent that he would doubt the reality of his pain:

[1] Although the Old Americans are equally interested in sports and athletic performance, the pain involved in it is expected but not accepted. It has been viewed as a necessary evil, and, accordingly, the participants in these sports are highly protected against pain by helmets and other devices. The participants in the rather violent Irish national game of hurling play totally unprotected.

That's what I was trying to figure out—what—what the—
what's the condition that's causing all this trouble, and I have
tried to cover every phase along that line. I was just wondering if the pain, which seems to be—uh—uh—there, but, I
thought maybe it was—the pain wasn't there. Maybe it was
a figment of imagination or it was something that I am
building up out of something smaller.

Under no circumstances, however, would the patient think
in terms of illness. When he reached a complete impasse in trying
to understand what was causing his pain by looking back to his own
experience, he would give up searching:

[Do you have any idea where your headache comes from?]
No, I have no idea. [Did you try to figure out something?]
No, Doc. [Have you ever tried to understand it?] Course. I
mean, if I—if I—did anything to injure myself, it would
have bothered me from the time I injured myself. That's the
way I look at it.

In recapitulating the various emotional reactions the Irish
patient experiences under pain, we discover a rather involved cycle.
At the onset of pain the patient does not worry. He tries to fight
the sensation silently and alone, ignoring it when possible, working
with it, and hoping that it will go away. He begins by minimizing it
and attributing it to insignificant causes. With the persistence of
pain, the anxieties begin to increase, especially when the pain begins to interfere with everyday activities. The anxieties are primarily
related to the incapacitating effects. To relieve these anxieties, the
patient tends to attribute the pain to injury, which eliminates its
threatening aspect. If he succeeds, he does not worry any more; if
he does not succeed, the worries increase until they reach the cul-
minating point, because nothing is worse than ignorance and lack
of knowledge as to the cause of the condition. When this point is
reached, it is time to consult the doctor.

Consultation with the physician seems to be the ultimate
conclusion of a long period of ignoring, fighting, suppressing, mini-

mizing, and interpreting the pain experience. In other words, it is the defeat or complete capitulation before pain. This defeat signifies a state that no Irishman would accept without a long and excruciating struggle—a state associated with doctors, medications, and hospitals and a state that he carefully avoids mentioning: the state of illness.

When this state is reached and when the patient is really downed by the pain, he stops fighting, he stops interpreting, he stops trying to understand it, and he surrenders himself to the doctor, leaving to him the task of determining the cause of pain, the treatment for it, and the responsibility for finding the cure for the illness. The constancy of pain may be one of the indications of illness, although the patient does not say so directly. He just goes to the doctor.

> I didn't worry enough to get the doctor. [And you say it was going on like that for about a year?] Off and on. This here shooting pains in the leg. [And you didn't go to a doctor?] For about a year, no. [Why?] Because it went away, see. [And when it became constant?] Constant I went to a doctor.

Determining the cause of pain becomes the responsibility of the man whose specialty is illness:

> I don't know why I have it. I know it exists. I know that where a pain exists, that there could be causes for the pain, but I don't know what it is. I leave it up to the doctor. That's what doctors are for. I mean, I'm not a doctor. I'm just a person.

> No, I got no idea what it would be. So, then I don't bother. I just have confidence in the doctors that they will find out.

As we shall see, it takes a long time before the patient decides to call upon a doctor's help—sometimes more than a year and, in extreme cases, several years. But, once decided, the patient becomes almost panicky in his appeal for the physician:

I keep going, trying till I suppose I'm on my back. Then I'll
say, "Get the doctor quick!"

The anxieties associated with the pain and the long period
of suffering alone must bring the patient into a state of extreme
tension. By calling the doctor, he finally achieves his peace of mind:

Well, that's what I do. I try to fight it like, yes. And if I
can't do it, why, you have to go to a doctor. Sure, because
I want to have peace of mind. When you have such pain, you
don't have peace of mind.

The peace of mind is achieved by entrusting oneself to the
doctor and becoming completely dependent on him:

[Now do you worry about this?] Uh—no, I don't think I do.
Because Dr. B— said the only thing he could do while I
was here would be to make me comfortable and relieve the
pain. I put my fate in his hands.

[And now, are you still worried about it?] No, I mean it's up
—it's up—it doesn't make any difference to me. It's all up
to them, what they decide to do. [Who are they?] The doctors.

The doctor becomes the absolute "boss," and the patient
blindly follows every order. He does not ask questions; he does not
even try to understand what he is given or why. He becomes the
most cooperative patient. There is no more question of refusing
help. The patient has arrived at the state when he knows that his
own fight is over and that he cannot depend anymore on his own
resources to handle his condition. However, as the help given by
the doctor is outside his experience and knowledge, he does not
attempt to find out what are the means the doctor uses to fight the
patient's battle:

I take anything. He is the boss while I am here. I follow him.
I figure he knows his business, and the quicker he can make
it better, the better I like it.

214

They Suffer Alone

I have taken so much stuff. I don't know whether it is a drug
or what. I never got them on the outside—any of that stuff.
I get them needles to kill the pain. [What kind of needles?
Do you know?] No, I don't know. He knows.

I get an injection, but I don't know what's for.

They give me some kind of shots in the arm. I didn't ask
what it was. Figured they were doctors, they knew what they
were doing.

When medical help is accepted, the Irishman lowers his
defenses. He does not try any longer to hide his pain:

When the doctor asks me how I feel, I tell him, of course,
because that's the only way he is going to find out how to cure
me.

This patient was the same one who had stated that he did not
want to tell the other guy all his troubles.

The Irishman may be much less articulate and much less
precise than the Old American in describing the symptoms, the
location, or the intensity of his pain (it is not easy to change the
lifelong patterns of communication), but he feels that he has to
cooperate with the man to whom he has entrusted his fate.

We have seen the Old American trying to avoid the threatening consultation with the doctor by using medical substitutes
such as pharmacists or chiropractors in order not to find out how
sick they were. The Irishman, being much less conscious of his
health and concerned only with the effects of pain, does not go
through all these stages. The only patient who had been to a chiro-
practor was not enthusiastic about his work, because he was too
gentle and did not hit hard enough.

Neither does the selection of a doctor present much of a
problem. All doctors are the same, and there is no point in shopping
around too much. When the time comes to call a doctor, the patient
goes to anyone who is close to his home or who was mentioned by
a friend:

[Did anybody recommend you to this doctor?] No, I just went. He was near the house one night and I had to get the doctor. And he was near the house. So I went there and he happened to be a neurologist.

Oh, through some people—they gave me a name—like they tell you about medicine. I took that medicine because a man told me it was good. I don't know whether it is good or not, and I try it.

The last quotation points in the direction of another difference between the Irish and Old American patients in their attitudes toward doctors. Whereas the Old American approached the doctor with a basic feeling of confidence in his expert knowledge, the Irish patient has a rather skeptical attitude, and his confidence is qualified: Doctors are human and therefore subject to mistakes:

Well, it is like anything else—sometimes they can do you good and sometimes they cannot. You got to consider that. They are imperfect as you are. Sometimes I can drive a truck for a year and never get an accident, and sometimes. . . .

The Old American does not shop around because doctors are experts; the Irishman does not shop around because physicians have their limitations.

It is rather difficult to reconcile the need for relying completely on the doctor with a skeptical attitude. The patient solves this conflict by developing a kind of a pragmatic approach. If one calls the doctor, one has to cooperate with him; cooperation is impossible without confidence. Therefore it is better to approach the doctor with a rational, if not an emotional, confidence. Besides, doctors do have knowledge:

[Do you have any confidence in doctors?] Well, certainly. Cause I figure they know what they're doing. I mean, he—uh —in other words, in order to—the way I look at it, in order to feel a lot better about things you got to have confidence in your doctor. If you don't have confidence, then, naturally,

216

you are not going to be able to cooperate with them. And it—
you are going to feel afraid, I think. I mean, I'm assuming
that the person would feel afraid if he didn't have confidence
in the person he was dealing with. And if Dr. D— or any
other doctor decided what they wanted to do, I'd be perfectly
willing to go along with them, because I feel that, after all,
they have the knowledge and—in the subject they are dealing
with.

The same patient added that, despite this reasoning, he
would still prefer to avoid doctors' help if it were possible:

What I want to tell you is what I've been trying to do to help
—help myself—not to depend on the doctors. [Do you think
that a man shouldn't depend on them?] If—if—if he can help
himself, I think he's much better off.

These ambivalent and often conflicting feelings about doctors, even in a situation when one has to depend on them, are also
expressed with regard to drugs, injections, or operations. It is true
that, once he is in the hospital, the patient takes it upon himself to
follow doctors' orders without question or resistance; nevertheless,
he does not give up his own opinion about medications, especially
about those he considers harmful, such as analgesics. They do not
voice these opinions on the ward, while speaking to the doctor, but
in the informal interview setting they were quite open about it:

They wanted to give me sleeping pills, but I don't like sleeping pills. I don't know why. I just don't care for them.

I don't like dope. You become an addict to it. I rather take
pain if I can—if I can—possibly stand the pain.

They give me sleeping pills and things of that sort but I
don't know. I just don't care to take them things. I just never
did like any sort of narcotics. It does away with pain, but, like
I say, habit forming.

The dislike of narcotics was especially strong when they

were administered in injection form. The Irish patients seemed to manifest singular apprehension and real fear:

> [Are you scared of a needle?] I always was. [What did you do in the Army when you had these different injections?] Looked the other way. [Did it happen to cause you to faint?] Yes, a couple of times I did. I don't mind the blood test—it never did annoy me when they took blood. But—uh—when I had a tooth pulled, I had to have gas—because of the—they couldn't put a needle in my gum. [Why?] I'd just pass out.

> When I get these injections, I'm a little nervous. I'm kind of tense. I just can't seem to relax. I seem to be tight. If I know I'm to get an injection, I—I—kind of tighten up. I just couldn't seem to relax enough.

It is difficult to explain the reason for this fear of needles. A psychoanalytic interpretation would relate the fear of injections to homosexual factors. Although in the case of Irishmen there seems to be some suggestion of homosexual tendencies in connection with their attitude toward sex and women, the interview material is insufficient in this respect and does not warrant this type of generalization. It is possible, however, that the fear of injections might be related to the apprehension expressed with regard to internal pain. The deep penetration of the needle may be seen as endangering the inside of the body. Thus the same patient who said that fear of an injection made him faint also said, "Injections are alright as long as it's in the arm." This attitude is understandable, because the arm does not contain any vital organs.

Very strong feelings are expressed against operations. Surgery is always seen as "cutting up"—as an attack on vital organs with a strong possibility of a negative outcome. In accordance with the Irish concern for the wholeness and strength of the body, the patient is primarily worried about the crippling effects of the surgery. He seldom expresses fears about the technical aspects of the operation, which consist of inflicting wounds and pain. As in the case of spontaneous pain, his anxieties are all related to the effects of the operation, which might result in a physical deformity or inability to work:

> If I need it (the operation), I would take it. [Are you scared of it?] Naturally. I'm not scared of the operation itself. Just —I'm scared of what's going to happen. I hope I'm alright, you know.

> [How do you feel about the operation? Are you scared?] I'd say yes. [Are you scared of the knife?] No, I don't think so. I'd be afraid of the outcome more than of the cutting, see.

A patient in his last days of cancer associated his physical state not with illness but with his operation.

> No, no, before I had that operation, I think I was quite a man. As far as health was concerned, I didn't think there was anything wrong with me—outside of that little back pain and stuff like that. That didn't bother me. But I was quite strong a man before the operation.

Conversely, a successful operation is judged in terms of one's being able to work after it. A colostomy patient told of his experience:

> Well, the doctor told me. He was going to cut me and told me what was going to happen. He said, "It will be the same as before. The only thing I'm going to change is the direction of the stool." Dr. K— was his name. He was a nice man. Smart man. And so, when I was turned out, I went to work. See, I had to stand on these tracks—we stand driving those electric trucks. And, of course, I know to take the shock in the knees so it doesn't hurt me. And I worked every day. I was never sick with it.

The ambivalence the Irish patient shows toward medical help may be partly understood as an interplay of two opposite trends: the traditional trend, stemming from the old country and entailing a disbelief in doctors, and the modern trend, developed by the children of immigrants in the process of acculturation, entailing a confidence in the skill of the medical expert. There is evidence in the comments of the Irish patients that, traditionally, there was little confidence in the physician in Ireland. This opinion persists among the elderly immigrants in this country:

[Did you go to the doctor in Ireland?] No, sir. You know, some Irishmen are no—there is no heart for the doctors. They call them donkeys. Some like myself—I never believed in doctors.

[Is it true that Irish people don't go to doctors?] My father and mother never used to. [Never?] No. This doctor treated them when they were there and everything, and they both died.

[When somebody was sick in the family, would your mother call the doctor?] No, no, no, no. I recall—probably heard people speak of it, years back. I am talking about thirty-five years ago. When a child was sick, the mother very seldom called the doctor. They used to take care of themselves. You can ask any old-timer here in New York especially.

On the other hand, occasionally we hear from a younger, American-born Irishman whose comments reflect the American opinion of doctors:

[Do you have confidence in doctors?] Yes, I do. Yes, I do. Because I figure that a man who has an education, like that— he learned it and should know what he is doing. I have confidence in him. [You mean a person who studied knows what he is doing?] That's right. That's right.

However, pure attitudes were rarely expressed in interviews. The impression obtained from the informant was that we are in the presence of an overlay of different attitudes that are being reconciled in a given situation; hence we see ambivalence and hesitation.

The behavior of the Irish patient in pain, which consists of pushing it down, or fighting it; the process of attributing it to non-threatening causes and waiting until it goes away; and an apparent traditional distrust of the medical profession and medical treatment cause long delays before a patient will consult the doctor. A number of physicians commented on the difficulties they have in treating patients of Irish origin because of their tendency to delay the visit to a doctor. Sometimes the disease has progressed to such an extent that it is too late for a successful treatment. Moreover, it is incorrect from the point of view of the American doctor to neglect the presence of a danger signal. The same feeling was expressed by the Old American patients who commented on the Irish negligence about consulting the physician.

The patients themselves speak about their tendency to delay the visit to the doctor, and some of them, after being hospitalized, feel guilty about having done so. Sometimes the delays were of several years' duration, during which the patient might have had agonizing pains:

> Oh, I had it about—well—about two weeks before I had the doctor.

> I didn't worry enough to see the doctor. For about a year I didn't see the doctor.

> Well, it was bothering me for—on and off—for the last maybe six or seven years.

A strong guilt was expressed by a patient who felt he had come too late to see the doctor, who diagnosed his condition as cancer of the stomach:

> It is wrong to push it down. Because I think it's dangerous. In fact, it was in my case—my original case. I pushed this abdominal pain aside for two, three, four months before I saw the doctor.

The reluctance to see the doctor does not stop after the first visit. It happens quite frequently that the patient who, in a moment

of weakness, went for a consultation decided to postpone his next
visit because the emergency had been taken care of:

> I went up to the doctor when I had to come down. Then I
> didn't go for a year. [You mean you had the pain for a few
> months, and what did you do about it?] Nothing.

> I went first to Dr. P—. He gave me pills to kill the pain, and
> I didn't go to him anymore. I still had the pain, but I just
> didn't bother. I neglected, I know that.

Even in most anxiety-provoking situations, the Irish patient
stubbornly refuses to think in terms of pathology. Pain is not perceived as a symptom, but as a sensation with possible harmful implications for the physique. The anxiety is closely associated with
the sensation. Once the sensation of pain is relieved, the anxiety is
also gone. This attitude allows for long periods of suffering before
he will consult a physician as well as between visits. Because not
many conditions are associated with a constant pain, and in most
cases the pain appears in intermittent waves, the patient may develop a cyclical pattern: onset of pain, anxiety, disappearance of
pain, relief of anxiety, and so on until the patient is hospitalized.

We have described the anxieties that the Irish patient in
pain experiences with regard to the physical effects. However, those
are not the only worries the patient experiences in his condition. At
the onset of pain there is the original feeling of annoyance with the
discomfort and the desire to get rid of it. The presence of pain in
itself is sufficient to affect the person's mood and temperament. The
patient expects a definite emotional effect of pain, which, in some
cases, would influence his personality. Everyone is expected to worry
when he is in pain and to want to be relieved of the discomfort,
especially when he goes to a doctor for help:

> Well—not that I'm worried about it—it's the fact that the
> pain is such a severe state that I think the pain will cause
> me to become quite emotionally unstable. In other words, the
> aggravation itself would bring that out. I worry about the

pain because the thing is, I don't want the pain. I mean, you have a toothache and you go to a dentist and have that tooth fixed. Otherwise, it would be real annoying, wouldn't it? Well, that is the way I feel about it. If anything can be done organically to take the pain away, and I think I would be able to do my work and take care of the family. If the pains are persistent, the fact that I can't bend down and do any work, I can't work on the grounds, I can't work and lift—the temperament has increased a great deal. I mean things annoy me. I'd just get mad or something or I swear.

[Now, did you worry about the pain?] Well, yeah, I imagine. Anybody will—people worry about it. Anything will give people pain—they'll worry about it. I want this damned thing fixed. That's my biggest objective. I wanted to get over with it. I mean, the pain was there bothering me and everything. I wanted to get rid of it in any ways I could.

It is interesting to note that, when the patient comes to the doctor with his anxieties about the sensation, the expectancy is that the doctor will relieve the condition in a very short time. Since it does not always happen, the patient is rather disappointed.

After I had the doctor—after I started taking the medicine he gave me, it still—it still did not do me any good. Woke up the next day. I was still the same way, so I knew—I didn't know—I didn't know what it was. I knew it was not just what he was treating me for because I would have been over it by that time. [Were you thinking of a disease?] No, not that way. [Now, let's say, if the headaches would have been relieved, then you wouldn't worry anymore?] I wouldn't have to worry about it, that's right. [Once the pain was relieved, you wouldn't worry?] No.

Any worry associated with the onset of pain is closely related to the concern with working capacities and, as expressed by a married patient, the fear of not being able to support the family. This feeling is found not only among the Irish. In every ethnic group men are concerned with the problem of how the illness will affect

223

their earning capacities and abilities to support the family. However, the Irish are not concerned with the effect of *illness* but with the effects of *pain* and with the loss of time in the hospital:

> [What are you worried about?] Supporting everybody at home. That's what gets me. I might lose time on the job, and I don't get paid when I get—you know. I don't like to stay out of work. I don't like it at all.

> I worry a little. I have a family to support, so I didn't know what to expect.

A description of the Irish behavior in pain would be incomplete without a few words about their attitudes toward hospitalization. We have seen how their suffering and pain anxieties bring them to the doctor. The visit to the doctor often results in hospitalization. In the hospital setting they finally realize how ill they are and begin to see their pain as a symptom. However, the idle life in the hospital and its regulations are trying experiences for the Irishman who values mobility and work, and these feelings were expressed quite frankly:

> I have a great dislike of hospital, period. I just don't like them, that's all. [Why?] Confining, for one thing—confining.

One of the ways to get out of this unpleasant situation is cooperation with the personnel:

> [Now, when you are in the hospital, what are you thinking about?] How soon I can get out of here. Get back to work. I just want to get out. I want to do everything the doctors tell me to get better as quick as I can. I try not to be any trouble to them (the staff). I help them as much as I can.

It is the impression of the researcher that the Irish patients' dislike for the confining routine of the hospital, along with their tendency to forget the original anxieties as soon as the pain is relieved, might result in a higher proportion of patients leaving the hospital against medical advice, as compared to any other group of patients.

The behavior manifested by the Irish patient in the hospital and reported on in the interviews and the attitudes expressed in answers to questions dealing with the pain experience reflect a pattern that has been learned in the culture, following the example of parents, siblings, or friends. The fact that the described pattern is common to so many patients of Irish origin, and only to them, is a strong enough argument in favor of a conclusion that it is an expression of specific cultural norms proper to the group and not to individual idiosyncrasies. However, the patients themselves, in commenting on the behavior of parents or siblings in similar situations, support our impression that their behavior and attitude are shaped within the family. The parents, whom as a child he looked up to as models of correct and approved behavior, have acted in pain in the same fashion in which he would tend to act as an adult. Their response to their pain experiences has been as inexpressive as his own. They have taught him not to complain and not to give in. Even the attitude toward medical care is based on the parents' skepticism about doctors:

> My mother is being treated right now at the Memorial. They are not sure what it is. [Did she have pain?] She did, yes. [How does she take her pain?] Very well. [What do you mean when you say "very well"?] She bore it, and she's the Spartan type. No, she never complained of her pain. [Was your father ever sick?] No, not that I can think of. He even—he is probably more hesitant about complaining about any pain than any person I've ever seen. He had a job for twenty-five years—as far as I know lost about four days in that time. He pushes himself.

Notice the use of work as a criterion.

> My mother always came when I had an operation. She did come with my sister. Mother never liked these operations. She—well—said, "You can take any pain." She said, "Four thousands of years they never had to cut a person. Why they

225

got to cut a person now?" I mean, she's kind of against medicine, you know. She thinks—well—a human being will fix theirselves up. As a matter of fact, she signed herself out of the hospital. She's never had a cast on her leg. She just had it up in a—one of them slings. She had them taken down and send her home.

The feeling about culturally correct behavior is shown in the contempt the patient has for a family member who does not live up to the expected pattern:

[Did anybody in your family have pain?] My mother, she's had sinus condition, but you'd never know it. She doesn't show it. [And what about the brothers?] Well, my youngest brother is a baby. I guess he's emotional. He gets hurt a little bit, and "Oh, oh, oh."

In attempting to understand the dynamics of responses to pain, which are only partly modified by acculturation among the younger, second or third generations, the opinion has been advanced that the taking of pain and the complex of suffering are closely associated with Irish Catholicism. According to this opinion, pain is seen as a Divine punishment. Therefore the individual accepts it voluntarily in the hope that, by long suffering, he will atone for his committed sins. Although this hypothesis is quite tempting, there is little evidence in the interviews to support it. However, there is enough evidence of feelings of guilt among the Irish patients, but they are not associated with Divine punishment. Moreover, although the nature of the interview did not allow for the exploration of patients' religious feelings, some comments were expressed that seemed to contradict the punishment theory:

Well, probably it's been—I deserve it because I didn't treat myself right. [You didn't treat yourself right?] Probably I got careless or something. Let myself get a cold in my shoulder, or something like that. That wouldn't be a punishment that would be—that would be a punishment for—through my own fault or something. [Through your fault?]

226

Not taking care of myself. [I see. But would you see some
other faults in you which would deserve some kind of punishment?] I don't think it would be any punishment be visited
on me like that. It would have to be damned serious, I tell
you that.

Without passing a final judgment on this hypothesis—that
the attitude of Irish patients toward pain is rooted in their religious
feelings—we feel that the research material offers sufficient data in
other areas that might help to understand the dynamics of Irish
responses to pain.

The most striking aspect of Irish response to pain is lack
of communication during the pain experience. The patient does not
share his feelings with anyone; neither does he expect any help in
his struggle with pain. The anxieties associated with the physical
effects of pain and the fear of losing his working capacities suggest
that the patient is extremely concerned with what will become of
him in the case of a permanent crippling. As long as he works, he
has a place in his family, he has status, and he is respected. The
strength of his body is his only tool in forming his social position.
The loss of physical strength is equated with loss of work and consequently with loss of status. There is nobody he can rely on in
case the physical strength is impaired by pain. He knows that, even
among the closest members of his family, he will not find a suppor-
tive action or word.

It is in the Irish family structure and its emotional atmosphere that these attitudes are shaped, and it is there that one can
hope to find the clues for understanding the patterns of lonely suffering.

A number of authors have commented on the tendency
among Irish males to remain bachelors or to marry late. The information offered by the Irish patients about their marital life not only
confirms these observations, but also points toward another phenomenon that seems to be characteristic of Irish intrafamily, interpersonal relationships: the centrifugal tendency of the Irish family.
It seems that even after marriage the ties between husband and

wife remain rather weak, as are the ties between parents and children and among siblings. At one point or another in the family life, its members tend to drift away from one another. The separation between members of the family might be temporary or permanent. Although divorces are infrequent because of religious interdiction, separations between husband and wife occur rather often. The ease and calm—indeed, almost indifference—with which these separations are accepted by husband and wife, regardless of who initiates the move, suggest that neither views the event as a traumatic experience. The same lack of emotion is expressed by children when they speak about leaving home or about their parents' separation. Members of the family leave one another; they stay away permanently, or they may come back after years of absence; all this occurs without causing too much upset, worry, or distress:

> To be quite truthful with you, Doc, I was away from her for a while. Just came back here about six or seven months ago. [For how long were you away?] For twelve years. [Why did you go away?] Well, she asked me. We had an argument, and I left, that's all.

> I walked out on her in '41—my first wife. Walked out in the middle of February. I didn't take care of nothing. Used to stay away.

> [Are you married?] I am, but separated. Well, that was mutual—not legal. About twenty-three years ago. There was no argument or nothing. I just got up and said, "Well, we can't agree. We might just as well as split up. You go your way and I'll go mine."

> I have been married twice. I married my first wife, and we were married eight years and I went to the Army. And I came back and got a divorce. She committed adultery. So the children were put into foster homes—three children. I had two more from the second wife. They are also in foster homes. I was married to the second wife four years. Once I came home and she was gone.

The same patient spoke about his parents:

They Suffer Alone

[Was your father supporting the family?] Oh, yeah, till he got old. Wanderlust, I guess you might call it. He wanted to go—take off. He was till he got that wanderlust, I guess. And then he just wanted to—he just took off. Said he was going to Jersey and that's that.

The same looseness of ties is characteristic of relationships between children and parents and among siblings:

No, I guess I haven't written to my family in about fifteen years. I lost track of them.

I say, we didn't see too much of Dad. He was home only maybe two or three months a year. Three months would be a long time, if he was home that much a year. I left home when I was fifteen—just walked out. Another kid and I. [Did you feel sorry about leaving home?] I didn't. I stayed away for four years, I guess—something like that. [Was your family looking for you?] Oh, no. I was going to see a little bit and then come back.

A respondent whose parents lived in the same city said, when asked how often does he see them:

No, not very often. Oh, well, once in three, four, or six months.

He said the following about his brothers:

I don't see them very often. The last time I saw them, oh, a couple of years ago. [Where do they live?] Uh—in Connecticut some place. I don't know where.

Again, speaking about his family relationships, he said:

I was home till about twenty-three, I guess. I was with my mother—my father wasn't home. I guess family differences. [Is your father home now?] That I couldn't say. I don't know the situation at home at all. [When did you see your father last?] Well, before the war. Sometime before the war. [You mean the Korean War?] No, World War II.

In an atmosphere of such loose relationships it is not surprising that the individual does not expect help from family members in case of a difficult situation—whatever the nature of the difficulty may be. There is no point in telling anybody about his difficulties, because nobody will help him anyway:

[When you feel that you are in need—you need help—would you go to your family for help?] No, I wouldn't go to my family. I mean, normally I wouldn't go. I mean, I don't expect them to—like I say, they go their way, I go mine.

[If you had any difficulties—any problems—would you count on your brothers?] I wouldn't count on my brothers. [On whom would you count?] Well, my friends, I guess. My in-laws.

This atmosphere of "everyone for himself" is conducive to the development of feelings of independence and self-reliance. However, it also fosters loneliness and isolation, with possible anxieties that, in case of a disaster, when one is incapable of helping himself, he is doomed to perish.

This feeling of isolation is reinforced by the specific relationship between son and father. As a child, the individual looks for a paternal advice and guidance. The Irish informant reports that he very soon becomes aware that he can expect neither advice nor guidance from his father. Many take it for granted; some resent it; but they all agree that the rapports between them and their fathers were never close:

We never—never been close. I don't think he's ever offered me a word of advice. I had a feeling that I had it coming—this advice—parental advice. And I never receive it. I suppose I resented it in that way.

The relationship between father and son seems to foster fear and hostility:

They Suffer Alone

Well, I wouldn't—I wouldn't dare have spoken in front of him until I was about eighteen. I'd be afraid.

Well, I'll tell you I—there was no love lost between him and me, if that's what you mean. No, I didn't have much use for him personally. We all feel about the same. He was too much for himself, I guess. He never bothered with us much.

An Irishman brought up in a traditional immigrant family summarized the differences between father-child relationships in his family and the expected American pattern:

Oh, he was very strict—very strict, yes. It was—Mama really praised us. Papa didn't bother at all. He read his paper, smoked his pipe, go and lay down in bed. [So he wouldn't be much with the children?] No, he didn't. You know, didn't see that stuff. Probably was foreign like other mothers and fathers, so he didn't. I think when they came from Europe—they don't run around with the kids as much as the ones here.

In their relationships toward the father, children naturally had respect for him as a father, but they did not "shower their love on him a hell of a lot." In their description of him, it is a lost cause to look for expressions of love or devotion. The only positive statements about the father refer to his working patterns or physical strength:

[What kind of a person was your father?] He was a strong, hard-working man. He was sixty-three years old, and I never seen him sick. He'd keep going—Sunday—and on Monday morning he was up.

[What kind of a person was your father?] Person? [Yes] Oh, hard worker—worked all his life.

Frequently the criterion for a favorable evaluation of a father's personality is his "correct" attitude toward alcohol:

My father is a stationery engineer. He—he is a very steady

drinker. He has been for as long as I remember, but he is not, as far as I know, an alcoholic.

He wasn't a drinking man. He had a drink—his glass of beer —home—never went in saloons. He went in, maybe for a pint of beer, and he come right out.

[You say your father was quite a man—a respectful man, huh?] Yeah, well, he drank, but—uh—I never seen my father what you call staggering drunk.

The extent to which a father's (and in general a man's) status depends only on his working and earning capacities is most strikingly revealed in the following statement:

Nobody would really pay any attention to the old man. He had to go along with things the way they were. He had no choice. See, he hasn't worked now in—oh, about twenty years. [So he hasn't much to say?] No, because, I mean— we're the ones that are supporting him.

The father image viewed by the child with fear and hostility suffers still more when he witnesses the unstable relationships between father and mother. The mother, toward whom the Irish patient expressed a great deal of love and for whose description he finds the most tender words—good-natured, very, very good, quiet and easygoing, the best of mothers—is often presented as the victim of an alcoholic father:

My father was a habitual drunkard. As far as I remember, he always spent his money. We hardly had anything to eat —made it rough for the Old Lady.

[How did he behave?] Mostly all the time rotten—bad. He used to beat Mother, but she knocked him stiff a couple of times. And there was a time—one of her brothers hit him.

It goes without saying that not all interviews present such a dark picture of intrafamily relationships. However, the type of descriptions quoted are by far the great majority. Significantly, one patient remarked:

> I don't remember Mom having an argument with Dad, never. Quite a good family—good ties and everything.

But we later found out:

> Father was on the road. He was on the road eight, ten months out of the year—South America, Cuba. So he wasn't home very much. Mom had to do all the bringing up—doing everything. We didn't see much of Dad.

Despite this negative image, the son nevertheless tends to identify with the father. Within the family the father is still the model for the child, regardless of the resentment he may feel because of his own rapport with him or because of the father's rapport with the mother. The man still possesses certain qualities that impress the child. The father drinks, but his drinking does not interfere with his work; the father is strong and healthy; he impresses the child with his independence and self-reliance; in one word, he is the *man*. The identification with father is clearly expressed by the adult patient:

> [Could you describe your father?] I would say on my order. About the same temperament as I am—strict. [Did he used to drink?] About the same as I do. We are similar. Look alike —all the way down. I take after him, I guess.

> [I guess you said he was selfish and irresponsible?] I guess headstrong. I'm headstrong, too, but I don't go to any extreme. I'm probably tenacious, but when I get something in my mind and think I'm right on it, I stay by it, that's all. But my father—he was right—that's all there was to it.

The awareness of negative features in the father's image and the child's observation of the poor father-mother relationship on the one hand, and the identification with father expressed in his own adult behavior toward his own wife and family on the other hand, may provoke feelings of guilt with regard to the family and, by extension, to people in general:

> [What would provoke your fears?] I suppose my own acts of omission toward other people. My obligations that I fail to perform for other people who have done things for me—parents and friends and relatives.

The expressions of guilt were especially frequent among patients who described their separation from wife and family. Invariably they tended to take the blame on themselves, pointing out the same faults they found in their fathers:

> When I found out about my wife's adultery, I was hurt—wondering what I did. In a way, yes, it was my fault. It was hard times then. She didn't have the right stuff. Bringing up a bunch of kids. I left her alone a lot—like during the night. Yeah, you get disgusted.

> [Do you feel sad about your children leaving you?] Yes, but there's no other way of seeing it. I must be wrong. Well, I can see it now. [Why were you wrong?] Just maybe I was taking a few drinks. And the oldest daughter died after she got through high school. Of course, I see it now. I was wrong. Because always they were very good children—they are the swellest, swellest children.

> I think it was about drinking. I used to drink pretty heavy. [Do you think it was your fault which caused the separation?] Absolutely, the experience was my fault. [Don't you blame your wife for it also?] No, naturally not. [You seem to think it was your fault in everything?] Absolutely. It was bothering me. I was just that stubborn type that I wouldn't ask to come back, that's all. She's strict Irish, too, and she wouldn't ask. That's Irish love—not to give in. There's nothing thicker than two Irishmen.

The feelings of guilt that the Irishman experiences with regard to his behavior and his relationship to his wife or children may be also manifested in his emotionality, which is identified as "soft-heartedness." This soft-heartedness is something that patient is not ashamed to confess; it brings tears to his eyes in the face of other people's trouble. It also permits him, through his identification with the sufferings of other people, to express indirectly feelings he might have about his own sufferings that he is unable to express directly:

> I'm a worrying type. [What do you worry about?] Oh, different things—everybody in trouble. I'm soft. If somebody is in trouble, maybe I should try to get him out of it. When I see a sad picture, I start crying. All through the family— they got the bladder near their eyes. Soft, you know.

These feelings of guilt, which are always present in the patient, are evoked when he is in a situation of stress, bedridden, or suffering from great pain and anxieties. The hospital provides the most adequate setting for the remorse and atonement, and the interview offers the opportunity to express it. Thus the patient can say with gratitude and with tears in his eyes:

> I thank you, Doc, for the talk. I feel the hospital has made a better man of me.

Among the four groups of patients of different ethnic backgrounds, the Irish patients presented the saddest, most depressing picture. Lacking the optimistic outlook of the Old American, the family support of the Jew, and the present orientation of the Italian, the Irish patient is worried, touchy, and frightened of the present and future effects of his painful condition. Not prepared to think in terms of illness and health care, he discovers in the hospital a world of human suffering of which he is a part. But he is unable to share his emotions, anxieties, and fears with a close person who would understand them and offer some comfort and support. Thus pain becomes an endless road of a lonely suffering, at the end of which is only death.

CHAPTER 6

Differences and Similarities

So far, data collected in our study were presented as patterns of behavioral and attitudinal responses to pain manifested and related verbally by patients of Old American, Jewish, Irish, and Italian origin. Our emphasis was on the regularities in responsive patterns for each ethnic group, and our aim was to document the original thesis stated in the introduction that responses to pain are learned and patterned as part of the individual's cultural heritage. The patient's information about his pain experience was seen as a description of a cultural experience, characteristic of each ethnic group; and, although no attempt was made to draw specific comparisons between the four groups, our approach was obviously crosscultural.

Differences and Similarities

Now, in this last chapter of the book, we summarize the results of the study in the form of a comparative exploration of what we have learned about all four groups in terms of their differential responses to specific elements of the pain experience, such as the intensity of pain, its quality and duration, and its interpretation and significance in illness and medical treatment. These comparisons, based primarily on the qualitative material collected in the process of our study, are, wherever possible, tested by statistical computations of the incidence with which identifiable responses to pain occur within each ethnic group.[1] These responses are grouped in a list of fifty items derived from our unstructured interviews, questionnaires, and direct observation of patients' behavior and their manner in describing their perceptions and feelings (see Appendix A).

First we shall examine how our four groups of patients compare in terms of such general background variables as age, education, occupation, socioeconomic status (SES), ethnicity (extent of cultural identification with the ethnic group), and, finally, the disease which is the cause of pain. Such an examination is helpful, as frequently questions are raised as to the effects which age, education, or disease of the patient might have upon his behavior in pain. The statistical analysis of the above variables for all patients suggests a number of differences in the composition of each of the ethnic groups.

All four groups were comparable in terms of age. However, there were significantly more Old Americans than Irish in the older age group (forty-six and over). The Jewish group included more higher-educated patients on the college level than any of the remaining three groups, which were comparable in terms of their education. The Jewish group included significantly more patients of

[1] All statistical computations were executed by Jack Cohen, Chief Research Psychologist at the Veterans Administration Hospital, Bronx, New York. Because of the complexity of the computations and their limited appeal to anyone but a small research minority, tables reflecting these computations have been omitted from the text. They are available on request from the author (Mount Zion Hospital and Medical Center, San Francisco, California 94115).

middle-class background than the Irish, Old American, and Italian groups, which did not seem to differ with regard to their socioeconomic background.[2] Significantly more Old Americans and Irish were in occupations requiring physical effort than Jewish and Italian patients, who tended to be blue-collar workers or in small businesses. Among the three immigrant groups, the Irish expressed less ethnic self-identification than the Jewish and Italian patients, who were much more emphatic about their cultural background in such areas as customs, values, food habits, and interpersonal relationships. This response may have occurred because there were relatively more Irish of a third American-born generation than Jews and Italians, who were mostly of first and second generations (see Table 3, Appendix B).

With regard to the pain-causing pathology, we differentiated among three major groups of patients—those suffering from herniated discs and backache; those whose pain was caused by migraine and other illness; and those whose pain was associated with a physical disability such as paraplegia, quadriplegia, or amputation. The statistical analysis of ethnic groups in relation to the disease revealed that there were relatively more patients suffering from a physical disability among the Old Americans than in any other group.

Thus, if there is a correlation between the patients' background variables and their responses to pain, there were sufficient differences among the four groups to warrant a detailed examination of such correlations, which will be attempted in the process of our crosscultural comparisons.

Altogether we explored statistically five sets of comparisons: (1) Jewish and Italian patients versus Irish and Old American; (2) Irish versus Old American; (3) Italian versus Old American; (4) Jewish versus Old American; and (5) Italian versus Jew-

[2] As the general patient population of a Veterans Administration hospital is of lower and lower-middle-class background, no attempt was made to assess rigorously the patients' SES. It was evaluated by the study group on the basis of the patients' education, occupation, and life style as revealed in the interviews.

ish. The reasons for such a selection of comparative sets derived from the analysis of the data as presented in the previous chapters. It seemed important to test the overall impression that most of the major differences in responding to pain were noticeable between the Irish and Old Americans on the one hand and the Italian and Jewish patients on the other. Another impression to be tested was that in spite of behavioral differences between the Old American and Jewish patients, in some areas their responses appeared to be similar. Finally, although the Jewish and Italian patients manifested many behavioral similarities, our observations suggested that their attitudes and orientations toward the experience were quite different; a similar reason underlay the sets of comparisons between the Irish and Old American patients.

The clinical impressions of medical practitioners that patients of Jewish and Italian origin tend to be more emotional while experiencing and expressing pain than the Anglo-Saxon—that is, the Old American—was confirmed by the observations derived from our study. Emotional description of pain experience occurred more frequently in the interviews with the Jewish and Italian patients than with the Old American and Irish. This emotionality was also expressed in the tendency of the Italian and Jewish patients to emphasize their perception of pain (to play up pain), whereas the Old Americans and Irish tended to deemphasize their perception (to play down pain). The former two groups also tended to describe the intensity of their pain as "very severe," whereas the latter two groups were more apt to differentiate between slight, severe, and very severe pain. The characteristic unemotional reporting on pain of the Old American which was commented upon earlier was confirmed by statistical computations, as also the vague and confused information offered by the Irish.

The literature on pain tends to differentiate between various qualities to the pain sensation, such as aching, pricking, or burning pain (see Hardy et al., 1952). Patients, on the other hand, tend to speak of sharp or dull pain, of a stabbing or aching sensation, or of a burning pain. Some of them try to convey their feelings by using illustrations from common experiences, such as sharp as if cut by a knife, burning like fire, or stabbing as with a needle. Our observations revealed that the Old Americans and the Irish were inclined more than the others to describe their pain as stabbing and sharp as well as to use comparative illustrations to describe their pain sensation. It is interesting to note that in identifying pain as burning, patients did not differ along ethnic lines.

Medical practitioners rely heavily on patients' descriptions of their pain in assessing its symptomatic significance. Such characteristics of pain as its intensity, location, and duration are important elements in the history of a disease and its etiology. It seems, however, that less precision can be expected from the Irish and the Italian patients than from the Old American and Jewish, who, despite their striking differences in behavior, tend to be more precise in describing their pain experiences. Among all the four groups, the Irish patients seem to be most confused in their description of perceptions and feelings about pain.

The perception of the time element in pain when defining its duration is probably affected by cultural time orientation. This impression seems to be supported by the fact that the Italian patients who were described earlier as present-oriented related more frequently than others that their pain was constant and present all the time, whereas patients from other ethnic groups described their pain as intermittent ("it comes and goes"), which clinically is probably more accurate.

The lack of inhibitions in exhibiting suffering manifested in the expressive behavior observed among the Italian and Jewish patients, and the nonexpressive behavior characteristic of the Irish and Old Americans was also documented statistically. Thus, while the Irish and American patients said that they prefer to hide their pain, the Jewish and Italian patients admitted freely that they show their pain and they do it by crying, by complaining about pain, by being more demanding, and by stating unequivocally that they cannot tolerate pain. Groaning and moaning in pain seemed to be common to all four groups; but our statistical computations suggest that they tended to be more frequent among the Italian and the

Jewish patients, whereas withdrawal from other people when in pain was most characteristic of the Old American patients.

The expressive behavior of Jewish and Italian patients, which suggested their desire to communicate their suffering to others, was manifested also in various motor responses to pain such as body movements, gestures, twisting, and jumping. Such communication through body movements has also been observed by other investigators of the function of gestures and body movements in the communication patterns in the Italian and Jewish cultures (see Efron and Foley, 1937).

Our observations suggested that anxiety and worry, which are usually associated with pain, are most frequently expressed by Jewish patients. This observation was confirmed statistically. They stated more frequently than others that pain was the primary reason for seeking admission to the hospital, and they, more than others, were concerned with the symptomatic significance of pain. On the other hand, the Old Americans, who, as stated earlier in the book, were also preoccupied with pain, denied seeking hospitalization because of pain and were more prone to rationalize their pain by attributing it to external reasons rather than to illness or other causes.

The preoccupation with the immediate sensation of pain which we found as characteristic of the Italian patients was illustrated by their tendency to speak primarily of their pain only, rather than in association with other symptoms of illness, and to be less preoccupied with the future effects of their pain—in contrast to the future-oriented Jews.

The Jewish patients' concern about the symptomatic significance of pain was further indicated by their tendency to seek immediate consultation with a physician. One may wonder whether the Jewish patients' higher level of education and economic comfort might not have influenced their readiness to seek immediate medical help. The statistical tests indicate, however, that neither education nor socioeconomic status seemed to influence significantly the patients' proneness to consult a physician as soon as they perceived pain.

241

The statistical tests suggest that both the Jewish and Italian patients tended to interpret their pain independently of the physician. The qualitative analysis of the interviews suggests that this tendency is more pronounced in the Jewish than in the Italian patients, even though this impression is not confirmed statistically. The preoccupation with the symptomatic meaning of pain so characteristic of the Jewish patients is also expressed in their insistence upon understanding the meaning of their pain, an insistence significantly more pronounced than even that of the rational and pragmatic Old Americans, who tended to leave it all to the physician and who in general seemed to have more confidence than the Jewish patients in the skill of the doctors.

The attitudes toward the doctor and his role in pain and illness seem to be strongly affected by the cultural background of the patient. Both the Old American and the Irish patients tended to express confidence in the doctor's skill—more so than the Jewish and Italian patients; the Jewish patients were significantly more likely to check up on doctors and shop around, thus suggesting a lesser degree of confidence in the physician.

The attitudes of the Irish and Old American patients toward pain, illness, and medical intervention, and their confidence in doctors and their skill were reflected in their total behavior in the hospital. They accepted their sick role as defined by the hospital and assumed what the hospital staff identified as a cooperative attitude. This attitude was reflected in their tendency to express satisfaction with the care they received as patients and their readiness to cooperate with the staff. Among all the patients the Irish seemed to stand out as most cooperative, which could be a manifestation of the resigned and defeated attitude that they seemed to adopt after a prolonged period of pain and illness. In contrast, the Jewish and Italian patients seemed to be more dissatisfied, more critical of the hospital care, and more demanding.

Looking back on the fifty items which were tested for statistical significance we find that the Irish and American patients differed from the Jewish and Italians on more than half of them, on the ones dealing with such aspects as pain description, attitude toward pain, and its meaning in illness, as well as with attitudes toward doctors, medical intervention, and hospital care.

The comparison between the Old American and the Irish patients supports much that was stated in the respective chapters. Thus, although both groups of patients tended to de-emphasize their pain by playing it down, the Irish more so than the Old Americans tended to describe its intensity as "very severe." This tendency may result from a lack of precision in relating their pain experience in general and a need to dramatize their pain, which allows them to legitimize their defeat in fighting pain.

The tendency to delay consultation with a physician, which was expressed by the Irish as well as by the Old American patients, seems to be more frequently stated by the Old Americans than by the Irish. This tendency would be consistent with the apprehensions which this former group seems to experience with regard to the doctors' ability to determine a major threat to their health.

Throughout the study the Irish patients expressed worry and pessimism about the outcome of their illness and its effect upon their body and masculinity. This worry was substantiated by their frequently expressed concern about the symptomatic significance of the pain they suffered in the course of their illness; this concern exceeded that of the more rational patients of Old American stock. It is interesting that in this respect the Irish attitude was more like that of the Jewish patients, from whom they differed in such a striking manner in relation to other behavioral and attitudinal aspects of their pain experience.

The tendency of the Old American patients to attribute pain and illness to external causes was evident when compared to the Irish, who tended to be rather helpless in explaining their illness and were prone to seek the cause within themselves. This helplessness as well as a resigned attitude toward the impact of illness seemed to be reflected in their passive and uncomplaining role as patients, which differentiated them from the cooperative but frequently griping patients of Old American background.

Finally, the Old American patients differed from the Irish in their detached and precise manner of describing their pain experience. The latter had greater difficulties in talking and describing their suffering.

Much like the Old American and Irish patients, the patients of Jewish and Italian origin frequently manifested similar behavior but differed in many attitudes toward pain. They were highly emotional and expressive in responding to their pain experience and tended to be less tolerant of pain than the other two groups, but here the similarities end. The Jewish patients expressed much more frequent concern about the significance of pain as a symptom of illness and therefore did not wait as long as the Italians to seek admission to the hospital or to consult a physician. In their desire to identify the pathological cause of pain, the Jewish patients cooperated with the physician in being more precise in describing their experience. The Italians tended to be more confused under the immediate impact of painful sensations and dramatized them more than the Jewish patients, who in comparison with them behaved almost like the "reporting" Old Americans.

In keeping with their cultural time orientation, the Italians unlike the Jews were mostly concerned with the immediacy of their sensation rather than with its future effects or its symptomatic significance. When in pain, they seemed to feel it all the time—as an ever-present, constant, intolerable sensation—and even more frequently than the Jewish patients claimed that they could not tolerate pain.

The Jewish patients, on the other hand, in their anxiety about the cause and future implications of pain, rather than about the sensation itself, were concerned with finding the most skillful physician to make the correct diagnosis and prescribe the best treatment. In many of these attitudinal responses to pain, the Jewish patients manifested many similarities with the Old Americans, with whom they shared many health values as well as their orientation toward the future, even though they behaved differently under the actual impact of pain.

The Jewish patients tended to describe their pain mostly as very severe, they openly manifested their pain, they tended to express their pain by groaning and moaning more so than the Old Americans and by tears and more frequent demands for help. In comparison with the Jewish patient, the Old American appeared to be unemotional and to be trying to play down his suffering. When in pain he tended to withdraw from other people in order not to show his pain, which he seemed to be able to tolerate better than the Jew.

From the point of view of the medical and paramedical staff in the hospital, the Old American patient lives up to the image of a desirable patient. He is not as demanding as the Jewish patient, and he has confidence in doctors and their skill, which is important in his role as an active member of the health team.

Many of the observations described and interpreted throughout the book were supported by statistical computation wherever it was possible to translate qualitative data into figures. The following summary of results will facilitate an overview of the responses which were analyzed and tested statistically:

COMPARATIVE LISTING OF STATISTICALLY SIGNIFICANT
DIFFERENCES IN RESPONSE TO PAIN

[OA = Old American, IR = Irish, IT = Italian, J = Jewish]

PAIN DESCRIPTION
Intensity of pain

reported by degrees (slight, severe, very severe)	OA	IR		
	(OA more than IR)			
reported usually as very severe			J	IT
Quality of pain				
stabbing, sharp	OA	IR		
aching, dull			J	IT
burning		no difference		
comparative description of pain	OA	IR		
Duration of pain				
constant pain				IT
intermittent pain	OA	IR	J	

245

Description of sensation

	OA	IR	J	IT
tendency to be precise in description of sensation	OA		J	
tendency to be vague and confused		IR		IT
emotional description			J	IT
unemotional description	OA	IR		
playing up pain			J	IT
reporting on pain	OA		(J)	
playing down pain		IR		
detailed spontaneous description	OA			
detailed answers to probing questions	OA			

BEHAVIOR IN PAIN

Expressive versus unexpressive behavior

	OA	IR	J	IT
showing pain			J	IT
hiding pain	OA	IR		
moaning and groaning			J	IT
crying			J	IT
motor responses and reactions	OA		J	
tendency to withdraw when in pain	OA	IR		
no tendency to withdraw when in pain			J	IT
demanding behavior when in pain			J	IT
complaining behavior when in pain			J	IT
uncomplaining behavior when in pain	OA	IR		

Tolerance of pain

	OA	IR	J	IT
'I can take pain'	OA	IR		
'I cannot take pain'			J	IT

Attitudinal response to being in pain

	OA	IR	J	IT
worry			J	IT
bothered by immediate effects of pain				IT
bothered by future effects of pain			J	
bothered by symptomatic significance of pain			J	IT
concern with understanding pain			J	IT

Reasons for being in pain

symptomatic interpretation of pain	no significant difference			
external causes	OA			

PAIN AND MEDICAL
INTERVENTION

pain and symptoms as reason for hospitalization			J	IT
Attitude toward doctor as related to pain				
immediate consultation			J	IT
delayed consultation	OA	IR		
	(OA more than IR)			
seeing doctor because of pain	OA	IR		
seeing doctor because of pain and symptoms			J	IT
Attitude toward doctors				
confidence in skill of doctor	OA	IR		
checking on doctors			J	
Attitude toward surgery				
confidence in surgery	OA	IR		
Attitude toward hospital care				
demanding attitude			J	IT
undemanding attitude	OA	IR		
satisfaction with hospital care	OA	IR		
dissatisfaction with hospital care			J	IT
cooperative attitude	OA	IR		
critical attitude			J	IT

In commenting on patient's responses to pain, most of the clinical practitioners tended to attribute differences in behavior and attitude to four major independent background variables: illness being the cause of pain, the patients' age, his education, and his socioeconomic status. In analyzing the results of our study we attempted to test these impressions with regard to the items that were our guidelines for testing the differences and similarities among the four groups. The logical procedure would have been to test the possible influence of these independent variables for each ethnic group independently. However, the rather small number of informants within each group disallowed this procedure, and we had to

247

test the interrelation between the independent variables and the patients' responses for all four groups.

There seems to be little doubt that the nature of a patient's illness seemed to affect to a great extent his behavior and attitudes with regard to his pain experience. In thirteen out of fifty items (26 per cent) on our list, the pathology influenced the patients' responses on a high level of statistical significance ($p < .05$ and less). Thus, it influenced their reasons for hospitalization. It made them more prone to show their pain by moaning and groaning, by crying, and by motor manifestation. Depending on the nature of their illness, they were more or less worried and more or less concerned about the immediate as well as symptomatic significance of their pain and the future effects of their illness. The pathology also affected the manner of presentation of their sensation (precise or confused) and their being more or less emotional and dramatic.

No other independent variable appeared to be as important in affecting the patients' responses as the nature of their illness. The age variable was important only in three areas: (1) whether the patients would show or hide their pain, the oldest patients being more prone to show pain than hide it; (2) how soon the patients would consult a doctor after experiencing pain, the middle age group tending to delay the least; and (3) the patients' feelings about their doctors, the oldest age group valuing the doctor's personality over his skills. The educational variable seemed to play a role only in two areas: it influenced the anxiety of the patient, the less-educated individuals seeming to worry more; also, the more educated seemed to have more confidence in surgery than the less educated. Finally, the socioeconomic status of the patient seemed to affect his response only in one area: the less privileged group tended to say that they visited the physician only because of pain.

As can be seen from this summary, the disease variable was clearly a major influence on patients' responses in those areas of their experience where differences were attributed to ethnic background. Hence, to assess the relative importance of the disease variable in comparison with the significance of ethnic background, we compared the responses of Irish and Old American patients with the responses of Italian and Jewish patients in those critical areas by keeping the disease variable constant. We selected all patients suffering from herniated discs and backache and compared their responses in relation to their ethnic background.

In response to six items, these two groups of patients suffering from pain associated with a similar pathology showed significant differences. The Italian and the Jewish patients tended to show their pain more than the Irish and Old American. Moaning and groaning, tears, and motor manifestations of pain were more frequently observed among the Jewish and Italian patients, who also tended to be more emotional and dramatic about their pain than the other two groups. Thus, we can conclude that, along with the major role which pathology might play in influencing a patient's response to his pain experience, the cultural background of the individual appears to be a most important, if not the determining, factor in shaping his behavior in pain and illness.

These same conclusions were reached independently by a number of social and medical scientists who investigated the role of ethnicity in affecting the patients' responses to pain and illness. During the years since we published the first results of our study (Zborowski, 1952), social scientists interested in health and human behavior (Croog, 1961; Mechanic, 1963; Suchman, 1964 and 1965) also found significant differences between ethnic as well as religious (Jewish, Catholic, and Protestant) groups in their responses to questions pertaining to health and illness.

An investigation of special relevance to our study was conducted by Sternbach and Tursky (1965), two scientists who explored the psychophysiological aspects of pain.

> . . . following Zborowski's (1952) findings, [they] interviewed and tested Yankee, Irish, Jewish, and Italian housewives, and corroborated the differences in pain attitudes. They found in addition that the Irish attitude involved deliberate suppression of suffering and concern for the implications of pain. Italian subjects had significantly lower pain tolerance to electric shocks and the Yankees demonstrated a more rapid

and complete adaptation of diphasic palmar skin potentials to repeated strong shock. In a latter report, Tursky and Sternbach (1967) presented additional physiological differences among the groups in noting mean heart rate, palmar skin resistance, and skin potential levels. *The differences among the groups in physiological activity seemed to parallel the culturally acquired attitudinal sets toward pain.* (Italics mine)

Pain symptomatic of illness

It is interesting to note that these findings were arrived at in a laboratory setting where subjects were responding to "experimental pain" without the complicating, anxiety-provoking elements experienced under the impact of the pathological (clinical) pain (Beecher, 1952).

Pain and illness are stress situations to which individuals respond as people, as humans equipped with intricate biophysical, biochemical, physiological, and psychological mechanisms which enable them to adapt to stress, whatever its origin (Dubos, 1965). However, stress is also a cultural experience in perception as well as in interpretation, and as such is responded to by behavior and attitudes learned within the culture in which the individual is brought up. To ask whether the man's biopsychophysical endowment or his cultural background is more important in allowing him to survive under stress is pointless and futile. The most we can hope to achieve is to assess the functions of different components in the biocultural process of man's struggle for survival.

Appendix A

❀❀❀❀❀❀❀❀❀❀❀❀❀❀❀❀❀❀❀❀❀❀❀❀❀

List of Items

❀❀❀❀❀❀❀❀❀❀❀❀❀❀❀❀❀❀❀❀❀❀❀❀❀

1. Patient in pain during the interview
   Patient not in pain during the interview
2. Pain only reason for hospitalization
   Pain primary reason for hospitalization
   Pain and other symptoms reasons for hospitalization
   Pain not the reason for hospitalization
3. Short experience of pain prior to admission
   Long experience of pain prior to admission
4. Pain associated with injury
   Pain symptomatic of illness
   Pain unexplained medically

5. Slight pain
   Severe pain
   Very severe pain
6. Stabbing pain
   Sharp pain
7. Aching pain
   Dull pain
8. Burning pain
9. Sharp pain
10. Comparative description of pain
11. Constant pain
    Intermittent pain
12. Pain with other symptoms
    Pain without other symptoms
13. Pain better at home
    No difference between pain at home and in hospital
    Pain better in hospital
14. Feeling of improvement
    Feeling of getting worse
    No change in condition since hospitalization
15. Hiding pain
    Showing pain
16. Resisting and fighting pain
    Passively taking pain
    Waiting until pain goes away
17. Expressing pain by moaning or groaning
18. Crying
19. Motor expressions of pain (such as jumping and twisting)
    Motor reactions to pain (such as clenching fists, teeth)
20. Demanding behavior in pain
21. Complaining about pain
    Does not complain about pain
22. Withdrawal when in pain
    Seeking people when in pain
23. Immediate consultation with doctor
    Postponing consultation with doctor
24. Seeing doctor only because of pain
    Seeing doctor because of pain and associated symptoms
    Seeing doctor only because of associated symptoms

Appendix A: List of Items

25. Can take pain
   Can take pain in general but not present pain
   Cannot take pain
26. Pain causes worry
   Denial of worrying about pain
27. Patient bothered by immediate effects of pain
28. Patient bothered by symptomatic meaning of pain
29. Patient bothered by future effects of pain
30. Optimistic orientation in general
   Optimistic orientation with reference to medical help
   Pessimistic orientation in general
   Pessimistic orientation with reference to medical help
   Skeptical orientation
31. Tendency to interpret pain
   No tendency to interpret pain
32. Concern with understanding the meaning of pain
   Concern with understanding the cause of pain
33. Symptomatic interpretation of pain
   Attributes pain to injury
34. Mechanistic interpretation of pain
35. Attributes pain to atmospheric conditions
   Attributes pain to intake of wrong substance
   Emotional interpretation of pain
   Religious interpretation of pain
   Scapegoating
36. Health conscious with protective patterns with regard to self
   Health conscious without protective patterns with regard to self
   Not health conscious with regard to self
37. Confidence in doctors
   Lack of confidence
38. Confidence in skill of doctor
   Confidence in personality of doctor
39. Checking on doctors
40. Reluctance to see doctors
41. Confidence in hospitals
   Reassuring effect of hospital
   Hospital apprehension
   Desire to get out of hospital as quickly as possible
   Depressing effect of hospital

42. Confidence in surgery
    Lack of confidence in surgery
43. Satisfaction with hospital care
    Cooperative attitude toward hospital
    Dissatisfaction with hospital care
    Critical attitude toward hospital and staff
44. Demanding attitude in hospital
    Undemanding attitude in hospital
45. Tendency to be precise in description of sensation
    Confused and vague description of sensation
46. Detailed answers to probing questions
    Vague answers to questions
47. Detailed spontaneous description of pain
    Confused spontaneous description of pain
48. Emotional description
    Unemotional description
49. Playing up pain
    Reporting on pain
    Playing down pain
50. Tendency to find a reason for pain
    Inability to find a reason for pain

$\mathbb{T}ables$

Table 1

DISTRIBUTION OF INTERVIEWS (242)

Interviews at the hospital

Irish, Italian, Jewish, and Old American patients (all male) 146
Other patients
    Men 24
    Women 6

        Total patients 176

Collateral interviews (relatives of patients and hospital staff).... 43

        Total hospital interviews 219

Appendix B: Tables

Table 2

THE ETHNIC GROUPS (146)

Ethnicity	Number	Percent-age
Irish	31	21
Italian	30	21
Jewish	45	31
Old American	40	27
Total	146	100

Place of birth, generation	Number	Percentage
(for Irish, Italians, Jews)		
Foreign-born	20	19
American-born		
1st generation	56	53
2nd generation	22	20
3rd generation	2	2
Undetermined	6	6
Total	106	100

Age	Number	Percentage
− 30	41	28
31–45	56	38
46–60 + ...	49	34
Total	146	100

Marital status	Number	Percent-age
Single	43	30
Married	82	56

People in Pain

Divorced, separated, or widowed	21	14
Total	146	100

Socioeconomic status

Lower class	87	60
Lower-middle	45	31
Middle	10	7
Undetermined	4	2
Total	146	100

Occupation

Physical	46	32
Nonphysical with physical exertion	39	26
Nonphysical and intellectual	58	40
Undetermined	3	2
Total	146	100

Education

No education	5	3
Grammar school	43	30
Grammar school and some high school	27	18
High school	25	18
High school and some college	24	16
College	14	10
Undetermined	8	5
Total	146	100

Religion

Catholic	67	46
Jewish	43	30
Protestant	27	18
No religion	2	1
Undetermined	7	5
Total	146	100

Cause of pain

Herniated disc and backache	65	45
Headache	9	6
Physical disability and other	64	44
No pain	8	5
Total	146	100

Table 3

Distribution According to Ethnic Groups

	Irish (31)		Italian (30)		Jewish (45)		Old American (40)	
	Number	Percentage	Number	Percentage	Number	Percentage	Number	Percentage
Place of birth, generation								
Foreign-born	3	10	7	23	10	22		
American-born:								
1st generation	9	29	17	57	30	67		
2nd generation	17	55	3	10	2	4.5		
3rd generation	1	3	—	—	1	2		
Undetermined	1	3	3	10	2	4.5		
Total	31	100	30	100	45	100		
Age								
− 30	8	26	12	40	11	24	10	25
31–45	12	39	11	37	21	47	12	30
46–60 + ...	11	35	7	23	13	29	18	45
Total	31	100	30	100	45	100	40	100
Occupation								
Physical work	13	42	7	23	5	11	21	53
Nonphysical with physical exertion	8	26	12	40	15	33	4	10
Nonphysical and intellectual..	9	29	10	34	25	56	14	35
Undetermined	1	3	1	3	—	—	1	2
Total	31	100	30	100	45	100	40	100

258

Education

No formal education	—	—	3	10	2	4	—	—
Grammar school	12	39	10	33	7	16	14	35
High school	15	48	9	30	14	31	14	33
College	3	10	6	20	21	47	8	22
Undetermined	1	3	2	7	1	2	4	10
Total	31	100	30	100	45	100	40	100

Socioeconomic status

Lower	23	74	22	73	15	33	27	68
Lower-middle	7	23	8	27	22	49	8	20
Middle	—	—	—	—	7	16	3	7
Undetermined	1	3	—	—	1	2	2	5
Total	31	100	30	100	45	100	40	100

Ethnicity

High	7	23	20	67	22	49	1	3
Low	22	71	10	33	21	47	39	97
Undetermined	2	6	—	—	2	4	—	—
Total	31	100	30	100	45	100	40	100

Presence of pain

No pain	1	3	—	—	5	11	1	3
Pain	30	97	30	100	40	89	39	97
Total	31	100	30	100	45	100	40	100

Cause of pain

Herniated disc and backache	17	56.5	17	57	18	45	14	36
Headache	2	6.5	—	—	5	13	2	5
Other	8	27	7	23	11	27	7	18
Physical disability	3	10	6	20	6	15	16	41
Total	30	100	30	100	40	100	39	100

259

Bibliography

ALEXANDER, L. "Differential Diagnosis Between Psychogenic and Physical Pain." *Journal of American Medical Association,* 1962, *181,* 855–861.

BABCOCK, C. G. "Food and Its Emotional Significance." *Journal of American Dietetic Association,* 1948, *24,* 390–393.

BARBER, T. "Toward a Theory of Pain: Relief of Chronic Pain by Prefrontal Leucotomy, Opiates, Placebos, and Hypnosis." *Psychological Bulletin,* 1959, *56,* 430–460.

BARKER, R. G. (in collaboration with B. A. Wright, L. Meyerson, M. R. Gonick). "Adjustment to Physical Handicap and Illness: A Survey of the Social Psychology of Physique and Disability."

(2nd ed.) New York: Social Science Research Council, Bulletin 55, Revised 1953.

BEECHER, H. K. "Experimental Pharmacology and the Measurement of the Subjective Response." *Science,* 1952, 157–162.

BEECHER, H. K. "Generalization From Pain of Various Types and Disease Origins." *Science,* 1959, *130,* 267–268.

BEECHER, H. K. *Measurement of Subjective Responses: Quantitative Effect of Drugs.* New York: Oxford University Press, 1959.

BEECHER, H. K. "Pain: One Mystery Solved." *Science,* 1966, *151,* 840–841.

BEECHER, H. K. "Pain in Men Wounded in Battle." *Bulletin of U.S. Army Medical Department,* 1946, *5,* 445–454.

BEHAN, R. J. *Pain: Its Origin, Conduction, Perception and Diagnostic Significance.* New York: Appleton, 1914.

BENEDICT, R. *Patterns of Culture.* New York: Penguin Books, 1946.

BIGELOW, H., HARRISON, I., GOODELL, H., AND WOLFF, H. G. "Studies on Pain: Quantitative Measurements of Two Pain Sensations of the Skin With Reference to the Nature of the Hyperalgesia of Peripheral Neuritis." *Journal of Clinical Investigation,* 1945, *24,* 503–512.

BINGHAM, J. A. W. "Some Problems of Causalgic Pain." *British Medical Journal,* 1948, *2,* 334–338.

BONICA, J. J. *The Management of Pain.* Philadelphia: Lea and Febiger, 1953.

BUTENDIJK, F. J. J. *De la douleur.* Paris: Presses Universitaires de France, 1951.

CANNON, W. B. *Bodily Changes in Pain, Hunger, Fear and Rage.* New York: Appleton, 1920.

CANNON, W. B. *The Wisdom of the Body.* New York: Norton, 1932.

CHAPMAN, W. P. "Measurements of Pain Sensitivity in Normal Control Subjects and in Psychoneurotic Patients." *Psychosomatic Medicine,* 1944, *6,* 252–257.

CHAPMAN, W. P., COHEN, M. E., AND COBB, S. "Measurements of Levels of Heat Stimulus Perceived as Painful and Producing Winces and Withdrawal Reactions in Patient." *Journal of Clinical Investigation,* 1946, *25,* 890.

CHAPMAN, W. P., AND JONES, C. M. "Variations in Cutaneous and Visceral Pain Sensitivity in Normal Subjects." *Journal of Clinical Investigation,* 1944, *23,* 81.

Bibliography

CLAUSEN, J., AND KING, H. E. "Determination of Pain Threshold in Untrained Subjects." *Journal of Psychology,* 1950, *30,* 299–306.

COLLINS, L. G. "Pain Sensitivity and Ratings of Childhood Experience." *Perceptual and Motor Skills,* 1965, *21,* 349–350.

COLLINS, L. G., AND STONE, L. A. "Family Structure and Pain Reactivity." *Journal of Clinical Psychology,* 1966, *22,* 33.

COOPER, I. S., AND BRACELAND, F. J. "Psychosomatic Aspects of Pain." *Medical Clinics of N.A.M.,* 1950, *34,* 981–993.

CRITCHLEY, M. "Some Aspects of Pain." *British Medical Journal,* 1934, *2,* 891.

CROOG, S. H. "Ethnic Origins, Educational Level and Responses to a Health Questionnaire." *Human Organization,* 1961, *20,* 65–69.

DALLENBACH, K. M. "Pain: History and Present Status." *American Journal of Psychology,* 1939, *52,* 331–347.

DEUTON, J. E., AND BEECHER, H. K. "New Analgesics." *Journal of American Medical Association,* 1949, *141,* 1051–1146.

DEVEREUX, G. "The Psychology of Feminine Genital Bleeding: An Analysis of Mohave Indian Puberty and Menstrual Rites." *International Journal of Psychoanalysis,* 1950, *31,* 237–257.

DUBOS, R. *Man Adapting.* New Haven: Yale University Press, 1965.

DUNBAR, H. F. *Emotions and Bodily Changes.* New York: Columbia University Press, 1938.

EDWARDS, W. "Recent Research on Pain Perception." *Psychological Bulletin,* 1950, *47,* 449–471.

EFRON, D., AND FOLEY, J. P. "A Comparative Investigation of Gestural Behavior Patterns in Italian and Jewish Groups Living under Different as Well as Similar Environmental Conditions." *Zeitschrift Fuer Sozialforschung,* 1937, *6,* 151–159.

ELHARDT, W. P. "The Effect of Emotions on the Occurrence of Pain." *Proceedings of American Society for Experimental Biology,* 1945, *4,* 19.

ENGEL, G. L. "Guilt, Pain and Success." *Psychosomatic Medicine,* 1962, *24,* 37–48.

ENGEL, G. L. "Psychogenic Pain." *Journal of Occupational Medicine,* 1961, *31,* 249–256.

ENGEL, G. L. "Psychogenic Pain and the Pain-Prone Patient." *American Journal of Medicine,* 1959, *26,* 899–918.

EWALT, J. R. "Pain from the Psychiatrist's Point of View." *Journal of Oklahoma State Medical Association,* 1948, *41,* 409–414.

263

FORD, C. S. "Society, Culture and the Human Organism." *Journal of Genetic Psychology*, 1939, *20*, 135–179.

FORD, F. R., AND WILKINS, L. "Congenital Universal Insensitiveness to Pain." *Johns Hopkins Hospital Bulletin*, 1938, *62*, 448–466.

FRANK, L. K. "Cultural Control and Physiological Autonomy." In C. Kluckhohn and H. Mowrer, *Personality in Nature, Culture and Society*. New York: A. Knopf, 1948.

FREEMAN, W., AND WATTS, J. W. *Psychosurgery*. (2nd ed.) Springfield, Ill.: Thomas, 1950.

FREIDMAN, L., AND FERGUSON, V. M. "The Question of Painless Childbirth in Primitive Cultures." *American Journal of Orthopsychiatry*, 1950, *20*, 363–372.

FULLOP-MILLER. *Triumph over Pain*. New York: The Literary Guild of America, 1938.

GELFAND, S. "The Relationship of Birth Order to Pain Tolerance." *Journal of Clinical Psychology*, 1963, *19*, 406.

GONDA, T. A. "The Relation Between Complaints of Persistent Pain and Family Size." *Journal of Neurology, Neurosurgery, and Psychiatry*, 1962, *25*, 270–281.

GOOD, M. G. "General theory of pain." *Anesthesia and Analgesics*, 1951, *30*, 136–150.

GREENBLATT, M., ARNOT, R., AND SALOMON, H. C. (Eds.) *Studies in Lobotomy*. New York: Grune and Stratton, 1950.

GUETZKOW, H. S., AND BOWMAN, P. H. *Men and Hunger*. Elgin, Ill.: Brethren Publishing House, 1946.

HALLOWELL, A. I. "Temporal Orientation in Western Civilization and in a Preliterate Society." *American Anthropologist*, 1937, *39*, 647–670.

HARDY, J. D., AND JAVERT, C. T. "Studies on Pain: Measurements of Pain Intensity in Childbirth." *Journal of Clinical Investigation*, 1949, *28*, 153–162.

HARDY, J. D., WOLFF, H. G., AND GOODELL, H. *Pain Sensations and Reactions*. Baltimore: Williams and Wilkins, 1952.

HART, H. "Displacement, Guilt and Pain." *Psychoanalytic Review*, 1947, *34*, 259.

HEARD, G. *Pain, Sex and Time*. London, 1939.

HEBB, D. O. *The Organization of Behavior: A Neuropsychological Theory*. New York: Wiley, 1949.

Bibliography

HENRY, J. "Environment and Symptom Formation." *American Journal of Orthopsychiatry,* 1947, *17,* 628–636.

HILL, H. E., KORNETSKY, C. H., FLANARY, G. H., AND WINKLER, A. "Studies on Anxiety Associated with Anticipation of Pain; 1. Effects of morphine." *Archives of Neurology and Psychiatry,* 1952, *67,* 612–619.

JEWESBURY, E. "Insensitivity to Pain." *Brain,* 1951, *74,* 331–353.

KAHN, E. "Some Aspects of Normal Personality Experiencing Disease." *Yale Journal of Biology and Medicine,* 1941, *13,* 397–408.

KEUR, J. Y., AND KEUR, D. L. *The Deeply Rooted.* Monographs of American Ethnological Society, 1955, *25,* 81.

KING, H. E., CLAUSEN, J. E., AND SCARFF, J. E. "Cutaneous Thresholds of Pain Before and After Unilateral Prefrontal Lobotomy: A Preliminary Report." *Journal of Nervous and Mental Disease,* 1950, *112,* 93–96.

KLUCKHOHN, C. *Mirror for Man: A Survey of Human Behavior and Social Attitudes.* New York: McGraw-Hill, 1944.

KLUCKHOHN, F. R. "Dominant and Substitute Profiles of Cultural Orientation." *Social Forces,* 1950, *28* (4), 350.

KOLB, L. C. "Psychiatric Aspects of Treatment for Intractable Pain in the Phantom Limb." *Medical Clinics of North America,* 1950, *34,* 1029–1041.

KROEBER, A. L., AND KLUCKHOHN, C. *Culture: A Critical View of Concepts and Definitions.* New York; Vintage (Random House), 1964.

KUNKLE, E. C., ARMSTEAD, G. C., AND GOODELL, H. "Spread of Pain." *Archives of Neurology and Psychiatry,* 1950, *63,* 187–188.

KUNKLE, E. C., AND CHAPMAN, W. P. "Insensitivity to Pain in Man." *Research Publication of the Association of Nervous and Mental Disease,* 1943, *23,* 100–109.

LEFEVER, H. D. "Bifrontal Lobotomy for Relief of Organic Pain." *Ohio State Medical Journal,* 1949, *45,* 128–131.

LERICHE, R. "Orientation Actuelle du Problème de la Douleur." *Journal of Psychological and Normal Pathology,* 1951, *44,* 497–509.

LERICHE, R. *The Surgery of Pain.* Baltimore: Williams and Wilkins, 1939.

LEVY, D. M. *Maternal Over-Protection.* New York: Columbia University Press, 1943.

LEWIS, C. F. *The Problem of Pain.* London, 1939.

LEWIS, T. *Pain.* New York: Macmillan, 1942.

LIBMAN, E. "Observations on Sensitiveness to Pain." *Transaction of the Association of American Physicians,* 1926, *41,* 305.

LIVINGSTON, W. K. *Pain mechanisms.* New York: Macmillan, 1943.

LUCK, J. V. "Low Back Pain." *Journal Indiana Medical Association,* 1944, *37,* 452–459.

LUDWIG, A. O. "Some Psycho-Social Factors in Cases of Severe Medical Disease." *Applied Anthropology,* 1948, *7,* 1–5.

MALINOWSKI, B. *A Scientific Theory of Culture and Other Essays.* Chapel Hill: University of North Carolina Press, 1944.

MATFUS, J. "Pain." *Psychiatric Quarterly,* 1951, *25,* 97–131.

MEAD, M. "National Character." In A. L. Kroeber, *Anthropology Today: An Encyclopedic Inventory.* Chicago: University of Chicago Press, 1953. Pp. 642–667.

MEAD, M. *New Lives for Old: Cultural Transformation, Manus 1928–1953.* New York, 1956.

MEAD, M., AND CALAS, N. (Eds.) *Primitive Heritage: An Anthropological Anthology.* New York: Random House, 1953.

MECHANIC, D. *Medical Sociology: A Selective View.* New York: Free Press, 1968.

MECHANIC, D. "Religion, Religiosity and Illness Behavior: The Special Case of the Jews." *Human Organization,* 1963, *22,* 202–208.

MEDVEI, V. C. *The Mental and Physical Effects of Pain.* Edinburgh: Livingston, 1949.

MERSKEY, H., AND SPEAR, F. G. *Pain: Psychological and Psychiatric Aspects.* Baltimore: Williams and Wilkins, 1967.

MINER, H. M. "Body Ritual among the Nacirema." *American Anthropologist,* 1956, *58,* 503–507.

MOLONEY, J. C. "On Oriental Stoicism." *American Journal of Psychiatry,* 1946, *103,* 60–64.

OGILVIE, H., AND THOMSON, W. A. R. (Eds.) *Pain and Its Problems.* London, 1950.

PAULETT, J. D. "Low Back Pain." *Lancet,* 1947, *253,* 272–276.

PETRIE, A. "Some Psychological Aspects of Pain and the Relief of Suffering." *Annals of New York Academy of Science,* 1960, *86,* 13–27.

PIERON, H. "Les Problemes Psychophysiologiques de la Douleur." *Annee Psychologique,* 1950, *49,* 359–372.

Bibliography

PLOSS, H. H. *Das Kind im Brauch und Sitte der Völker, Anthropologische Studie.* 2 vols. Stuttgart: Auerbach, 1876.

RANGELL, L. "Psychiatric Aspects of Pain." *Psychosomatic Medicine,* 1953, *35* (1).

REIK, T. *Masochism in Modern Man.* New York: Farrar, Strauss, 1941.

RITZENHALER, R. F. "Chippewa Preoccupation with Health: Change in a Traditional Attitude Resulting from Modern Health Problems." *Microfilm Abstract 1950,* 10 (4), 324–325. Abstract of Ph.D. thesis, 1950, California University.

ROMANO, J. "Emotional Components of Illness." *Connecticut State Medical Journal, 7,* 1943.

ROWBOTHAM, G. F. "Pain and Its Underlying Pathology." *Journal of Medical Sciences,* 1946, *92,* 595–604.

RUESCH, J. *Chronic Disease and Psychological Invalidism.* Berkeley and Los Angeles: University of California Press, 1951.

SCHAMP, J. R., AND SCHAMP, H. M. "Variability of the Pain Threshold in Man." *Journal of Dental Research,* 1946, *25,* 101–104.

SCHILLING, R. F., AND MUSSER, M. "Pain Reaction Thresholds in Psychoneurotic Patients." *American Journal of Medical Sciences,* 1948, *215,* 195–197.

SHIELDS, C. "The Mechanism and Physiotherapeutic Relief of Pain." *Lancet,* 1951, *261,* 459–462.

SILVERSTEIN, A. B. "Age Differences in Pain Apperception." *Perceptual and Motor Skills,* 1963, *16,* 169–170.

SMITH, M. W. "Different Cultural Concepts of Past, Present and Future: A Study of Ego Extension." *Psychiatry,* 1952, *15,* 395–400.

SPERLING, M. "A Psychoanalytic Study of Migraine and Psychogenic Headache." *Psychosomatic Medicine,* 1950, *12,* 381–391.

STERNBACH, R. A. *Pain: A Psychophysiological Analysis.* New York and London: Academic Press, 1968.

STERNBACH, R. A., AND TURSKY, B. "Ethnic Differences Among Housewives in Psychophysical and Skin Potential Responses to Electric Shock." *Psychophysiology,* 1965, *1,* 241–246.

STEWARD, J. H. (Ed.) *Handbook of South American Indians,* vol. 1. Smithsonian Institution; Bureau of American Ethnology Bulletin 143. Washington, 1946.

SUCHMAN, E. A. "Social Patterns of Illness and Medical Care." *Journal of Health and Human Behavior,* 1965, *6,* 2–16.

SUCHMAN, E. A. "Sociomedical Variations Among Ethnic Groups." *American Journal of Sociology,* 1964, *70,* 319–331.

SZASZ, T. S. *Pain and Pleasure: A Study of Bodily Feelings.* New York: Basic Books, 1957.

TURSKY, B., AND STERNBACH, R. A. "Further Physiological Correlates of Ethnic Differences in Responses to Shock." *Psychophysiology,* 1967, *1,* 151–162.

WALKER, A. E. "The Relief of Facial Pain." *Medical Clinics of North America,* 1945, *29,* 73.

WALKER, A. E., AND CULBRETH, G. C. "Surgical Treatment of Pain and Motor Disorders." *Progress of Neurology and Psychiatry,* 1949, *4,* 372–388.

WATTS, J. W., AND FREEMAN, W. "Frontal Lobotomy in the Treatment of Unbearable Pain." *Research Publication of the Association of Nervous and Mental Disease,* 1948, *27,* 715.

WATTS, J. W., AND FREEMAN, W. "Unbearable Pain Relieved by Brain Surgery." *Scientific Newsletter,* 1945, *48,* 388.

WEISS, E. "Bodily Pain and Mental Pain." *International Journal of Psychoanalysis,* 1939, *5,* 10.

WHITE, J. C., AND SWEET, W. H. *Pain: Its Mechanisms and Neurosurgical Control.* Springfield, Ill.: Thomas, 1955.

WOLFF, H. G. *Headache and Other Head Pain.* New York: Oxford University Press, 1948.

WOLFF, H. G. "Personality Features and Reactions of Subjects with Migraine." *Archives of Neurology and Psychiatry,* 1937, *37,* 895.

WOLFF, H. G. "Some Observations on Pain." *Harvey Lectures,* 1943, 1944, *39,* 39–95.

WOLFF, H. G. *Stress and Disease.* Springfield, Ill.: Thomas, 1953.

WOLFF, H. G., AND HARDY, J. "On the Nature of Pain." *Physiological Review,* 1947, *27,* 167–199.

WOLFF, H. G., AND WOLF, S. *Pain.* Springfield, Ill.: Thomas, 1951.

ZBOROWSKI, M. "Cultural Components in Response to Pain." *Journal of Social Issues,* 1952, *8,* 16–30.

ZBOROWSKI, M., AND HERZOG, E. *Life Is with People: The Jewish Little-Town of Eastern Europe.* New York: International Universities Press, 1952.

I*ndex*

A

Age factor in pain response, 17, 189–190, 248

Anxiety reactions: in Jews, 113–122, 241 *passim;* in Old Americans, 66–73 *passim,* 83–88 *passim*

Attitudes towards pain and time-orientation, 45–46

B

BEECHER, H. K., 16, 250
BENEDICT, R., 44–45

Biological function of pain, 24–25 (*see also* Warning function of pain)

C

CALAS, N., 41, 42
CHAPMAN, W. P., 20, 27
Communication function of expressing pain, 41–43, 53–56, 102–104, 241

Crying Old Americans, 50; Jews, 100–104; Italians, 137–139 (*see also* Emotionality; Expressive-

269

Index

271

Index

Index

Punishment interpretation of pain, 38–40, 226–227
Purification function of pain, 39–40

R

Reflex reactions, 18–19 *passim*
Religious functions of pain, 39–40
Response to pain: age factor, 17, 189–190, 248; behavioral responses, 18–19; conflict in, 28–29, 32–33, 108–110; communicative functions, 41–43, 53–56, 102–104, 241; cultural differences, 1–9 *passim*, 32–48 (*see also* Cultural dimension); denial, 56–57; education and, 248; generational differences, 6; of Indians, 44–45; in initiation rituals, 40–41; of Irish, 187–245 *passim;* of Italians, 136–386 *passim;* of Jews, 97–135 *passim;* nature of illness and, 10, 248–249; of Old Americans, 49–96 *passim;* personality and, 19–20; "personification," 83–84; physiological reactions, 15–19 *passim*, 57–58; of schizophrenics, 27n; sensory vs. emotional aspects, 15–19 *passim;* time orientation and, 46–47; types of, 18–19, 245–247; violence and, 45–46; withdrawal, 60–61, 105, 144 (*see also* Emotionality; Expressiveness and stoicism; Verbalization of pain)

S

Sample of the study, 6–7, 10, 12–13; distribution of interviews; pathology of respondents, 257; socioeconomic characteristics,
98, 137, 187–188, 237–238, 256–259
Schizophrenic response to pain, 27n
Sensory aspect of pain, 15–19 *passim,* 24–27 *passim*
Sex factor, 17
SMITH, M. W., 46
Social relationships (*see* Family structure; Family relationships)
Social sanction function, 38–40
Socioeconomic characteristics of sample, 98, 137, 187–188, 237–238, 256–259
Socioeconomic factors in pain (*see* Cultural dimension)
Statistical interpretations, 237–249
STERNBACK, R. A., 15, 16n, 25n, 26n, 249–250
STEWARD, J. H., 40, 45
Symbolic aspects of pain, 25–27, 41–42
SUCHMAN, E. A., 249
Suffering (*see* Punishment interpretation of pain; Response to pain)
Surgery (*see* Treatment attitudes)
SZASZ, T. S., 3

T

Time orientation and response to pain, 45–47, 92–94, 117–119 *passim,* 149–157 *passim,* 240
Treatment attitudes: cultural differences, 242, 247; of Irish, 218–220; of Italians, 161–163; of Jews, 131–134; of Old Americans, 85–87, 95 (*see also* Doctors; Medication attitudes)
TURSKY, B., 249–250

V

Values related to pain, 27–28, 31–33, 45–46, 47 (*see also* Cul-

273

Index

tural dimension; Health and illness attitudes; Medication attitudes; Treatment attitudes)

Verbalization of pain, 17–18, 240; by Irish, 188–192; by Jews, 98–104; mechanical analogies, 84-85; "personification," 83–84; by Old Americans, 81–85 (*see also* Expressiveness and stoicism)

Violence and pain attitudes, 45–46

W

Warning function of pain, 24–25, 62–66, 72–76, 110–121 *passim*, 150–152, 205, 241, 242, 244

WATTS, J. W., 25

Withdrawal, 60–61, 105, 144

WOLF, S., 20

WOLFF, H. D., 15, 16–17, 20

Z

ZBOROWSKI, M., 249